PETERSON'S®

Teens' Guide to College & Career Planning

Your High School Roadmap to College and Career Success

JUSTIN ROSS MUCHNICK

About Peterson's®

Peterson's has been your trusted educational publisher for more than 50 years. It's a milestone we're quite proud of as we continue to offer the most accurate, dependable, high-quality educational content in the field, providing you with everything you need to succeed. No matter where you are on your academic or professional path, you can rely on Peterson's for its books, online information, expert test-prep tools, the most up-to-date education exploration data, and the highest quality career success resources—everything you need to achieve your education goals. For our complete line of products, visit **www.petersons.com.**

For more information, contact Peterson's, 4380 S. Syracuse St., Suite 200, Denver, CO 80237; 800-338-3282 Ext. 54229; or visit us online at **www.petersons.com.**

Contents

Contents

How to Approach This Book

Whether you picked this guide up because you're highly motivated on your own or you're reading it because someone in your life told you that you should, you're probably wondering what exactly this book can do for you. In short, it can help you create a roadmap to the kind of future you want to have. As you explore the information here, you'll be prompted to think about your interests and skills, contemplate numerous potential paths forward for both your education and your career, and evaluate what your priorities are in life.

The Short and Sweet Version

No matter how motivated (or not) you may feel at the start of this book, you can be sure that by the time you finish it, you'll feel ready to take on your future. That's because each chapter is loaded with tons of tips, advice, explanations, examples, and guidelines to help you make sense of your options both during high school and after.

Whether you're planning to go to a four-year college or university, go to community college, apprentice to learn a trade, undergo vocational training, or enter the workforce right after graduation, you'll find everything you need to know laid out in this book. For instance, if you have no idea what you'd like to do, our skills inventory and reflection questions in Chapter 2 can help you start to figure it out. Perhaps, you know exactly what kind of path you'd like to take, so you can use this book to make an effective timeline of the tasks you'll need to complete to get there.

No matter what your parent(s), guardian(s), teachers, or guidance counselor might imply, it's totally normal to be anxious, confused, or unsure when the question of your future comes up. Most teenagers don't have all the answers worked out right away and that's both okay and developmentally expected. However, questions about your future will be coming up a lot these days because they *are* important to ponder. The approach laid out in this guide makes it easy to ponder them.

As you read this book, try to keep an open mind and be honest with yourself. There are no right answers, nor will you be encouraged to take one path over another. Instead, consider the options laid out before you and try your best to figure out which one feels right for the kind of life you want to have one day. You have lots of time to figure things out and you only need to take things one step at a time; this guide can help you through each step of that journey.

Often throughout this process, you will be asked to consider questions about yourself, some of which you may have never thought of before. You can answer these questions in your head, but it can be even more useful if you take notes or journal about the thoughts they bring up so that you can reference those notes when evaluating your education and career options. By the end of the book, that process of self-discovery will have landed you on a tentative plan for your future so that you are prepped and ready to use the tools laid out in this guide.

Another thing this book can do for you is help calm any nerves, worries, or anxieties you have about the transitions you'll undergo as you move from middle school to high school, from high school to college, vocational training, or the workforce, and ultimately, into your long-term career plans and adult life. No matter how old you are coming into this book, there are tools within these pages to help you steer your ship. If you're starting early, such as the summer before high school, then you might even find it useful to periodically return to this book over the years to refresh yourself on what you need to know for different stages of your life.

Assuming you purchased this book and it's yours to mark up, taking notes in the margins is absolutely encouraged! Don't be afraid to jot down your own ideas as you read along, since your notes could prove useful later. In fact, you will occasionally see places to take notes sprinkled throughout the book for this very reason. Of course, if you borrowed this book from a library or from a friend, it's better to take notes in a notebook. Just don't be afraid to write out your thoughts *somewhere*, as this has been proven to help people process information.

THREE WAYS TO READ THIS BOOK

There are, of course, more than three ways to read this or any book, but considering this is a guide, there are three main approaches that prove most useful for most people. Figure out which approach (or combination of approaches) works best for both the way you absorb information and the period of education and career planning you're at when you pick up this guide. There's no one right way to read this book so long as you get the information you need.

Option 1:
The Read-Through

One approach is to read straight through from beginning to end. This approach is useful for those who are starting early, for those who like to understand the big picture, or for those who are starting late, such as seniors who want to see if there's anything they haven't thought of yet. As you might expect, this is the most thorough approach that ensures you don't miss a single tip contained here. The sequence of chapters is designed to become more and more relevant over the course of high school, but that doesn't mean that reading the later chapters earlier is a bad thing. Instead, doing so means you'll know what's in store for you in the years to come. This can help you get ahead on thinking about your plans.

Option 2:
The Skim & Find

Option 3:
The Handbook

Another way to approach this book is to skim through the entire contents while looking out for information that pertains to you. This is likely to be a useful approach if you are coming to this book later, such as during your junior or senior year of high school, or if you are someone who struggles to have the attention span to read every word.

At points in this book, you may find that some information is less relevant to you. For instance, if you know you want to enter the workforce after high school graduation instead of going to college, then some of the sections that focus on college will be less useful to you. They may still contain tips that would apply to your life, such as offering information on how to handle conflict with roommates, but you won't need to read every single word closely to glean useful information from them. If this is the case, then "skimming" through the text looking mainly for information that's relevant to you might work best. You need to look through the whole book, but skip sections that are less applicable to your life and focus only on those that you need.

Yet another approach is to not try and read the entire book at once but instead to come to different sections over the course of your high school career and address them one at a time. In this approach, you might use Chapters 1 and 2 during your freshman year to help you figure some early plans out, come back to other chapters throughout high school as they become relevant, then look at Chapters 10–12 during your senior year or after when you're planning for your life in the "real world." The timeline in Appendix A, which is a simplified version of a more in-depth college timeline in Chapter 3, is also a useful reference that can help prompt you to undertake certain tasks, such as when to start searching for colleges. The benefit of using this guide as a handbook is that it makes the different sections more digestible.

A combination of the above approaches is likely to yield the best results. You might read through all the way when you first get the book, return to sections to re-read them handbook style as they become relevant, and later flip through to skim and find certain pieces of information you remember being in the book when you need them. It's a good idea to keep this book on a shelf in your room or anywhere else where you can find it and reference it later.

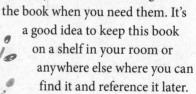

WHAT'S INSIDE THIS GUIDE?

Each of the chapters is jam-packed with useful information to help you make the most of college and career planning. That said, it can be overwhelming to look at so much information all at once. Here are some of the ways the book breaks down information to make it more approachable for you.

The Short and Sweet Version

At the beginning of each chapter, you'll notice a graphic guide called "The Short and Sweet Version." Think of these breakdowns as chapter summaries to help you get a sense of what the chapter will include. If you have read the book before, you can treat these sections like brief recaps of the most important parts of each chapter. If the prospect of reading this entire book sounds daunting, quickly reading through the "Short and Sweet Version" for each chapter can give you a digestible way to think about the book as a whole. These guides are useful if you are using the "Skim & Find" approach to reading since they're a quick way to see exactly what is covered in each chapter. Basically, these brief breakdowns are there to help you if you need them!

Topical Chapter Breakdown

In addition to the summaries at the beginning of each chapter, use this table as a quick reference to figure out which kinds of information can be found where. If you are using the "Skim & Find" or "Handbook" options outlined earlier, this breakdown is an especially handy reference point to help you home in on which sections to read first.

Topical Chapter Breakdown

	This chapter is about…	It contains information on…
Part 1: Setting the Stage for High School Success		
Chapter 1: Getting Hyped for High School	what to expect in high school, especially during your first year, and how to make the most of your high school experience.	• choosing classes • navigating high school social dynamics • adjusting to high school workloads • setting meaningful high school goals • your freshman year and how to crush it
Part 2: Figuring Out Your Future		
Chapter 2: Finding a Path to Your Future	how to evaluate your skills, interests, values, and priorities so you can start thinking about what kind of career you'd like to have one day.	• conducting a skills assessment • thinking about your future plans in terms of skills, interests, careers, and personal development • how to plan for the future even if you aren't planning on a four-year college or university
Chapter 3: Planning Your Education While in High School	what to do over the course of high school to achieve the goals you set for yourself, including a detailed timeline.	• what to do each year of high school to set yourself up for success • study skills that lead to higher achievement • choosing classes based on your future plans, whether they include college or not

	This chapter is about…	It contains information on…
Chapter 4: Other Options During and After High School	the variety of options available to those who aren't planning to go to a four-year college or university.	• community college, trade and vocational schools, and other options that exist for recent high school graduates • entering the workforce right after high school • careers that don't require a four-year degree
Chapter 5: Considering the Military Option	weighing your options around enlistment in the military.	• deciding if enlistment is right for you • choosing a branch • preparing for basic training • planning for the military while in high school
Part 3: Continuing Your Education with College		
Chapter 6: The College Search	figuring out which of the thousands of colleges out there you should apply to.	• conducting a college search • determining what you want in a college • figuring out what you need to know about each school you're considering • figuring out which type of college suits your needs • deciding if trying for a highly competitive college is right for you • campus visits, interviews, and more
Chapter 7: Applying to College	the college application process and everything that goes into it, including information on how colleges will evaluate you.	• navigating the college application process • creating a brag sheet • early decision and other admission types • taking a gap year • tackling admissions essays
Chapter 8: College Entrance Exams	all the different exams you're likely to encounter and tips on how to get signed up and prepare effectively.	• the PSAT/NMSQT, SAT, ACT, TOEFL, GED, and other exams • making sure you know what to expect on the day of your exam • exam best practices and helpful tips for bringing home the scores you want
Chapter 9: Financing Your College Plans	finding the best sources of financial aid for your situation, navigating the scholarship and financial aid application process, and paying for school in a way that's sustainable for your future.	• applying for scholarships and grants • applying for federal and private loans • weighing your options on how to pay • when to start looking for sources of aid (and how) • making good financial decisions surrounding financial aid • spotting a scholarship scam

This chapter is about…		It contains information on…
Part 4: Success in College and in Your Career		
Chapter 10: Academic Expectations in College	the transition from high school to college and what you need to know to succeed at college academics.	• choosing college courses • planning for a degree • the types of majors available to you • making the most of self-motivated learning • the types of resources campuses have to help students succeed • attending college with a disability
Chapter 11: Preparing for College and Adult Life	adjusting to the social aspects of college life, plus tips on navigating adult life that are helpful for anyone (not just those going to college).	• managing stress • moving out • taking care of yourself as a young adult • mental health, identifying signs of abuse, and other "big" topics that could come up when you're out in the real world • setting and respecting boundaries • navigating roommate relationships
Chapter 12: You and the Workplace	how to put your best foot forward when you finish high school or college and start your career.	• choosing a career • writing a résumé and cover letter • searching for jobs • nailing your job interview • finding a mentor • what employers tend to expect

Goal-Based Chapter Breakdown

There's useful information throughout the entire book for people who are thinking of pursuing a variety of post-high school paths. If you aren't sure which path you'd like to follow, we recommend preparing for the college path since it will prepare you for any of the other options, as well. Consequently, like many guides for teens, we've structured most of the book around this path. However, as you start to develop a clear sense of what you'd like to do, you may find that college isn't likely to be where you end up right out of high school. If that's the case, this book also has plenty of information to help you prepare.

Information for all kinds of teenagers can be found throughout each chapter. That said, use the chart on the next page to help you determine which chapters you'll want to pay closest attention to based on your chosen path.

Goal-Based Chapter Breakdown

	1	2	3	4	5	6	7	8	9	10	11	12
If you are planning to go to a 4-year college or university, your most relevant chapters are…	✓	✓	✓			✓	✓	✓	✓	✓	✓	✓
If you are planning to attend community college, learn a trade, or engage in vocational training, your most relevant chapters are…	✓	✓	✓	✓				✓	✓	✓	✓	✓
If you are planning to enlist in the military, your most relevant chapters are…	✓	✓	✓		✓			✓			✓	✓
If you are interested in entering the workforce right after high school, your most relevant chapters are…	✓	✓	✓	✓							✓	✓

Appendix A: College Timeline

In Appendix A, you'll find a condensed version of the more expansive timeline outlined in Chapter 3. Students can use the appendix as a quick reference for what they need to do each year of high school to ensure a smooth transition to college. Some of the tips are also relevant to those who will not be headed to a four-year university.

Appendix B: Additional Resources for Underserved Student Populations

This guide defines "underserved student populations" as those with unique needs that require extra support and/or those who have historically been inadequately served by the existing resources on college campuses. Students of color, students who identify as religious or ethnic minorities, immigrant students, and students with developmental, physical, or learning disabilities will be able to find extra resources to support their college and career plans here.

YOU'RE READY FOR SUCCESS!

Now that you know a bit about the different ways to approach reading this book, the type of content you'll find in each chapter, and some of the strategies (like note-taking or journaling) that can help you optimize your reading, you're ready to begin your journey toward college and career success. Get excited—your future awaits!

PART

1

Setting the Stage for
High School Success

CHAPTER 1

Getting Hyped for High School

You know what TV and movies say about it—being in high school should be cool! You'll be able to join clubs, try out for sports, learn an instrument, go to dances and other events, take part in meaningful school traditions, and experience whatever else there is to experience as part of your high school's community. But what will it really be like? Will you be able to figure it all out? Rest assured that you will . . . especially since you are reading this book! It's true that high school will be like nothing else you have experienced and, as a freshman, you're going to have questions about everything. Luckily, you'll have people around to help, like teachers and guidance counselors, but you'll also be able to get answers right here. Whether you're wondering about keeping your stuff organized, choosing your classes, or figuring out what a GPA is, this guide has you covered.

The Short and Sweet Version

Here you are, about to start high school. Wow! How do you feel? No, seriously, take a second to think about how you're feeling. Are you pumped? Nervous? What kinds of concerns are on your mind? What questions do you have? Hopefully, no matter what they are, by the time you get through this book, you'll have answers.

Some people say that high school means "the best years of your life" while others talk about it more like a prison sentence to be endured. Your own high school experience will probably be somewhere in the middle of those two extremes. It will also be uniquely yours because no matter what others have told you, their experience is only their own. You will be forging your own path as a high school student, and a lot of how well high school goes depends on your mindset.

There is so much growth that awaits you during this period of your life, so a lot of the advice you'll find in this chapter is about setting goals, being kind and honest with yourself about your needs and desires, recognizing how your priorities may shift over time, and finding ways to take on more independence and responsibility as you mature. As a teen, it can be hard to imagine that adulthood is just around the corner, but high school will likely be exactly what you need to prepare yourself for that transition.

Just by reading this book, you're demonstrating that you're the kind of teenager who takes their future seriously, so you can be certain that you're probably more primed for high school success than you even realize. Try to breathe, relax, and remember that you've overcome new challenges before, and you will continue to do so in the future. This guide may be the roadmap to a successful future, but you're the one who gets to plot the course.

MENTALLY PREPARING FOR HIGH SCHOOL

There is a good chance that thinking about entering high school is or was at least a little scary for you right after finishing middle school. As a recent middle school graduate, you have a vague awareness that things are going to be different. Your teachers, older siblings, or neighbors might have prepared you for some of what to expect, but chances are that you have a lot more questions swirling around in your head than you do answers. Consider these common questions that might be coming at this point.

Common Questions about High School

- Just how much bigger is my school going to be and how will I find my way around?
- What happens if I get lost?
- What if my friends don't have lunch when I do?
- What happens if I can't open my locker or don't remember my locker combination?
- What happens if there aren't any lockers at my school?
- Will all those books fit in my backpack?
- What if my best friend isn't in any of my classes?
- What if I don't know anyone in my classes?
- What if I don't know where the bathroom is or have enough time to go between classes?
- What if I forget where to go for my class or how to navigate from one class to another in the time I'm allowed?
- Will I have enough time to get my lunch and eat it during my lunch period?
- What if the older students are scary or mean to me?
- What if my teachers are intimidating?
- What if I miss my bus?
- *What if ... what if ... what if?*

Just looking at that list of questions probably got you thinking of even more that aren't listed here. If you're feeling overwhelmed, that's understandable! Luckily, a lot of those questions will be answered within the first few days of getting to high school, usually during any kind of freshman orientation you might have. It makes sense to be buzzing with questions because in middle school you probably knew where everything was. You had a routine and knew the expectations of your school. You knew exactly who would be sitting next to you at lunch and you knew all your teachers. As an 8th grader, you might have felt like you were at the top of the heap. Even if you struggled in middle school (or just hated it), you probably got to a point where you could at least predict what your day-to-day life would look like. Now, suddenly, you're back where you were at the start of middle school—beginning all over again with a new routine, a new school community, and a boatload of unanswered questions.

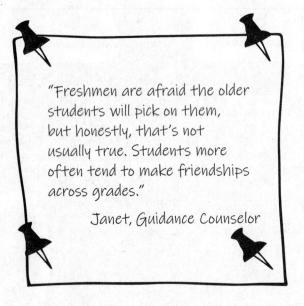

"Freshmen are afraid the older students will pick on them, but honestly, that's not usually true. Students more often tend to make friendships across grades."

Janet, Guidance Counselor

First of all, if you *are* freaking out, take a few deep breaths, sit back, and realize that it's okay to have the ups and downs, the doubts, and the feelings that zip back and forth between "I can't wait to go to high school" and "I'm hiding under my bed and never coming out." In the first few weeks of high school, you'll be surrounded by kids who are older and oftentimes

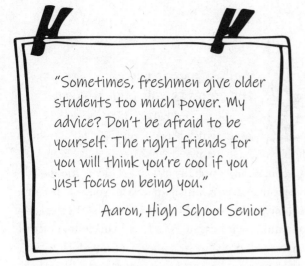

"Sometimes, freshmen give older students too much power. My advice? Don't be afraid to be yourself. The right friends for you will think you're cool if you just focus on being you."

Aaron, High School Senior

bigger, who are familiar with the school, and who seem to know an awful lot more than you do. You'll wonder what it will be like to try out for sports teams or shows and activities with the 10th, 11th, and 12th graders, and you may even start to feel inferior, even though you're definitely not.

If anxiety is getting the best of you, part of you may want to shell up and hide from anything that seems like a risk, such as talking to an older student. Instead of withdrawing, try to keep an open mind and remain optimistic. You might find that when you overcome those anxieties, the very people you feared (like those older students) can become great sources of assistance and reassurance. For instance, once you muster the courage to talk to friendly

"My son was nervous about starting 9th grade, but after the first two or three days, he felt so much better. He learned the best route to all his classes so he'd be on time, and he made a good number of new friends right away. So, the things he worried about the most were no longer a concern."

Beatrice, Mother of a High School Sophomore

11th and 12th graders, they will likely give you lots of advice on how to navigate high school, and your teachers and other adults in the school will likely be warm and welcoming, ready to help freshmen like you get their bearings. Be open to the assistance and friendliness of others in your community.

Second, remember to take any feedback you've already gotten about high school with a grain of salt, especially if it was negative feedback. The friend of a friend's brother who told you he hated 9th grade isn't you, and most likely, he didn't go to high school at your exact school or take your exact classes with your exact teachers. Everyone adjusts to high school in different ways and at different speeds. Furthermore, every high school culture is slightly different, even for high schools within the same school district. That means that your experience will be uniquely yours.

For some teens, the transition from middle school to high school takes a short time—days or weeks. They may find that they immediately feel at ease in their new environment and don't have many "growing pains." For others, the adjustment takes longer, especially for those who avoid sharing their feelings or letting others help them get over their insecurities. If you experience a bumpier transition to high school, look for opportunities to seek advice from teachers, guidance counselors, and older students with whom you feel at ease. It's easier to make the transition to high school if you have support.

Third, remember that you are not alone. All those older students ahead of you have had the same fears and feelings. They made it through, and so will you. In fact, it's very likely that the sophomores, juniors, and seniors at your school are too busy dealing with the problems of being sophomores, juniors, and seniors to be concerned if you forgot your locker combination and have to slink off to the school office to find out what it is. People probably won't notice your mistakes since they're focusing on what's going on with them, including their own mistakes that they're hoping *you* won't notice. Remember that you are human and so are all the people around you—everyone has insecurities, no one is perfect, and it's okay to mess up now and then. Just learn from your mistakes and chalk it up to building wisdom.

WHAT'S SO DIFFERENT ABOUT HIGH SCHOOL?

The biggest adjustment is that when you get to high school, the guidelines for success all change. This can be overwhelming, especially if you feel like you only just got the hang of succeeding in middle school. To prepare you, here are six of the major differences you'll likely notice when you get to high school.

1 **YOU ARE MORE INDEPENDENT AT SCHOOL.** In many middle schools, students are put in some sort of group. Perhaps the same cohort of students travels from class to class together or students are grouped within their grade to match a particular set of teachers. Because of this group-based scheduling being so common in middle school, there's a good chance that you and all your immediate peers did the same things together—ate lunch, took the same classes, goofed off. Therefore, it could be a big adjustment to realize that you'll have your own schedule of classes in high school that could be very different from your best friend's. You'll be in classes with people you don't know because there are different levels of classes, such as math classes attuned to your learning level rather than your grade. You may also end up taking electives that combine students from various grade levels. To succeed, you'll have to learn to manage your schedule independently and make friends in classes where you might not know anyone yet.

2 **YOU ARE MORE INDEPENDENT OUTSIDE OF SCHOOL.** Your growing independence will likely extend outside of the classroom to your social and home life. Unless your parent(s) or guardian(s) lean toward being very strict, you'll probably find yourself gaining more and more freedoms at home over the course of high school. You can expect the adults in your life to give you opportunities to prove that you are mature and capable of handling these new freedoms—things like driving safely, running errands, or managing your own schedule. Don't let this progress toward independence overwhelm you. Instead, embrace any opportunities to demonstrate your growth and maturity. When someone has enough trust in you to grant you new freedoms and space for independence, rise to the occasion.

3 **YOU HAVE MORE SAY IN THE COURSES YOU TAKE.** In middle school, you probably had fewer choices about which classes you could take. In high school, you have many more choices to make about your education, especially as you get older. You'll also have more electives, which are classes you take because the topic interests you rather than because it's a specific graduation requirement. As a freshman, your choice of electives will probably be somewhat limited. However, by the time you are a junior or senior, you'll likely have a wider variety of choices to make, all depending on your goals and interests. The bigger your school, the more likely you are to have a lot of electives to choose from, so be aware that if you go to a tiny high school, your elective options may still be somewhat limited.

"If keeping your grades up is important to you, the most important thing you can do is turn your work in on time. It's easier to ask to redo an assignment than to get credit for late work, and having a "0" in the gradebook will sink your grade fast. Teachers also have huge volumes of grading. If your work is turned in on time, it will be graded with the rest, but if you turn it in late, it could be a while before a teacher can get around to grading it and putting it in the book, meaning your "0" could be sitting there for a long time. If you must prove eligibility for sports or your parents check grades a lot, this could cause trouble for you."

Summer, High School Tutor

YOU ARE GRADED DIFFERENTLY. Your teachers in middle school were probably more lenient when it came to things like late homework or not following the directions of an assignment. Because you were growing as a person and student, they were more likely to look at your past record of trying your best and give you a little leeway. Teachers in high school are just as interested in seeing you succeed, but they aren't as likely to accept excuses. "I forgot" simply won't work anymore, so you'll be expected to keep a calendar and stay on top of your assignment deadlines. In high school, teachers will likely deduct points if you don't get your homework done and turned in on time. They may even refuse to accept your work altogether past a certain point. You will also have to pay closer attention to things like rubrics (documents showing how you will be graded on a particular assignment) and course calendars. Large projects will require more of your time, so you'll need to get started well in advance. Pushing things to the last minute probably won't work out the same way it used to.

If you do fall behind, you can of course talk to your teacher about getting caught up. While high school teachers are indeed usually more strict than middle school teachers, they are also still compassionate educators who generally want to see students do well. However, it will likely be on you to recognize when your grades are slipping and initiate those conversations with your teacher. High school teachers typically have hundreds of students at a time and can't "hand hold" every single one through the process of getting their grades up, so you will need to take the initiative. Keep track of your grades, recognize when they're slipping, and ask for help putting in the work to catch up. Demonstrate that you take responsibility for your grades and want to make things right and put in the effort.

YOU TAKE ON MORE RESPONSIBILITY. Because you are more independent in your classes, managing a larger workload, and are ultimately more in charge of your education, you're also generally expected to take on more responsibility in high school, both in and out of class. Increasingly, you will be expected to handle things for yourself rather than having someone else handle them

for you. You may find yourself taking on new responsibilities you haven't in the past, such as caring for younger siblings or accepting babysitting jobs, working part-time, getting yourself to and from school, minding the house while your parents are gone, or any other number of tasks. Your job will be to exhibit the maturity you've developed when taking on new responsibilities.

YOU HAVE TO SPEAK UP FOR YOURSELF AND ADVOCATE FOR YOUR NEEDS. In middle school, your parents probably helped you if you got into a tough situation, academic or otherwise. In high school, you may have to deal with new situations on your own, such as speaking with a teacher about homework, talking to a counselor about getting into a course level better suited to your skills, or making your voice heard in clubs and activities. The less you can rely on adults to handle things for you, the more you'll develop confidence in your own ability to stand up for yourself and communicate when you have a need. To succeed, you must develop the ability to figure out how to identify a problem, come up with a solution, and then act. This doesn't mean that you can't or shouldn't reach out for help if you're in over your head, only that you must recognize that knowing when to reach out for help is part of advocating for yourself.

"I love making friends with the freshmen; it reminds me of giving advice to my younger sister. As a teen, sometimes it's weird talking to adults about stuff, but you can talk to older kids and they'll be there for you. Other teens know things parents and teachers don't, like how to handle situations with other kids on social media. My advice to freshmen is to try and make friends with an older student who will have your back and look out for you if you're in a tough spot."

Leah, High School Senior

EXPLORING YOUR INTERESTS

One of your underlying goals throughout high school should be to develop your interests. That means trying out new things that intrigue you but with which you don't yet have experience. There's no harm in trying something and determining it's not for you, but you might surprise yourself if you remain open-minded in pursuing new interests. Here are some meaningful ways to explore your interests as a high school student.

Elective Classes

One easy way you can dig deeper into your potential interests is by taking elective classes. Although you'll be required to take a variety of core classes such as math, English, history, and science, your choice of electives can point you in the direction of a future college major. Not to say that your core classes cannot spark a life-long interest, but electives offer you more personal choice and the freedom to try new topics on for size.

Most schools offer electives in areas such as computers, art, economics, foreign language, or music. Some schools offer very high-level or specialized English, history, science, or math topics as electives, as well. Examples of these could be an in-depth study on medieval literature or an exploration of how forensic science plays into crime scene investigations. Still other electives may be connected to participation in clubs or special programs, such as a public speaking course you might take alongside participation in the debate team or a business course you're expected to take as part of a school-to-work program.

You can get the most out of elective classes if you have an inkling of what you might want to do when you grow up. For example, you may think you'd like to be in business someday, sitting in an office overlooking the city. You can begin to realize that dream by taking economics as an elective. Or perhaps you think you'd rather be building high-rises instead of sitting in them. If your high school offers an architecture class or technology courses geared toward future engineers, these could be great options for you! Other electives, such as Spanish, graphic design, or coding, can help you develop other widely marketable skills, giving you an edge no matter what you decide to do later.

Clubs and Activities

Explore your interests via clubs and activities. High schools offer many extracurricular activities that allow you to learn beyond the four walls of your classroom. You may think these activities are there just so you can have some fun and make friends. While that's certainly true, they also give you the opportunity to find out what your interests are. Extracurricular activities can help you determine which goals you want to set and then figure out how to reach them. Every school is different, so you'll have to find out what your high school specifically offers, but here is a list of clubs and activities commonly available at high schools.

"As a freshman, I got into band camp and got to know kids in the band. When I was walking through the halls, I knew more people than just my fellow freshmen. If you know people around you, you'll feel more comfortable. Then, you'll be more willing to do new things."

Maddy, High School Junior

Options for Clubs and Activities

Bands and Choirs

- Marching Band
- Pep Band
- Orchestra
- Jazz Band/Jazz Choir
- Show Choir
- Women's and Men's Choirs
- Acapella Groups/Glee Club

Chess Club

Speech and Debate
(sometimes called "Forensics")

Student Council

Computer Club

Homecoming/Prom Committees

Knowledge Bowl/Trivia Club

Future Business Leaders of America (FBLA)

Peer Mediators

Theater and Performance Groups

- Musical Theatre
- Drama Club
- Improv Comedy Troupe
- Dance Teams
- Color Guard (Marching Band)

Athletics (including Cheerleading)

Mock Trial

US Army Junior ROTC

Model United Nations

School Newspaper

Science Club

Yearbook

"I wish I had joined more clubs and done more activities in my freshman year. If you join a club as a freshman, you can be a leader of the club when you get to be a junior or senior. If you wait to join when you're a junior, you'll be at the bottom end. Colleges want you to be a leader, so you have to start trying out activities when you're a freshman."

Desi, High School Junior

Often, there is some form of "Clubs and Activities Night" offered at the beginning of the year for students to see what's available at their school. Your school may also have ways for students to start their own clubs, so if it has always been your dream to have an Anime Club or a Teen Birdwatcher's Society, it might just be a matter of asking your counselor how you can start one.

Explore in Your Free Time

Don't forget that your school isn't the only place where you can explore your interests! It might not seem like you have a ton of time to explore interests on your own with the increased workload that comes with high school classes, but if you manage your time wisely, you should still have plenty of time for yourself on evenings or weekends. Whether you're trying to perfect a complicated move on your skateboard or spending an afternoon watercolor painting just for fun, any time you devote to developing your personal hobbies is a wise investment. Try and carve out a little time outside of school each week for your personal interests.

"Some kids that I counsel know what they want to be. Others don't have a clue, and some have an inkling. Your high school courses can help you reach that goal and, if you don't have a goal, they can help you explore what you want to do. No idea? Then go nuts...take whatever sounds interesting!"

Manuel, *Guidance Counselor*

"All of my very, very best memories from high school are from clubs—I was in track, theater, color guard, and yearbook, so I was always busy but I loved that! Now that I'm a high school teacher, the best part of my week is coaching the trivia team. Clubs are amazing because they don't have the same rules and restrictions as classes, so students get to be themselves and form meaningful bonds with each other over something they love. Extracurriculars enrich your high school experience, no question!"

Cameron, *High School Art Teacher*

Volunteer Work

High schools often offer opportunities for you to do volunteer work. Are you interested in working with younger kids? In being a lawyer? In helping those who are sick? You can volunteer to help out at a preschool, in a law office, or at a hospital, for instance. Some schools may even require you to submit a certain number of volunteer hours as a condition of graduation, but you are free to volunteer well beyond those required hours. By volunteering and working alongside people who are doing the things you may like to do, you can quickly judge if you really do like a given field. You are also developing critical skills related to empathy, communication, and service that will prove useful in your adult life.

BUILDING MEANINGFUL RELATIONSHIPS IN HIGH SCHOOL

For many teens, one of the most overwhelming aspects of their first year of high school has to do with the sheer number of people they meet. You'll have a whole slew of new teachers, counselors, administrators, coaches, peers, and more to meet during your first few weeks of school. Besides the stress of trying to remember that many names, it can be overwhelming trying to figure out how to navigate all these new kinds of social relationships. The tips here can help you consider a few of the common types of relationships you'll need to develop.

"I participated in two different volunteer opportunities during high school. One was through my school and involved tutoring middle school students who struggled with reading. The other was a program each summer through my church where we would help do various home repairs for low-income families. I learned a lot about myself and the world through both opportunities. Now I'm hoping to go into non-profit work involving building literacy in low-income communities, so those experiences definitely shaped me."

Priya, College Sophomore

Making New Friends

Entire books have been written on the topic of making friends as a teenager, but the basics come down to this: be brave! Worry less about the idea that your friendship could be rejected and more about mustering the courage to ask to sit with someone at lunch, invite someone from class over to play video games, or introduce yourself to the person next to you in the assigned seating arrangement. One of the beautiful things about high school is that there are endless opportunities to make friends, so long as you are willing to make the effort to talk to people in your classes, clubs, and activities. If you do struggle with overcoming shyness or social anxiety, your counselor may be able to offer you some tips for dealing with concerns that arise. However, even the shyest person can find a kindred spirit if they look for opportunities to talk to people who seem like they have similar interests. Sometimes, all it takes is a shared love of the same TV show or musician to spark a lifelong friendship. The worst that can happen is you get a no. Just remember that what other people think of you is none of your business! Brush it off and invest your energy into someone who wants to be your friend.

"My school didn't have a hockey team, so I played through a club in town on nights and weekends. It was cool because some of the other kids on the club were from my school, but lots were from other high schools. I liked making friends from other schools so I could get to know different kinds of people. I even ended up going to another school's prom with a close friend from my club and now we're dating!"

Flynn, Recent High School Graduate

Establishing Strong Teacher Relationships

Your teachers are real-life adult human beings who are *not* your parents and who you get to see all the time! This means they can be some of the most insightful voices. As a person who is essentially learning how to be an adult during high school, you can turn to your teachers for wisdom and support while you work things out.

When you first meet your teachers, they will likely have activities designed for you to get to know them, them to get to know you, and the students in the class to get to know each other. Don't blow these activities off as unimportant because when you participate, your teacher can start to understand you beyond your face and name. If your teacher has office hours, it's a good idea to attend early in the year just to get to know them a bit and talk about school outside of the classroom.

As you become more and more comfortable with certain teachers or other adults in advising positions, such as coaches, librarians, and counselors, you may start to think of some of them as mentors. When this happens, recognize that you don't have to restrict your conversations with them to school stuff. If you find yourself comfortable with a particular adult in your school, look for opportunities to get to know them in appropriate settings outside of class, too, such as by coming to their office hours to say hi or asking if you can visit their classroom to share lunch one day. They may be busy, so it might be hard for them to find time for stuff like that, but don't take it personally. Truthfully, hanging out with students is one of the best parts of the job for most high school teachers. They understand and appreciate teenagers for who they are and will probably be pumped that you want to get to know them or ask for advice.

Getting to Know Your Guidance Counselor

Similar to the advice for getting to know teachers, you will want to make it a point to establish a relationship with your guidance counselor early on in your high school career. If something happens, whether it be a scheduling issue, a concern about a standardized test, or a conflict with a close friend, the guidance counselor is the person trained to do exactly what it sounds like, which is guide and counsel you through the issue. Your guidance counselor is also the person you'll want to share your hopes and dreams with so that they can help you plan a course toward achieving your goals. For instance, if you know you want to get into a highly competitive college like Stanford University, that's the kind of thing you'd want to share with your guidance counselor during your first year so they can help keep you on track with the steps you'll need to complete to reach that goal. Don't be afraid to ask your guidance counselor any question about navigating high school life. Their job is to guide you, so let them do that!

Come to my office hours, students! I am sitting there waiting to talk to students during that time no matter what, so it's much more fun if they show up. I don't care if you just want to tell me about a cool movie or show me pictures of your new puppy or whatever...come to office hours!

Amy, High School Journalism Teacher

CHOOSING CLASSES

Some of the most critical decisions you're going to have to make during high school concern the classes you take. Both the types of classes you take and the level at which you take them have an impact on your education experience.

Standard Courses

Most students will take standard courses in all their core subjects. At your school, standard courses probably will not have any special name, since they are the base-level courses that the majority of students will take. They are designed to ensure that every student at the school meets the same graduation requirements by the time they get through high school.

Accelerated ("Honors") Courses

If your high school offers them, some students may opt to take "honors" courses instead of standard courses. These classes may be called something different at your school, but the term generally refers to accelerated, advanced courses aimed at students who perform above the average for their grade level in a given topic. They tend to cover more material in greater detail and at a faster pace than standard courses, allowing students who excel in that topic to stay better engaged by challenging themselves.

Honors-level classes require more from you. You'll do more reading and writing that demands deeper, more complex understanding of the subject matter. Classes at this level develop advanced critical thinking skills by asking you to interpret situations, texts, and events and to analyze the information you are given. Honors classes allow you to really delve deep into a subject and are especially important if you are looking to apply to competitive colleges where students are expected to have such advanced skills upon admission. In an honors class, teachers will expect you to participate actively in class discussions. Your goal as an honors student is generally to develop a deep enough understanding of a topic that you can speak freely about it in a sophisticated manner.

Some students are on what is often called an "honors track," meaning that their education plan includes taking honors courses in as many subjects as possible, whenever possible. Other students prefer to pick and choose which subjects they might like to challenge themselves in, like taking standard English and social studies courses while opting for honors math and science. Still other students may try to take honors courses only to find that the pace is too much for them to handle when combined with the rest of their workload. In this situation, students may then decide to move from an honors section to a standard section for one or more subjects.

No one decision is a better approach to the topic of honors courses, so long as you are making choices that allow you to make the most of your education without spreading yourself too thin. Your parent(s) or guardian(s) and guidance counselor can help you make decisions about which course level to take, but remember that *you* are also an important voice in that conversation. If you feel like you're drowning in an honors class, don't stay in it just because your parents want you to or you've been told that it's a good idea for college. Ultimately, you need to be in the class that is ideal for your learning needs and where you are mastering the material while still being challenged. If you're unsure which level would be a good fit, ask to meet with your teacher since they will have a good sense of how you perform in that subject.

> When I was a freshman, I was intimidated by the older kids' appearance of greatness and their academic accomplishments. I thought, 'Wow, I can't get to their level.' But don't give up on working toward a challenge because you think there's too much competition, especially if it's something you really want to do.
>
> Fabian, High School Senior

Advanced Placement (AP®) Courses

Advanced Placement (AP®) courses are a type of accelerated course specifically designed to help prepare students for college. They may be offered in addition to honors courses, or they may be the only type of accelerated courses available at your school. While there are 38 AP exams offered by the College Board, the courses available to you will depend on your school, so talk with your guidance counselor to see which options you have. Different schools and districts also have different rules about AP courses. Some schools may allow you to start taking as many AP classes as you want as early as your freshman year, but most will either limit the number of AP classes you may take in a year or restrict the courses to students above a certain grade level.

This guide covers AP exams more in depth in Chapter 8, but the basic thing you need to know is that they're a great way to potentially earn college credit while still in high school. That's because when you take an AP course, you have an AP exam at the end of the year. The scores required for credit vary depending on the college, but if you earn a high enough score, many colleges will give you college credit for AP exams. If you earn enough of these credits, you may even be able to shave time off your degree later. On top of that, you'll also impress college admission offices with the fact that you're taking AP classes. Colleges look favorably on students who work hard in high school and are not afraid to challenge themselves in the classroom.

The AP exams are given to students across the United States in May and are scored on a level from 1–5, with 5 being the best. Most colleges want you to get a 3 or above in the exam to earn college credit. While most AP exams are about the same level of difficulty, there are a few (like AP Studio Art and AP Music Theory) that are notorious for being difficult to pass—your guidance counselor can help paint a realistic portrait of which AP courses have tough exams and what kind of work is required to do well.

During the college admission process, some colleges "weight" the different levels of classes you take. For instance, they'll give you more GPA points for an A in an honors or AP class than they would for an A in a regular class. Your high school may also do the same with your transcript, depending on their policies. An A in a class at a regular level may count as a 4, while an A in an honors or AP class would count as a 5, and a B in an honors or AP class would count as a 4. With enough A's in standard courses and AP courses, some students even graduate high school with a GPA above 4.0, meaning an A++ grade average.

Other Types of Accelerated Courses

Your school may have accelerated courses outside of the honors and AP framework. For instance, they may allow advanced students to conduct independent studies or take online courses to challenge themselves. They may also have concurrent enrollment courses, meaning courses that are designed to give students credit from local community colleges. If you are generally interested in accelerated learning, ask your guidance counselor which specific opportunities exist at your school.

Planning for Accelerated Courses

Even if your school's policies won't allow you to take many honors or AP classes until your junior or senior year, the time to start planning for this high academic level is in your freshman year. For instance, if you know that you'd like to enter AP classes as a junior or senior, you can better prepare for this likelihood by taking honors level courses as a freshman or sophomore. AP and honors classes are very competitive and sometimes there is competition to get a spot in one, so there is little wiggle room for poor grades or performance as you move from freshman, to sophomore, to junior year. That doesn't mean that you're sunk if you struggled earlier in your high school career—especially if you're motivated—but it does mean that if you can, you'll want to start thinking about challenging yourself and developing strong study habits early on so that you're ready for AP when you get to it.

Are You Ready for an Accelerated Course?

Sometimes, you don't even have to worry about this because it could be determined for you by a placement test, teacher selection, or some other placement method. Occasionally, students can apply or petition to take an honors class if they feel they are up to the challenge but haven't been identified for one by a teacher. If your school allows you to take the initiative, you should consider whether taking an accelerated course is the right choice for you. Many students do well in accelerated classes. Others struggle, even though they may have done very well in a regular-level class. It may be hard to tell which type you are before you get to the course, but being honest with yourself and having some frank discussions with your guardian(s) and teachers can help you figure out if it's a challenge worth undertaking for you.

Just to repeat for emphasis: You must be honest with yourself and with your parent(s) or guardian(s). Sometimes, parents see their kids through rose-colored glasses and think they're geniuses. Meanwhile, their child may be smart but nonetheless struggling to cope with the transition to high school and may have fallen behind. Or perhaps science seemed easy and intuitive until they got to physics and now it's throwing them for a loop and they need to slow down. Your mindset has a lot to do with how well you'll do in high school, so it's important to take courses at a level that fits you so

you can stay positive. Trying to force yourself into an honors class that's above your current abilities or letting yourself become bored out of your mind in a standard course when you should be in honors are equally good ways to quickly burn yourself out.

If you only want to take an honors course here and there rather than trying to stay on an honors track, a good rule of thumb is to take accelerated classes in the subjects that "come easy" to you or that you feel more passionately about and stick with the regular track for classes that aren't necessarily your forté. If you've never taken honors before, start out by adding one honors course in your best subject. If you find that your workload can handle it, you can always talk to your guidance counselor about adding more later. Just don't take an honors course or stay in a standard course only because your friend decided to do so…you are not your friend, so pick the classes that are right for you!

"I had been on the honors track all through middle school, but when I got to high school, I couldn't keep up with math anymore. I ended up having to talk to my counselor to ask to repeat Algebra 2 in a regular class instead of honors. I felt ashamed at first—I'm supposed to be an 'honors' student!—but honestly, I was so relieved to finally be learning the concepts for real again. None of my friends cared what math class I was in, and I was a lot less stressed once I was in the right class. It's no big deal if honors classes aren't right for you."

Mylee, Recent High School Graduate

"Remedial" Courses: Removing the Stigma

In addition to accelerated types of learning, like AP or honors, your school may also have remedial courses. These are courses designed to help students who are struggling or performing below the average of their peers in a given topic. Remedial courses tend to move at a slower pace and focus on the most important information students need rather than going into as much detail as a standard or honors course would. Assignments may be modified to accommodate the slower pace. Generally, students must be recommended for the course by their teacher or other school personnel—you can't just take a remedial course because you want an "easier" version of a class (and the students who genuinely need these courses wouldn't usually consider them easy).

Many schools are moving away from using the term "remedial." While it is accurate that these courses are meant to remedy various learning challenges, the term has become associated with being less intelligent, which is extremely inaccurate. Therefore, if these types of classes do exist at your school, it's very likely that they are called something different. Your school may also offer courses that are not themselves slower-paced versions of standard courses but rather specialized support classes designed to help students develop abilities needed in any subject. For example, students who struggle with reading or who do not speak English as a native language may end up in literacy development courses so that they are better prepared to do the reading and writing necessary for all their classes.

If you are placed in one of these courses, don't let any sense of stigma get you down! These courses are designed to offer structure and support to help you reach the standards you need to get a high school diploma. There is no shame in needing extra help or in benefitting from a slightly slower pace. It's critical that you learn the basics of the subject before you graduate, so if a remedial course can get you there, that's excellent! In fact, teachers for these courses are often specially trained to help students who are overcoming different types of learning difficulties. It can be

"My school has this program called STAR. Everyone knows they're the slower-paced classes, so I was kind of freaking out when I got put there after I had a bad car accident and missed part of sophomore year. I didn't want my friends to make fun of me. No one did, though, and because of those classes, I had help to catch up on everything I missed when my broken back was healing. I'm glad that program existed for me and the other kids who needed it."

Kwan, High School Senior

beneficial to end up in a course where there is more space and awareness to help you succeed. You may find that having individualized attention matched to your learning style even allows you to eventually move back into a standard education classroom, should you desire to do so. In short, don't think of it as a bad thing if you are recommended for a course like this. Instead, see it as an opportunity to be supported in your learning.

YOUR GPA AND TRANSCRIPT

Your GPA and your transcript are both related to what you've probably always called a "report card." Simply put, the word *transcript* describes a document that contains information on all the courses you have taken or are currently taking during your time in high school. Most transcripts include the grades you received for each course and your grade point average (GPA), which is a numerical representation of the average grade you received across all the courses you've taken. Both the transcript and GPA are important because they can influence college applications and future employment alike.

Your GPA (Grade Point Average)

In short, the GPA is the average of all your grades starting from your freshman year. A little planning in your freshman year can go a long way toward a better GPA when you graduate. There's no getting around the fact that your GPA is important to your future. It affects what college you can attend, the kind of accelerated courses you can take, your ongoing eligibility for clubs and sports, your ability to apply for certain academic and athletic scholarships, and the career or college programs for which you may be able to qualify. It is important to think of your GPA as a reflection of your total effort throughout all of high school, including freshman year. The best way to have a good GPA as a senior is to take things seriously from the start.

One good way to stay on top of your GPA is to understand how it is computed. Different schools have their own ways of totaling a GPA, but in general, here is how most high schools do letter grades:

Letter Grading Scale

A = 4 points   C = 2 points   F = 0 points

B = 3 points   D = 1 point

On this scale, a grade point average of 4.0 represents straight A's. Some schools give higher points for grades earned in honors or AP courses. Some schools or colleges may also weight + and − grades, meaning that a B+, a B, and a B− would all be weighted slightly differently. At schools that do this, the scale might look something like this:

The scale that weights + and − grades is the scale typically used by colleges, while the more simplified scale is most common in high schools, where students may also have a point added for certain accelerated courses (for example, a B in an AP course would receive 4 points instead of 3). It's important to speak with a guidance counselor to determine what sort of scale your GPA is calculated on at your high school.

GPA SCALE	
Letter Grade	**4.0 Scale**
A+	4 Points
A	3.67 Points
A−	3.33 Points
B+	3 Points
B	2.67 Points
B−	2.33 Points
C+	2 Points
C	1.67 Points
C−	1.33 Points
D+	1 Point
D	0.67 Points
D−	0.33 Points
F	0 Points

To understand why these points matter, let's look at a hypothetical student's grades for one semester.

Understanding Grade Point Average

GIORGIO STUDENTMANN – SOPHOMORE, FALL 2021		
Honors English	A	(4 points)
World History	B	(3 points)
Web Design	A	(4 points)
Geometry	C	(2 points)
Spanish 2	B	(3 points)
Physical Education	A	(4 points)
Jazz Band	A	(4 points)
Chemistry	C	(2 points)
Old Cumulative GPA:		3.75
Term GPA (Fall 2021):		3.25
New Cumulative GPA (Fall 2021):		3.5

- The grades total 26 points. Divide that by the number of classes, which is 8, and you get a GPA of 3.25 for one semester. Usually, your GPA is rounded to no more than 2 decimal places.
- This is the student's GPA from their freshman year. You will not have a cumulative GPA until after you complete your first semester of high school.
- This is the student's GPA from the current term, which in this case is Fall 2021.
- This is the student's new cumulative GPA. It's an average of the old cumulative GPA (3.75) and the new term GPA (3.25).

GIORGIO STUDENTMANN – SOPHOMORE, SPRING 2022		
Honors English	A	(4 points)
World History	A	(4 points)
Advanced Drawing	A	(4 points)
Geometry	B	(3 points)
Spanish 2	B	(3 points)
Woodworking	A	(4 points)
Jazz Band	A	(4 points)
Chemistry	B	(3 points)
Old Cumulative GPA:		3.5
Term GPA (Spring 2022):		3.63
New Cumulative GPA (Spring 2022):		3.57

Now, imagine our hypothetical student, Giorgio, wants to apply himself to raising his GPA the next semester. To do so, he would need to receive a term GPA above 3.5, meaning that he has to get mostly A's with a few B's.

Let's take a look at the next semester report card and see how he did.

- The grades total 29 points. Divide that by the number of classes, which is 8, and you get a GPA of 3.625 for one term. Rounding his GPA to 2 decimal places, Giorgio's GPA for this term is 3.63.
- This is the student's cumulative GPA from the end of the last term, Fall 2021.
- This is the student's GPA from the current term, Spring 2022.
- This is the student's new average. Giorgio did it—he raised his GPA!

"Yes, GPA is important, no doubt. If your GPA is lower than you hoped when you graduate, though, remember that it's not the only part of your application! Our job is to look at the total package, not just reduce you to one number. It's an important factor but not the only factor."

Adaeze, College Admissions Officer

To be even more accurate, many schools do not simply average term GPAs together to create a cumulative GPA, as in the example from the graphic. Instead, they would consider the total number of courses you have over all the terms you've attended high school and then calculate accordingly. In this case, let's say that Giorgio earned 60 total points for 16 classes during his freshman year. Then, if we look at the two report cards here, we can see that Giorgio earned 55 total points for 16 classes during his sophomore year. That means he had 115 total points over a total of 32 classes, so $115 \div 32 = 3.59$ cumulative GPA. You'll notice that this is very close to but slightly different than the way of calculating cumulative GPA from the graphic, so make sure you know which way your school uses. Remember to also ask your guidance counselor about courses that may be weighted "heavier" (meaning worth more grade points) and whether your school assigns different values for plus and minus grades.

Your Transcript

An official transcript is a history of the classes you took and the grades you achieved in those classes. Some transcripts may also include other data, such as test scores, the names of teachers you've had, data on absences, comments about classroom behavior sent home on report cards, and any other information that may be included in report cards. Your official transcript is one of numerous things colleges ask for to assess what kind of a student you are. You may also be asked to provide a transcript for certain types of employment.

An unofficial transcript will generally contain all the same information as your regular transcript but in a less secure format so that it's easy for you to look at and not official enough to submit to a school. Whenever a school or employer asks for an official transcript, which is more common when verifying a college degree than a high school diploma, make sure you do what's necessary to have an official version sent.

All schools send a school profile along with your transcript to colleges, showing pertinent information, including the community in which the school is located, the student population, how many honors and AP classes are offered, the number of periods in a day that classes are offered, socioeconomic demographics of the school, and more. When colleges look at your transcript, they're looking at not only your final GPA but also the kinds of courses you took and to see whether you challenged yourself enough during your high school years. Did you take courses that stretched you academically, such as honors and AP classes, or did you take only those classes you were required to take? Students are evaluated based on what courses they have taken within the confines of what their school offers, meaning admissions officers will know if you didn't take AP courses because you didn't want to take them or because they simply didn't exist at your school.

Sometimes, transcripts tell admissions officers a story. For instance, if they see that you had low grades freshman year but really bounced back sophomore year, that can reflect well on you. Or if they see that you got a B in an honors English class the year after getting an A in a standard English class, then that likely shows that you're a person who is willing to take a risk if it means challenging yourself to grow. Don't assume that having a perfect 4.0 GPA is the only way to make an impact with your transcript, though it certainly doesn't hurt!

Important Things to Know About Transcripts

Your transcript is basically a one-page report card that records all the grades you have earned from 9th grade on, including summer school, community college courses you may have taken, etc. If you took any high school classes before high school, such as an advanced math or language class in 8th grade, you will also most likely get credit for those classes on your high school transcript, but not always—so check with your school counselor. When a college reviews your transcript, they consider who you are in the context of your own school. Your school profile informs colleges of every class and offering at your school. By matching your courses up with the school profile (and reading your teacher and counselor recommendations), colleges have a good idea of how you fared within the course selection offered in your school. Did you take the most rigorous courses offered at your school? Did you shy away from challenges in certain areas? Did you struggle to overcome learning challenges but eventually succeed? Ideally, your transcript can answer these questions.

Transcripts differ from school to school. You need to find out what data your school records on your transcript. For example, say you got good grades but missed a lot of classes because you just didn't feel like showing up. If you're gunning for a top university but your transcript shows how many unexcused absences you had, suddenly your great grades might not look as good.

Questions to Ask Your Guidance Counselor about Your Transcript

- Does it include tallies of excused and unexcused absences?

- Are we graded on a quarter, trimester, or semester system, and how will this be demonstrated on the transcript?

- Will the transcript show plus grades (like C+) and minus grades (like B–), and if so, will those be weighted differently than regular letter grades?

- Is any information about classroom behavior or school discipline included on the transcript?

- Some schools don't count the freshman year, or the first semester of your freshman year, when adding up your GPA. Will my freshman year count?

- Will my class rank be shown on my transcript, and if so, how?

- Will my GPA be "weighted," meaning that I get an extra point for certain classes (like AP)?

- Will information from outside of school, such as volunteer work, be documented on my transcript?

- How is cumulative GPA calculated—based on total number of classes or by averaging term GPAs?

Another thing to be on the lookout for when submitting a transcript to a college is whether they allow you to explain parts of your transcript. For instance, on the part of your application with essay prompts, one prompt may include an opportunity to clarify any information that is necessary for interpreting your high school grades. This isn't the place to try and explain away any slacking off you did, but if you experienced a setback outside of your control, such as recovering from a car accident while in school, dealing with a mental health episode, or going through a traumatic home event, it may be useful to indicate where in your transcript this could have impacted your performance. If the admissions committee knows that the term you got a 2.8 GPA was also the term when your dad passed away or when you were first diagnosed with social anxiety, they are likely to give you some leeway for a few "off" grades. Recently, so many students had their grades affected by the switch to remote learning during the COVID-19 pandemic that many schools are also giving students a chance to respond to essay questions on that topic specifically. Note that not all schools will give you options for explaining your grades, so be aware of that going into the application process.

How Does a College Evaluate Your Transcript?

Like many things you'll encounter in this book, the answer to that question depends largely on the colleges you're applying to. However, here are a few things colleges commonly consider when looking at a student's high school transcript.

- **DEGREE OF DIFFICULTY:** This refers specifically to the degree of difficulty of the coursework you took within the context of what was available to you at your school. Did you get straight A's but never take a single honors course? If so, it might seem to some schools that you didn't push yourself enough. Be sure to reach further in classes and challenge yourself in areas that come easier to you when you are able. Again, don't take advanced classes just for the sake of it, but look for subjects in which to challenge yourself, or stretch yourself to take a difficult elective now and again.

- **GRADE PATTERNS:** Colleges look at how you did in school—from your first semester to the next, year by year, and class by class. Did your grade go up, stay the same, or go down from the first to second semester? One single low scoring term won't sink you if they can see that your overall pattern involves achieving good grades.

- **GRADE TRENDS:** Did things continue to improve as you advanced each year? Did they stay the same? Or as school got more challenging and you got older, did your grades drop in some or all subjects? Did you seem on track until the end of junior year, when your grades suddenly took a dive? How you progress is a key indicator to colleges of the kind of student you might be on their campus.

- **EXTRA ACADEMIC ENRICHMENT:** Did you go beyond what was offered in your school and seek additional academic experiences (community college, summer programs, independent study, research, etc.)? Are you academically curious outside of the classroom?

TIPS FOR A SMOOTH START TO HIGH SCHOOL

There is no magic formula for succeeding at high school. Sure, there are plenty of guides (including the one in your hands!) that can help you figure out the best way to take on high school life, but a lot will depend on where you live, what your school is like, the kind of activities you get involved in, your own personality, and about a million other factors. No two people have the exact same high school experience, so a lot of what you figure out will simply come with time—as you move from freshman to senior year, you'll get older and wiser. Eventually, you may even find the tables turned, meaning you'll be the one handing out advice to incoming freshman. High school is largely about the experience, so first and foremost, try and make the most of that experience. That said, these tips can help make your transition to high school a smooth one.

Use Goal setting to Motivate You

Goals are important because if you have a rough idea of where you're headed, you'll have an easier time getting there. As a teenager, you've probably already set some goals in your life before. However, the idea of intentional goal setting may still seem new. Here are some ways to maximize your high school goal setting.

Start High School with a List of Goals

Write down a list of things you want to accomplish in high school, both academically and in your social life. You might even want to put your list away somewhere so you can return to it later and see what you've accomplished or how your goals have changed. Try and set a timeline for these goals, but remember that those timelines should be tentative, meaning "not set in stone," because it's okay to be flexible with yourself. Obviously, your goals will likely shift over time, but having a list of goals will help you stay motivated and give you something to work toward.

Make Your Goals Specific

Many people are tempted to be vague when setting goals because they think that a vague goal will be easier to achieve. In fact, the inverse is true—specific goals are easier to break down into a series of steps than vague goals. Because you can make a plan for how to accomplish them, it's easier to measure progress and envision success. See the graphic in this section for examples.

As you might notice, many of the specific versions of goals include potential timelines or details about frequency. For instance, while "I want to ride my bike

VAGUE VS. SPECIFIC GOALS	
Vague Goal	**Specific Goals**
I want to be a better student.	• I want to turn in all my homework on time this year. • I want to take notes during every class. • I want to maintain a 3.5 or higher GPA this term.
I want to be healthier.	• I want to increase my activity by trying out for football in the fall and track and field in the spring. • I want to ride my bike to school at least three days a week this semester. • I want to try a new way of cooking vegetables every week.
I want to be more creative.	• I want to practice drawing for one hour every weekend. • I want to write a new short story in my journal every week. • I want to take a digital photography class and learn how to edit my photos.

more often" is a more specific goal than "I want to be healthier," it is even more specific to determine a frequency for the activity and a timeline for measuring if you were successful. If your goal is "I want to ride my bike to school at least three days a week this semester," then at the end of the semester, you'll have a clear way of determining if you met that goal or not.

Think Backwards

If you don't know what your short-term goal should be, it may help to think backwards from a long-term goal. Start by considering where you'd like to end up and then trace backward through the steps you'll have to take to get there. For example, if your goal is to someday live in a different country for a year, then you might first try to get specific by narrowing it down to a country. If the answer is France, then your next step is to think about what goals you might need to reach to get there. As a freshman in high school, "Go live in France for a year" is a great long-term goal, but you might first need to also set the short-term goal of "Take a French class as a freshman" to get there.

Set Both Short- and Long-Term Goals

Speaking of long-term and short-term goals, it's important to have both. Many times, they will be interrelated, such as the example of learning French being a short-term goal that helps achieve the long-term goal of one day living in France. If all your goals are long-term, it can be disappointing to feel like you're never accomplishing milestones along the way. Conversely, if all your goals are short-term, you won't have a big picture idea of where you're heading. You need to set both kinds of goals so you can break your dreams down into accomplishable steps.

Get Involved

If you're a naturally outgoing person, then you might not need to be reminded of the importance of getting involved in your high school community. However, if you're shy or tend to keep to yourself, it can be tempting to stay on the sidelines of high school life. There's no doubt that some aspects of high school social life are high stakes, so the idea of getting involved might even

be intimidating. However, getting involved with activities, events, and traditions at your school is also an important way to make friends, learn life skills, and feel integrated into your community. You'll get the most out of high school if you find comfortable places to knit yourself into the social fabric of your school.

Get Started on Sports, Clubs, and Activities Early

We've already talked about how clubs and activities help narrow your interests and focus you on what you want to do in the future. But extracurricular activities also serve an important social function for high school students. Through extracurriculars, you'll find friends who like the same things you do. You'll be with older kids, so you'll get to know some juniors and seniors. You'll gain confidence in yourself as you work together with your peers. You'll become comfortable with being in high school a lot quicker than if you hang around on the fringes looking in instead of

> "If a student is struggling in my class but I can see that they're trying to participate every day, I'm more likely to give them leeway if they ask for a second chance to redo an assignment or turn something in late. I know they aren't just making an excuse because it's obvious they're engaged with the class based on how often they participate in discussion.
>
> Michelle, High School English Teacher

being in the middle of the action, whether it's on a soccer team, chess club, or any other activity. Because these social parts of school help you adjust to life as a high school student, you can get the maximum benefit from them by getting involved early. However, even if you join your first club as a senior, you'll still benefit from it.

Speak Up in Class

A big part of high school grading revolves around participation. In fact, your teachers might even explicitly indicate that participation in class is one of the grades you'll receive. If a teacher makes participation 10% of your grade, that might not sound like a lot, but it means that you can't get an A in the course without participating on a regular basis. You don't have to deliver a TED Talk every time you speak up, but make it a goal to contribute at least one comment or question per class. If you do, you'll find yourself more involved with classroom learning, less bored (since you're paying closer attention to what's going on), and typically better prepared come exams or big projects. Oh, and it will make you look good to your teachers, which never hurts.

Stand Up for Important Causes

In high school, you're likely to find more opportunities to speak up and get involved with causes that are important to you. You may have the opportunity to join clubs or activities that align with your ideologies, such as the recycling club, or you may have the opportunity to get involved with events and fundraisers that benefit charitable causes. If you are politically minded, you may also want to write to local politicians to discuss causes that matter to you. As you start to identify what your priorities are, don't be afraid to get involved in the causes that stand out to you.

Put Yourself Out There

Listen, if you're shy, you've probably been told dozens of times now that you just need to "put yourself out there" and things will go better. Suffice to say, it's easier said than done. However, high school is an important time for practicing this very skill. There are lots of low-stakes ways to practice this skill if it's something you need to work on. Maybe asking your crush to homecoming with a grand gesture feels high-risk. However, asking that hilarious person in your science class who you want to make friends with to be your lab partner is a much lower-risk way of practicing a similar skill. Keep an eye out for tiny moments when you can push yourself to make connections. Look for opportunities to put yourself out there and take social risks. If it doesn't work out, it might feel bad at first, but you'll ultimately be fine and recover. If it works out, though, you'll feel proud for making the effort, and it will be easier to take similar risks in the future.

Don't Skip Out on Traditions

There are certain aspects of high school that might seem cheesy to some, like school dances, graduation ceremonies, and pep rallies. If those don't seem like your thing, it can be difficult to imagine why you should participate. No one is telling you that you *must* get involved in your school's spirit week or help plan the prom, but you might find that participating in traditional events ends up being more fun than you thought. Your first homecoming dance only happens once. Sure, you and your friends might have just as much fun doing something else that night, but you might actually have fun at the dance, and participating in these events helps you be part of a shared high school experience.

Support Your Own Growth

The four years you spend in high school will be some of the most transformative years of your life. In a very literal sense, your body is likely to be unrecognizable to your middle school self by the time you get through high school. In a mental and social sense, you will also increasingly be stepping into your own identity as you draw closer to adulthood. At times, your hormones will make you feel like you're on an emotional roller coaster and it will seem that much harder to make sense of who you are and what you want to accomplish. Friendships will change and evolve. Your interests will shift and deepen. Throughout it all, there are a few ways to help support your own growth and development as a person.

Practice Self-Sufficiency and Self-Advocacy

Self-sufficiency and self-advocacy are two life skills that go hand in hand. Self-sufficiency essentially means being able to handle your responsibilities, schedule, and life for yourself, without anyone's assistance. Things like learning to make your own doctor's appointments, getting yourself up for school without a parent's help, and learning to do basic errands and chores for yourself are all examples of self-sufficiency. Self-advocacy involves recognizing when you can no longer be self-sufficient and need help. Speaking up to a teacher about your learning accommodations, asking your parents to help you accomplish a task you're stuck on, and reaching out for help when you're having a health crisis are all examples of self-advocacy. It means speaking up and being a voice for yourself when you need one. If you practice self-sufficiency and self-advocacy whenever possible, you are practicing critical skills for adulthood. You will also feel more confident in your independence, making it easier to enter the adult world after high school.

"As you transition to high school, it's important that you develop self-advocacy skills. If you need or want something, you will have to seek out the resources to get the help or support that you desire. If you are struggling academically in a particular subject, you need to seek out your teacher for extra help. Your school counselor is an excellent resource to help you develop your self-advocacy skills and to help problem-solve other situations. Once you are in college, your parents won't be there. It's important to start early so you will feel comfortable asking for what you need."

Kehlani, Guidance Counselor

Learn How to Set Your Boundaries

Whether you're setting boundaries for yourself, such as by practicing self-discipline around schoolwork, or with others, like when you ask your friends not to tease you about a topic you're sensitive about, high school is the perfect time to practice boundary setting. Learn to say "no" to things when you're spread too thin already. Learn to enforce routines with yourself, like going to bed by 11 p.m. nightly even though it's tempting to stay up all night playing video games. Practice telling your friends what you need or how they've hurt your feelings so you can have frank discussions rather than doing passive things like giving them the silent treatment or talking behind their back. Figure out which kinds of behaviors you will tolerate and which you will not, then communicate your needs fairly. The more you practice doing these things, the easier they'll be when the stakes are high.

Take Care of Yourself

There are many ways to take care of yourself, and all of them are important. One is by making sure your basic needs are met: drink water, eat enough food to be satiated and with enough variety to get the nutrients you need, move your body in ways that feel good whenever you can, tend to your personal hygiene on a regular basis, and get a solid 7+ hours of sleep every night. Other ways include self-care, such as tending to your emotional needs and knowing when you need extra rest. You can also look out for yourself by trusting your gut when a situation doesn't seem right. If you feel like you are unsafe or in over your head with a situation, such as an adult person making you feel uncomfortable, a loved one harming you, or personal struggles like an intense desire to restrict your food intake, caring for yourself also means reaching out to a trusted adult who can help.

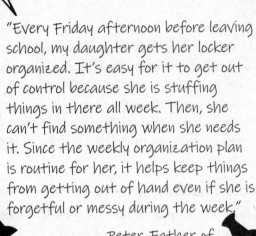

"Every Friday afternoon before leaving school, my daughter gets her locker organized. It's easy for it to get out of control because she is stuffing things in there all week. Then, she can't find something when she needs it. Since the weekly organization plan is routine for her, it helps keep things from getting out of hand even if she is forgetful or messy during the week."

Peter, Father of
a High School Junior

These are some basic things that organized students always know:

- What was assigned in each class
- When the homework is due
- When the next test, paper, or major project is scheduled
- What they need to bring to each class
- Where the supplies they need are in their backpack or locker
- What books or supplies they need to bring home each night
- Who (besides their teacher) they can get notes from if they missed a class
- What the procedure is for missed or late assignments when they do happen

Get Organized

In high school, being organized does not just mean showing up to class on time with your teeth brushed. This may have been enough to get by in middle school, but in high school, the complications of a fuller schedule will make it much harder to fly by the seat of your pants. To stay on top of all your assignments, deadlines, events, and other responsibilities, you will likely need to keep some kind of calendar or agenda, have a filing system for assignments and notes, and make sure you have all the learning materials you need ready to go. For instance, remembering your laptop won't be enough if you also forget the charger, so you might need to have a system in place for making sure everything you need ends up in your backpack before school. Organization is highly individual and depends largely on the kind of tasks you personally need to accomplish and your own weak points, but look for ways to become a more organized person over the course of high school.

The best way to get organized is to set up a system. It can be someone else's system or your own. The important thing is to have some way to keep track of when assignments are due, when tests are coming, and on what nights you are committed with practices or meetings. Each week, go through and set up a new schedule for the coming week. It sounds like a lot of work, but when Thursday hits and your head is spinning, you'll be glad you have a schedule to follow. For instance, you could have three tests on the same day. Wouldn't it be helpful to know that way ahead of time instead of remembering the day of the tests? Having a system is especially important if you struggle with ADHD or any other condition that can make organization a challenge. If you do, develop a system you can fall back on and practice it until it feels like a routine.

Handle Yourself Like a Professional

This is primarily important when dealing with adults at your school but is good advice in general. Make sure you know all your teachers' and administrators' names, use their correct titles, and use proper greetings when emailing them. If one of your teachers or administrators has a Ph.D. and goes by "Dr.," always use that title unless they tell you to call them something else. It is especially common for students to forget to use titles with women, so demonstrate mindfulness when addressing a woman with an earned title, such as Principal. Similarly, do not assume a woman prefers the married title "Mrs." unless they introduce themselves that way. When in doubt, use the less specific title "Ms." for a woman.

In emails, make sure you say hello and close your email properly; don't just say "Hey when is the paper due?" like you might in a text message to a friend. If someone is taking a while to get back to you, say by not responding to an email, it's okay to follow up, but do so respectfully and with an understanding that working people are very busy and often swamped with emails, especially when working in a school setting. Demonstrating basic professional courtesy to the professionals who work at your school is a way of showing the adults in your life that you see and respect them as people.

Celebrate Your Milestones

When you reach a goal or experience something for the first time, celebrate it! Gather some friends together and get lunch to celebrate your first kiss or go bowling as a reward for acing that biology exam. It's easier to keep following your goals if you celebrate what you accomplish along the way. Marking important events in your life is also a way of making memories and giving yourself milestones to look back on to see how you've

grown as a human. The four years of high school will go by faster than you expect, so take time to celebrate the moments you spend becoming your adult self along the way.

Develop Good Study Habits

If your study habits are lacking, you still have time to improve them. Studying should not happen only in the days or hours—or minutes!—before a test. As a high school student, it's your job to attend class, pay attention to your teachers, recognize what you don't understand, and get the help you need to be able to understand it.

> "An email to a teacher is not the same as texting your friend! It's more like a letter. It should have a proper opening and closing and contain the information a person needs to answer you. Nothing makes me want to scream more than when I get an email that just says, 'what did we do in class,' with no punctuation or identifying information. I have 160 students across 6 class periods and can't always remember every detail off the top of my head. It's even worse when someone wants a favor but didn't take the time to properly ask. Students, I beg of you, take the time to write a proper email...your teachers will appreciate it!"
>
> Andie, High School History Teacher

Review Class Notes Regularly

Reviewing your notes daily, even if just a quick skim, is the best way to start committing your learning to long-term memory. It can also be helpful to create flashcards or do more in-depth reviews periodically. To amp up your retention rate, you can jot down pertinent questions or pull out main ideas as you skim over your notes from the week. If you only do so right before a test, you're limited by what your short-term memory can retain.

Think Like a Teacher

When you are taking and reviewing notes, imagine that you are going to have to teach them to someone else. If you had to teach the information you are currently learning, what would you focus on to make sure your student understood? You'll probably figure out pretty quickly that the things you'd highlight as important are the exact same things your teacher thinks are important, meaning those are the things you need to write down. You can anticipate a lot of what will come up on tests or projects by thinking this way as you study. For instance, if you take the time to write yourself some "practice" exam questions, you might be surprised to find that the questions your teacher ends up asking are very similar. If a teacher takes the time to repeat themselves often on a topic, that also means they are using repetition as a teaching technique, hoping that repeated exposure to the information will help it "stick" for students. Thus, keeping an eye out for repetition is a great way to take solid notes.

Consider Taking Notes by Hand

Studies have shown that physically writing notes also helps you retain information later, so it can be a way to keep your brain engaged with a lecture as well. You'll also be able to draw diagrams or graphs related to the content you're learning, which can be especially important for certain subjects. If keeping a digital copy of your notes is important, you can consider retyping them later or get a smart device or app designed for classroom notetaking, such as a tablet with a pen designed to mimic handwriting. There may also be some courses, such as speaking-intensive language

Practice Taking Useful Notes

One of the most important study habits to develop is notetaking. Notes don't always have to be in written form, and they definitely shouldn't just be transcripts of every single thing your teacher says. This is especially true if your teacher provides slides or other materials that have exactly what they displayed written down for you already. In that case, your goal is to take notes that add information to what's on the slides. Instead of trying to write down every single thing a teacher says, try to focus on main ideas and details that seem important for later, like the information that might come up on an exam. Even if your teacher has no visual aids to help you take notes, if you determine the main idea of the lesson, you need only record the details that support that idea. If you're a visual learner, try adding drawings or idea maps to your notes related to different concepts. Color-coding notes with pens and highlighters of different colors can also be helpful to those who need information organized visually.

courses where students are up and out of desks a lot, where teachers or professors may not allow you to take digital notes. You need to be able to take paper notes when digital notes are not available to you.

Use Shorthand When Writing Notes

Whether you prefer to take notes the more traditional way or on a computer, get comfortable with writing and reading your own personal "shorthand." It's hard to write down every word the teacher has to say—and that's not even the correct or most efficient use of your time—so it's very helpful to use "w/" for *with* and "b/c" for *because* and draw an upward arrow for *increasing*. The more you practice shorthand, the more you'll find little unique ways to shorten things so that everything makes sense in your own head.

Manage Your Time

In high school, you have to learn how to balance your schedule by determining what you have to do and how much time you have to do it. Your workload increases as you move into the upper classes. If you don't learn how to manage your time as a freshman, you'll just struggle that much harder as you move up the grades. Start early with learning how to manage your schedule. The best way to do this is to figure out the average amount of time it takes you to do something, then create blocks of time to help you accomplish tasks. For instance, if you know that your chemistry homework always takes you an hour each weekend, then you'll know to schedule that hour into your weekend at a time that works well.

Use Your Accommodations If You Have Them

Some students are on what's called an Individualized Education Plan, or IEP. This could be because they are performing above or below the average of their peers, because they have an impairment that impacts their learning, or simply because teachers identified them as someone who needs a more individualized approach. Students with certain conditions that affect school, like ADD/ADHD or dyslexia, almost always have an IEP. Usually, an IEP comes with individualized accommodations

that are designed to help support a student's learning, such as extra time for tests or a designated notetaker, usually a peer who takes thorough notes and shares them with the student. The specific accommodations available to you will depend on your own conditions and IEP, but if you have an IEP, it is smart for you to know exactly what your accommodations are so you can make sure to self-advocate in the classroom. This is especially important in high school classrooms because teachers often have dozens of students on IEPs and may occasionally need to be reminded of the accommodations you specifically get. If you have accommodations, find out what they are, ask for them when you're not getting them, and use them—they're there to help you!

Get Comfortable Asking Questions

You've probably heard the saying, "There are no stupid questions." Whether you went down the wrong hall and can't find your classroom, you need help signing up for a club you really want to join, or you didn't understand what the teacher was saying, speak up and ask questions. Guidance counselors and teachers are there to answer these questions and point you in the right direction.

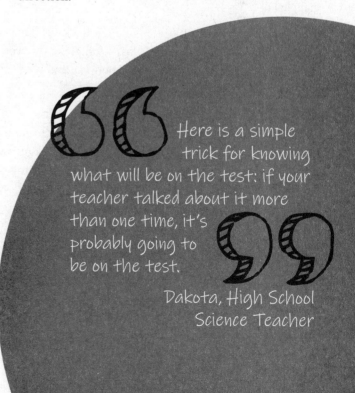

Here is a simple trick for knowing what will be on the test: if your teacher talked about it more than one time, it's probably going to be on the test.

Dakota, High School Science Teacher

FRESHMAN YEAR DO'S AND DON'TS

Everyone makes errors, but if you can avoid these mistakes as you begin your freshman year, you'll be in great shape.

Don't do this:	Instead, do this:
Assume freshman year doesn't "count" because senior year is so far away.	Use freshman year to build a strong foundation and create a cushion for any genuine slip-ups or setbacks you might face later.
Choose classes based on your friend's schedule or because you heard they were easy.	Choose the classes that make the most sense for you. Taking one or two classes with a friend isn't bad, but center your own needs and interests when choosing classes.
Skip class or show up late here and there—what difference does a day make?	Attend classes every day and be on time unless you have a genuine need for an absence or tardy. Missing means making work for yourself and your teacher later…it's easier to just stay caught up. Furthermore, excessive absences and tardies can hurt your grades and possibly your ability to get into the college you want.
Assume your genius brain is a steel trap that never needs reminders.	Recognize the need to write down your assignments, deadlines, and important information…in more than one place, if need be. If it's important enough to remember, write it down.
Forget to do a homework assignment and then just pretend the assignment never happened.	If you miss an assignment, whether for absences or just because you forgot or couldn't do it, always follow up on it. You may be able to turn it in late, get partial credit, or talk to your teacher to make it up.
Say no to every opportunity because you have to study OR skip studying altogether so you can fit all your clubs and social activities in.	Exhibit work/life balance. Too much work and too much fun can be equally harmful. Make sure you are managing your time to accommodate both your schoolwork and your social and personal needs.
Zone out thinking about what you're going to have for lunch while in class, completely miss what's going on, and then say nothing.	For one, try not to zone out in class. However, it happens to the best of us, so if you do zone out, own up to it and ask a peer or a teacher to clue you in. If you need something repeated, politely ask for that.
Sit around hoping the teacher notices that your half-finished assignments are a cry for help.	Teachers aren't mind readers and they have a lot of students. If you are struggling, take the initiative to talk to your teacher and ask for help. It really is okay to ask—teachers love to teach, and part of teaching is helping students understand things.

Don't do this:	Instead, do this:
Keep a situation that is making you uncomfortable to yourself or hide it from adults.	If something is upsetting you, speak up. It's good to talk to friends but recognize when you may need to bring in adult assistance, such as if you or someone you know might harm themselves or others. Teachers, counselors, parents—all are there for you!
Stay up all night studying or binging the new season of your favorite Netflix show because you're young and don't need that much sleep.	Teenagers need a lot of sleep! More than they tend to get. The temptation to stay up late is strong, but a good night's sleep helps restore your brain power. Sleep well so you can learn well.
Clam up and refuse to speak in any of your classes or to any of your teachers.	Pump yourself up so you're ready to get to know a lot of new people. Make an effort to remember people's faces and names for when you see them again. Be friendly and kind whenever you can. Practice empathy by trying to picture yourself in another person's shoes whenever possible.
Assume that you're the only one going through what you're going though.	Everyone is going through something. No one has a perfect life. No matter what you're experiencing, no matter how unique, there is someone in your community who can empathize in some way. Try and have empathy for others and be a good listener and the same will come back to you.
Have a meltdown because you don't know what exactly to expect in new situations.	Remember to breathe and take each new experience in stride. You don't have to know everything perfectly that first year. You just have to show up and do your best.

YOUR HIGH SCHOOL EXPERIENCE WILL BE UNIQUELY YOURS

It's been said, but it still bears repeating: Everyone has a different high school experience. Try not to compare yourself to others, but focus instead on making the most of the opportunities that come your way. There are sure to be challenges, many of which you may have never encountered before, but there is also sure to be a lot of laughter, joy, adventure, achievement, and fun along the way. High school is but one of many chapters in your life, but like all the others, it's a chapter that you get to write. This guide can help you make the most of high school and college—just remember that all the most important answers are within you.

PART

2

Figuring Out Your Future

CHAPTER 2

The First Steps to a Career

Chances are you haven't spent much of your teen years thinking about career planning yet, so when someone asks you what you want to do when you "grow up," you're likely to draw a complete blank. Sure, maybe you've known you want to be a pediatrician since the day you got your doctor playset back in preschool, but for many teens, the question of who they want to be has mostly been about daydreaming, not making a roadmap for the future. If you add in that you're likely to change your mind or vacillate between options a bunch between now and starting your first job, it can feel premature to think about your career now. However, even if you change your mind a dozen times between the start of high school and your college graduation, it's good to have at least a potential path in mind at the beginning of and throughout high school so that you can make the most of your time there prepping for the kind of career you might like to have. It's not like you'll be locked in—you can always change your mind and start a new path—but any prepping you do for one path will hopefully make it easier to switch to another if you choose to do so later. The key is to start thinking about your future *now*, while you have plenty of time and potential routes to get there.

The Short and Sweet Version

The sheer number of careers out there can be super overwhelming. Maybe you've got a few different ideas in mind or maybe you're not sure where to start. First, take the self-assessment inventory to get a better sense of your skills, strengths, and interests. We outline a few careers that might be a good match depending on which types you fall into. Use your results as a starting point to help you figure out what options might make the most sense for you.

Once you have your self-assessment results, consider how these might help you narrow your options and figure out next steps. As part of this process, you'll need to start researching what jobs are out there and which sound interesting to you. Once you've found a few that pique your interest, consult the US Department of Labor, Bureau of Labor Statistics for more detailed information on the median salary, requirements and responsibilities, education or training needed, and outlook for the careers you're considering.

Remember that deciding on your future path goes beyond picking a job title. You are a whole person with hobbies, friends, family, goals, and dreams. A job is just one facet of your life, and it's important that your career makes it possible for you to do the things you love. As you decide on your next steps, consider who you want to be and what your priorities and values are. We've included a list of questions for you to consider as you research the careers you're interested in and decide on the path that's right for you.

Regardless of which path you choose, you'll need to think about what your next steps should be. Generally, this boils down to whether you want to attend college or pursue a vocation or trade instead. Each option affords you different opportunities, and you'll want to seriously consider your career goals before making a decision. It's okay if you're still uncertain— not everyone knows exactly what they want to do while they're still in high school. But now is the time to start thinking about your options and what you're most excited to do next. Your future is bright!

INTERESTS AND STRENGTHS INVENTORY

Here, we've included a brief inventory for you to complete to get a better sense of your personality, skills, and interests. Using Dr. John Holland's theory of occupational choice, we've created a general inventory of six different categories of careers you can pursue. However, keep in mind that there are a lot of other resources and tools out there that can also help you get a better sense of what career paths might be a good match for your unique qualities and characteristics. Use this inventory as a starting place to begin thinking about the types of jobs that might align with your goals.

Self-Assessment Inventory

Directions: This self-assessment inventory contains 60 statements and should take about 5–10 minutes to complete. Next to each question, there are five options, and each is worth a certain number of points: Strongly Agree (2), Agree (1), Neutral (0), Disagree (-1), and Strongly Disagree (-2). Pick the answer that best reflects your level of agreement with the corresponding statement. At the end of the quiz, you'll add up your points for each section to determine which career opportunities might be a good fit for your personality, skills, and interests.

Section 1

	Strongly Disagree	Disagree	Neutral	Agree	Strongly Agree
1. I prefer tasks that I can do independently.	(-2)	(-1)	(0)	(1)	(2)
2. I can easily learn how to operate a tool or machine.	(-2)	(-1)	(0)	(1)	(2)
3. I prefer activities where I'm outdoors.	(-2)	(-1)	(0)	(1)	(2)
4. I am a physically active person.	(-2)	(-1)	(0)	(1)	(2)
5. I'm direct and straightforward when I communicate with others.	(-2)	(-1)	(0)	(1)	(2)
6. I would consider myself a realistic person.	(-2)	(-1)	(0)	(1)	(2)
7. I value skills with a clear practical application.	(-2)	(-1)	(0)	(1)	(2)
8. I enjoy working with plants and/or animals.	(-2)	(-1)	(0)	(1)	(2)
9. I'm good at taking things apart and putting them back together.	(-2)	(-1)	(0)	(1)	(2)
10. I don't mind getting my hands dirty.	(-2)	(-1)	(0)	(1)	(2)

_____ _____ _____ _____ _____

Section 2

	Strongly Disagree (-2)	Disagree (-1)	Neutral (0)	Agree (1)	Strongly Agree (2)
1. I tend to think abstractly or theoretically.	(-2)	(-1)	(0)	(1)	(2)
2. I like to research things so that I can learn more.	(-2)	(-1)	(0)	(1)	(2)
3. I prefer to work independently instead of with others.	(-2)	(-1)	(0)	(1)	(2)
4. I thrive in an environment where I can be curious.	(-2)	(-1)	(0)	(1)	(2)
5. I am an observant person.	(-2)	(-1)	(0)	(1)	(2)
6. I enjoy analyzing and interpreting data.	(-2)	(-1)	(0)	(1)	(2)
7. I approach things in a precise and logical manner.	(-2)	(-1)	(0)	(1)	(2)
8. I excel at investigating complex ideas and problems.	(-2)	(-1)	(0)	(1)	(2)
9. I seek knowledge to gain a deeper understanding of the world around me.	(-2)	(-1)	(0)	(1)	(2)
10. I would consider myself a serious person.	(-2)	(-1)	(0)	(1)	(2)

____ ____ ____ ____ ____

Section 3

	Strongly Disagree (-2)	Disagree (-1)	Neutral (0)	Agree (1)	Strongly Agree (2)
1. I can often intuit important information.	(-2)	(-1)	(0)	(1)	(2)
2. I like to engage with works of art, like poems, paintings, or films.	(-2)	(-1)	(0)	(1)	(2)
3. I enjoy expressing my thoughts, ideas, and emotions.	(-2)	(-1)	(0)	(1)	(2)
4. I need the freedom and space to experiment and try new things.	(-2)	(-1)	(0)	(1)	(2)
5. I would consider myself a sensitive person.	(-2)	(-1)	(0)	(1)	(2)
6. I like to develop new and original ideas for solving problems.	(-2)	(-1)	(0)	(1)	(2)
7. I thrive in an environment where I can explore my creativity.	(-2)	(-1)	(0)	(1)	(2)
8. I prefer following my own rules.	(-2)	(-1)	(0)	(1)	(2)
9. It's easy for me to see things from other people's perspectives.	(-2)	(-1)	(0)	(1)	(2)
10. I value aesthetics more than others do.	(-2)	(-1)	(0)	(1)	(2)

____ ____ ____ ____ ____

Section 4

	Strongly Disagree (-2)	Disagree (-1)	Neutral (0)	Agree (1)	Strongly Agree (2)
1. I am a friendly and outgoing person.	(-2)	(-1)	(0)	(1)	(2)
2. I enjoy helping others however I can.	(-2)	(-1)	(0)	(1)	(2)
3. It's important that I make a difference in the world.	(-2)	(-1)	(0)	(1)	(2)
4. I excel at building and maintaining relationships with other people.	(-2)	(-1)	(0)	(1)	(2)
5. I can communicate openly with others.	(-2)	(-1)	(0)	(1)	(2)
6. I enjoy promoting teamwork and cooperation.	(-2)	(-1)	(0)	(1)	(2)
7. I would consider myself a patient person.	(-2)	(-1)	(0)	(1)	(2)
8. It's easy for me to empathize with other people.	(-2)	(-1)	(0)	(1)	(2)
9. I am eager to support and encourage others.	(-2)	(-1)	(0)	(1)	(2)
10. I prefer working with others instead of on my own.	(-2)	(-1)	(0)	(1)	(2)

_____ _____ _____ _____ _____

Section 5

	Strongly Disagree (-2)	Disagree (-1)	Neutral (0)	Agree (1)	Strongly Agree (2)
1. I am comfortable with making decisions.	(-2)	(-1)	(0)	(1)	(2)
2. I prefer teaming up with others to complete projects.	(-2)	(-1)	(0)	(1)	(2)
3. I am passionate about promoting ideas or new ways of thinking.	(-2)	(-1)	(0)	(1)	(2)
4. I enjoy leading others.	(-2)	(-1)	(0)	(1)	(2)
5. I can persuade someone to see my point of view.	(-2)	(-1)	(0)	(1)	(2)
6. I am willing to take risks.	(-2)	(-1)	(0)	(1)	(2)
7. I am usually the person who initiates a project or task.	(-2)	(-1)	(0)	(1)	(2)
8. I enjoy debating or negotiating with other people.	(-2)	(-1)	(0)	(1)	(2)
9. I like motivating other people to do a good job.	(-2)	(-1)	(0)	(1)	(2)
10. I bring energy and enthusiasm to most situations.	(-2)	(-1)	(0)	(1)	(2)

_____ _____ _____ _____ _____

Section 6

	Strongly Disagree (-2)	Disagree (-1)	Neutral (0)	Agree (1)	Strongly Agree (2)
1. I thrive in an environment with structure and clear expectations.	(-2)	(-1)	(0)	(1)	(2)
2. I value stability and predictability.	(-2)	(-1)	(0)	(1)	(2)
3. I am generally averse to taking unnecessary risks.	(-2)	(-1)	(0)	(1)	(2)
4. I enjoy processing, organizing, and managing information.	(-2)	(-1)	(0)	(1)	(2)
5. I have higher standards than most when it comes to my work.	(-2)	(-1)	(0)	(1)	(2)
6. I enjoy sticking to a specific routine.	(-2)	(-1)	(0)	(1)	(2)
7. I believe that rules are there for a reason and should be followed.	(-2)	(-1)	(0)	(1)	(2)
8. I complete tasks with accuracy and precision.	(-2)	(-1)	(0)	(1)	(2)
9. I would consider myself an organized person.	(-2)	(-1)	(0)	(1)	(2)
10. I am more efficient when there are existing protocols and procedures in place.	(-2)	(-1)	(0)	(1)	(2)

_____	_____	_____	_____	_____

Answer Overview

In the blanks below, add up the points for each section of the test. Each section corresponds with a type. Following this self-assessment inventory, we cover the different types along with career choices that might be a good fit for each type.

_____ Total for Section 1: Realistic (Doers)

_____ Total for Section 2: Investigative (Thinkers)

_____ Total for Section 3: Artistic (Creators)

_____ Total for Section 4: Social (Helpers)

_____ Total for Section 5: Enterprising (Persuaders)

_____ Total for Section 6: Conventional (Organizers)

The section where you scored the highest will be your primary type. The section where you had the second highest number of points will be your secondary type. Finally, the section with the third highest number of points will be your tertiary type. Your top three types can offer insight into what careers might be a good fit for you. If you have a tie, feel free to revisit your answers for each section: Do certain answers resonate most with you? Was there a statement you weren't sure about that you might want to change your answer for? Are there statements you initially agreed with strongly but maybe aren't sure about now?

Primary Type: _____

Secondary Type: _____

Tertiary Type: _____

Holland Code Type Descriptions

Here, we include an overview of each of the six types: Realistic (Doers), Investigative (Thinkers), Artistic (Creators), Social (Helpers), Enterprising (Persuaders), and Conventional (Organizers). Review the types you had the most points for and scan the list of suitable careers to see if anything piques your interest.

1 Realistic (Doers): Doers enjoy being active and engaging in physical activity. Realistic types "learn by doing" and are often task-oriented and driven by results. Jobs that doers might enjoy are more tactile or kinesthetic in nature, involving craftsmanship and physical challenge. These roles usually require practical skills, including hands-on work and using either tools or machines. In these positions, a doer might be working outdoors with real-world materials, plants, or animals.

2 Investigative (Thinkers): Thinkers are typically observant people who enjoy doing research to find the answers to complex problems. Thinkers seek to understand how things function and often value a flexible environment with minimal structure where they are free to be curious. Generally, thinkers prefer to work independently instead of on a team. The jobs that are best suited for thinkers involve intellectual and research-oriented tasks, including analysis, investigation, and exploration. In these positions, thinkers use and apply ideas, theories, data, and facts to solve problems.

3 Artistic (Creators): Creators generally value self-expression and creativity and avoid stifling or conventional roles in favor of a flexible and unstructured environment where they can be independent and experimental. Creators value the opportunity to communicate openly and honestly while developing their creative competencies. Artistic types are usually free-spirited, intense, and imaginative. Jobs for creators typically involve the creation of something new or original in a specific medium, like graphics, text, audio, or video. In these positions, creators often use designs, patterns, and forms in order to convey a thought, idea, or emotion.

"When I took the Holland Codes inventory, my highest scores were in artistic and investigative. It gave me a lot to think about and helped me feel more confident that my career interest in becoming a web designer or video game developer was probably a smart fit for me, since both those jobs combine creative and technical know-how."

Colleen, High School Sophomore

4 Social (Helpers): Helpers are most concerned with helping other people in some capacity. Their top priority is making a concrete difference in the lives of others and having a positive impact on the world at large. People in these roles are often empathetic, compassionate, and outgoing, and they excel at building relationships. As such, helpers enjoy working as part of team and are effective at promoting cooperation and communicating tactfully. In these interpersonal and service-oriented positions, helpers might be offering support by communicating, healing, counseling, training, or teaching.

5 Enterprising (Persuaders): These jobs focus on starting projects and bringing them to fruition. In these positions, you'll likely be leading people, making decisions, and persuading others to see things from your perspective. People who pursue these types of roles tend to be natural leaders who are motivated, driven, and adventurous. Persuaders also tend to be motivational, influential, and adept at negotiation, with the desire to climb the ladder and advance to more powerful positions. As such, roles in business, sales, and management are often a good fit. Persuaders thrive in careers that always offer new challenges and allow them to shake up the status quo.

6 **Conventional (Organizers):** Organizers value structure and are logical, efficient, and detail-oriented. Conventional types prefer to blend into their environments instead of standing out or shaking things up. Organizers are conscientious and dependable, so they work well with others and are also easy to manage. Organizers would do best in a job with structure, direct communication, and clear expectations. As such, jobs that are well-suited for organizers typically involve precisely implementing or following a given procedure or set of rules. In these roles, conventional types are generally responsible for managing details, data, and protocol.

Realistic (Doers)

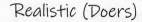

- Aerospace Engineering and Operations Technician
- Aircraft or Avionics Equipment Mechanic or Technician
- Airline or Commercial Pilot
- Architect
- Automotive Technician
- Boilermaker
- Cardiovascular Technologist or Technician
- Carpenter
- Chef
- Conservation Scientist
- Civil or Electrical Engineer
- Diagnostic Medical Sonographer
- Electrician
- Electrical or Electronic Engineering Technician
- Elevator Installer and Repairer
- Fitness Instructor
- Forester
- Firefighter
- Law Enforcement Officer
- Material Moving Machine Operator
- Medical Lab Technician
- Paramedic
- Physical Therapist
- Plumber
- Surveyor
- Veterinarian or Veterinary Technician
- Welder, Cutter, Solderer, or Brazer
- Wind Turbine Technician

Investigative (Thinkers)

- Aerospace Engineer
- Biologist
- Chemical Engineer
- Clinical Psychologist
- Computer Programmer
- Computer Systems Analyst
- Dentist
- Detective
- Economist
- Educator
- Food Scientist
- Forensic Scientist
- Historian
- Instructional Designer
- Journalist
- Lab Technician
- Librarian
- Mechanical Engineer
- Medical Doctor
- Optometrist
- Pharmacist
- Podiatrist
- Software Engineer
- Statistician
- Surgeon
- Veterinarian
- Web Developer

Artistic (Creators)

- Architect
- Art Director
- Art Therapist
- Choreographer
- Copywriter
- Craft, Fine, or Performing Artist
- Digital Animator
- Editor
- Educator
- Event Planner
- Fashion Designer
- Film Director or Producer
- Graphic Designer
- Interior Designer
- Interpreter or Translator
- Journalist
- Landscape Architect
- Marketing Coordinator
- Museum Curator
- Music Director, Composer, or Producer
- Pastry Chef
- Photographer
- Social Media Specialist
- Technical Writer
- Video Editor
- Web Designer
- Writer or Author

Social (Helpers)

- Barber, Hairstylist, or Cosmetologist
- Chiropractor
- Dental Hygienist
- Dentist
- Doctor
- Educator
- ESL Teacher
- Financial Advisor
- General Practitioner
- Genetic Counselor
- Home Health and Personal Care Aide
- Human Resources Professional
- Librarian
- Massage Therapist
- Mental Health and Substance Abuse Social Worker
- Nurse Anesthetist, Nurse Midwife, or Nurse Practitioner
- Occupational Therapist
- Physician Assistant
- Physical Therapist
- Preschool or Kindergarten Teacher
- Psychiatrist
- Radiation Therapist
- Respiratory Therapist
- Social Worker
- Special Education Teacher
- Speech-Language Pathologist
- Surgeon
- Teacher Assistant
- Therapist
- Training Manager
- Travel Agent or Consultant

More Options for Self-Assessments

If you feel like you are struggling to pinpoint a career path that's right for you, investing some time into these types of assessments can help you narrow down your options a bit. The Holland Code Careers Test is just one option you can use to pinpoint your strengths, skills, and interests. Here, we've made a list of a few other options you can try. Note that there are a lot of different versions of these tests out there on the internet, some paid and some free.

- **Myers-Briggs Type Indicator:** This test is based on Carl Jung's theory of 16 distinct personality types. Your personality type consists of a combination of 4 letters: Extroversion or Introversion, Sensing or Intuition, Thinking or Feeling, and Judging or Perceiving. Generally, proponents of the Myers-Briggs test think that your type indicates your different preferences for how you perceive the world and interact with others, which can help you figure out the careers that might be a good fit for your needs and strengths.

- **Strong Interest Inventory:** If you want to dive more into John Holland's theory of career codes, then consider taking the Strong Interest Inventory. This test expands on Holland's career codes by focusing on your preferences in five key

Enterprising (Persuaders)

- Air Traffic Controller
- Arbitrator, Mediator, or Conciliator
- Architectural or Engineering Manager
- Compensation or Benefits Manager
- Computer and Information Systems Manager
- Customer Service Manager
- Education Administrator
- Financial Advisor or Manager
- Human Resources Manager
- Immigration or Customs Inspector
- Insurance Sales Agent
- Lawyer
- Logistics Manager
- Management Consultant
- Occupational Safety and Health Inspector
- Paralegal/Legal Assistant
- Personal Trainer
- Public Relations Manager
- Real Estate Agent
- Recruiter
- Sales and Marketing Manager
- Sales Engineer
- Sales or Retail Buyer
- Social Services Director

Conventional (Organizers)

- Accountant
- Auditor
- Budget Analyst
- Claims Adjuster or Investigator
- Computer Network Architect
- Database Administrator
- Economist
- Editor
- Event Planner
- Financial Analyst or Advisor
- Immigration or Customs Inspector
- Information Security Analyst
- Insurance Underwriter
- Interpreter or Translator
- Medical Technician
- Librarian
- Loan Officer
- Notary
- Nursing Assistant
- Occupational Health and Safety Technician
- Paralegal/Legal Assistant
- Pharmacist
- Project Manager
- Quality Inspector
- Radiologic and MRI Technologist
- Statistician
- Systems Analyst
- Web Administrator
- Web Developer

work-related areas: work style, learning environment, team orientation, leadership style, and risk taking. Note that it might be easier to complete this test once you have some work experience and start to develop preferences about your work environment.

- **Career Beliefs Inventory:** This is a tool used in career counseling to help individuals identify and overcome attitudes that can be a barrier to choosing a career. If you feel stuck when it comes to finding a career path that interests you, this tool can help you work through any assumptions, biases, or generalizations you might hold about yourself or about work itself.

- **Personal Values Assessment:** This test can help you pinpoint what you need from your work and what motivates you. In other words, if you're not sure what matters to you most when it comes to choosing a job, this test can be useful in identifying what priorities you have and which careers might be most fulfilling.

- **Kiersey Temperament Sorter:** The Kiersey Temperament Sorter divides people into four temperaments: Artisan, Guardian, Idealist, and Rational. Your temperament results can give you a better sense of your personality type and core characteristics, which can help you figure out the types of roles and workplaces that might be a good match.

TRANSLATING YOUR INTERESTS INTO A CAREER PATH

The real value in these assessments is that they can help you figure out what strengths and interests you have and what jobs exist that might be a match. Of course, you don't have to do a particular job just because a strengths test told you it would be a good fit for you. Here is how you can translate your interests into a career path.

1 First, use your assessment results to identify a job, or even two or three jobs, that sound compelling to you. If there are jobs you've never heard of, look them up to see what they involve. If there are jobs you already know you don't want to do, cross them off the list. If the jobs you're most interested in are similar to each other, then that might give you a good indication of which direction you'll want to pursue for your career. If you find that you're gravitating toward one or two jobs in particular, that can give you a good starting point to look for similar, related jobs. For instance, if you know that you might be interested in something to do with publishing, then you could consider being a writer, editor, book designer, or project manager, or even go into something like sales and marketing. Doing this kind of job research can also help you pick a major if you've already decided to attend college but haven't yet figured out exactly what job title you want.

2 Now that you've identified a few positions of interest to you, start researching the jobs themselves and what qualifications you should have. Sometimes, a job sounds good on paper, but when you learn what it actually requires—what tasks you'll be doing, how much education or training is necessary, what your day-to-day routine will look like, how much money you can expect to make—it may not be what you actually want. As you research what's involved, make sure to consult the US Department of Labor, Bureau of Labor Statistics website, where you can find job outlooks for positions you might be interested in. There will usually be an overview of what the job entails, how much education or training is required, and what the median salary is for workers with that job title. If you're researching more than one position, you can use a spreadsheet to organize information so you can compare different jobs at a glance.

3 Consider how your desired lifestyle, priorities, finances, and personal mindset will influence your decision. Some jobs require many years of education, which can be expensive and time consuming. Other jobs might only require a year or two of additional training after high school, but the tradeoff might be a lower salary. Depending on what field you go into and what position you pursue, you'll need to consider what you want your workload to be like, how much money you want to make, where you want to live, how much education you're willing to pursue, and more. In the next section, we list some questions to think about as you choose a career path. Remember, choosing a job that makes you happy involves more than just your job title or your salary. You'll need to think about how your job will help you be the person you want to be, live the life you want to live, and achieve the goals you want to reach.

4 **Remember that it's okay to change your mind.** Maybe you research a few careers and want to keep looking at other options. Maybe you try out a music major in college but decide to switch to business or history instead. Maybe you graduate and spend a few years as a high school teacher, social worker, or nurse and eventually feel burnt out. A lot of people end up switching majors or careers because as much as you research and try to prepare, it's hard to truly know what a job is like until you actually do it. Don't freak out if this ends up being you. You don't want to be stuck in a job that you hate, so don't be afraid to explore your options and find a new path.

"My entire life I wanted to be a teacher, so I became one. Everything was going great at first and I adored my students, but the working conditions were awful. I hardly ever had weekends or evenings to myself because of all the planning and grading, the administrators at my school weren't very supportive, and it was frustrating to deal with parents who didn't understand what the job was actually like. After 10 years, I got serious burnout and had to give it up. Now, I work at a publishing company that creates educational materials for schools, so I'm still teaching in a way. It's been a very happy career transition for me and it wasn't as scary changing careers as I thought it would be. Sure, it was hard at first but much better than staying in a job that made me miserable."

Maureen, Former
Middle School Teacher

THINKING ABOUT YOUR FUTURE: WHO DO YOU WANT TO BE?

A lot of times when people talk to teens about future planning, they're thinking primarily about education and career. However, your future is more than just the classes you'll take and the labor you'll one day do. Thinking about your future includes several things, such as the kind of environment you might want to live in, the lifestyle you might want to lead, the person you want to be, and the people with whom you might like to associate in your everyday life. For instance, if you know that you love being surrounded by children, you might be considering a career in early childhood education. Or maybe you know that no matter what, you want to use your exceptional math skills to build something spectacular, so while you aren't sure what kind of engineer you'd like to be yet, you know generally that you're interested in engineering fields.

Of course, maybe you don't have the faintest clue what you want to do later or how you'll want your adult life to look, and honestly, that's totally fine, too! It's okay if you don't know all the answers now or if your goals and priorities shift over time; in fact, it's both normal and highly likely that they will. The person you are now is different than the person you'll be five, ten, or twenty years down the line. However, starting to think about who you are at your core and beginning to ask yourself questions about the future now will help you stay attuned to your goals and priorities as they shift over time. Furthermore, if a clear picture of how you want your future to look emerges now, you'll be all the better equipped to start setting goals and planning the necessary steps to make that future a reality.

Here, we've provided some questions to ask yourself so that you can start envisioning the life you want. While the interests and skills assessment was designed to get you thinking about what you might be good at or enjoy doing in your future career, that is only part of the picture. To get a full view, you'll also need to think about yourself as a person and the kind of lifestyle you might like to lead, since any career you undertake will be but one piece in a total

Questions to Ask Yourself When Considering Future Plans

Lifestyle

- Would you rather live in an urban environment, like a big city, or a more suburban environment? Or, perhaps, would a secluded or rural environment be best for you?

- Would you prefer to work in a team environment, or do you prefer working solo?

- Do you think you may potentially want to have a spouse, live-in partner, pets, or children one day?

- Is owning a forever home or building a life in one place important to you, or could you see yourself moving around a lot to experience different places?

- How important (or not) do you want travel to be to your work or personal life?

- Is having flexibility enough for a particular lifestyle (like "van life" or living on a boat) important to you?

- Do you have a strong desire or need to work remotely (i.e., from home) rather than going into an office or job site?

Finances

- What kind of financial situation will you be in after graduating high school—is your family likely to offer some support or are you going to be on your own?

- Is there money set aside for you to go to college or will you need to find sources of funding?

- Is finding a job with a high income a priority to you, or would you rather prioritize other aspects of your job experience?

- What size of a family would you like to potentially be able to support one day, how soon would you like to start it, if so, and what sort of financial planning might you need to do after high school or college to make that happen?

- Is having money enough for a cost-intensive hobby (like world travel or equestrianism) or certain luxuries (like a sports car or boat) important to you?

- Do the jobs you're interested in pay enough to support the kind of lifestyle you want?

- Is the career you're interested in financially stable or will your income be unpredictable?

mosaic that makes up your day-to-day life. You want to make sure that the career you pursue matches the kind of lifestyle you want or need. Or, alternatively, if the kind of career you would like is your highest priority, then you'll need to consider how the rest of your life might need to look to accommodate the demands of that career. If you want to be an on-call obstetrician and deliver babies, for instance, that might be at odds with having a jetsetter lifestyle where you're out of the state for long periods of time.

Use these questions in conjunction with the potential career paths you identified through the interests and skills inventory so that you can weigh the pros and cons of various career options. As you research the different career paths you're interested in pursuing, consider how your answers to these questions might inform the choices you make. This will help you filter out the jobs that won't mesh with your expectations and priorities and will give you more direction in terms of what you're looking for out of a career.

Questions to Ask Yourself When Considering Future Plans

There's nothing magic about this list of questions—think of them simply as prompts to get your mental juices flowing. Take some time to get quiet, breathe deeply, and think honestly to yourself about what you envision happening in your adult life. Then, ask

Priorities

- Is having children an important goal for you and, if so, how would you want your future career to look in terms of parental work/life balance?

- Is having pets or animals an important goal for you and, if so, how would you want your future plans to look in terms of being able to provide for the needs of that type of pet? (Hint: You probably don't need to factor in something like a goldfish, but if you wanted to have a horse, for instance, this comes with a lot of factors to consider).

- Is having a particular size of home or amount of space important to you, or could you live anywhere?

- Which is more your style: the nicest home or job in a location that's less exciting to live in or a boring home or job in an exciting location?

- How important is it to you to be near your family or closest friends during college or when settling into a career?

- What sort of work/life balance seems important to you—are you willing to work long hours doing something you love, or would you rather work 9-to-5 with plenty of time for your hobbies and social life?

Personal Mindset

- What do you believe spiritually? Politically? Ethically? Philosophically?

- What markers of your identity as a human are most important to you?

- Which of your identities and beliefs are most central to who you are?

- What makes you uniquely you?

- What are some of your best skills that you think could be useful in a career situation?

- Which identities and beliefs have the greatest impact on how you make decisions or plan for what's to come?

- What sort of friendships do you hope to foster as an adult?

- What sort of romantic relationships do you hope to foster as an adult?

- What are some aspects of your personality you value and want to continue to grow as you develop?

- What are some aspects of your personality that you might like to work on as you grow and develop?

- What personal goals do you have right now that reflect how you might like your future to look?

yourself these or similar questions. We recommend taking some time to journal or map out your responses in a visual way that you can return to later. Once you've figured out your priorities, you'll know what to look for in potential future careers, colleges, or other endeavors.

"For a long time, I wanted to be a firefighter because it just seemed like the coolest job in the world. Once I started reading up on what it takes to be one, I realized that it might not allow me to be home with my family for dinner every night. I have a super close-knit family, so family is one of the most important things to me and I know I want to have at least four kids one day. Now, I am thinking about physical therapy. I would still get to help people, but the lifestyle and salary that come with being a physical therapist will be a better way to live the way I want to."

Gideon, High School Senior

WHAT IF I'M *NOT* GOING TO A FOUR-YEAR COLLEGE OR UNIVERSITY?

Chapter 3 will cover a lot of what you need to do in high school to prepare for a career generally, but a lot of the advice is centered on college preparation. However, as you've probably figured out by now, preparing for college is not the only way to make the most of high school. If you're thinking about what kind of career you want and what kind of lifestyle you might like to lead, your pondering could include asking yourself some hard questions about whether a traditional four-year college path is truly right for you. If you have started thinking about options early and determined that college probably isn't what you want to do right after graduation, you might approach things differently according to the advice laid out here. If you have truly no idea what to do, try planning for at least community college; this option keeps a variety of paths open.

Planning for Community College

A lot of time and energy gets devoted to preparing teens for four-year universities and colleges, and this can make students who are more interested in community colleges feel overwhelmed. The good news is that a lot of that college prep information is just as useful for preparing a student for community college. However, the difference is often in the time and degree of preparation necessary to succeed. While getting into a four-year college or university can take a lot of advance planning,

significant effort, and detailed attention to things like your GPA, your test scores, and college interviews, getting into community college is generally less significant of an undertaking. For one, most community colleges have open admission, meaning that anyone who has completed high school (or its equivalent in the form of a GED) can enroll. Another reason is that most community colleges recognize that not everyone in high school was a straight-A student—they are open to a wider range of students purposely to make opportunities (and the second chances that might come with them) available to all.

That said, whether you are planning to get a two-year associate degree before moving into the workforce or to attend community college for a while before transferring to a four-year program, there are a few things you can do while still in high school to prepare for success.

Ask Your Guidance Counselor about Concurrent Enrollment Opportunities

Many high schools these days have a relationship with one or more local community colleges for the purpose of helping high school students get credits for community college before they even finish their senior year. These courses, called concurrent enrollment in some school districts, allow high school students to gain community college credits that they can use after high school, provided they pass the minimum grade requirements necessary for credit (usually a C). Depending on the program, your school may even pay tuition fees and other associated costs, such as textbooks, allowing you to essentially earn community college credits for free. While these credits may or may not transfer to four-year universities, they would allow a student, after high school graduation, to seamlessly move into the local community college having already completed required courses. If a student has taken enough concurrent enrollment courses, they may even be able to earn an associate degree in fewer semesters.

Students in concurrent enrollment programs will usually take classes onsite at their high school either with high school teachers trained to fulfill the needs of the community college program or with college instructors who visit the high school. Occasionally, particularly for classes where certain types of lab equipment may be necessary (such as welding or other technical training), students may also be excused from their high school for part of the day to travel to a community college for a course. Alternatively, students may attend a community college course online as part of a concurrent enrollment opportunity. The guidelines for programs like these vary from district to district, so talk to your guidance counselor about the options specifically available to you.

Pick At Least One Challenging Course per Year

Students who are planning to go to four-year colleges or universities are told to take as many challenging courses as possible, but there is less necessity for an intense workload if you are planning to start off at community college. That's because when you transfer, your college GPA will be weighted as more important than your high school GPA. Of course, that doesn't mean you should forget about your GPA or let your grades slip on purpose, especially since financial aid for community college could be based on academic merit, but it does mean you don't have to bust your hump fitting in a bunch of AP classes unless they genuinely interest you.

Since you don't have to be as worried about your GPA as someone who is trying to get into a competitive college, you don't have to worry as much if you take a challenging course and don't get quite as high a grade as you're used to. This means you have incentive to try out new topics even if you aren't positive that you'll be awesome at them. You have more room to experiment with finding subjects that interest you and that might light the way for a potential career path. Here, we outline three major benefits of taking a challenging course as a future community college student.

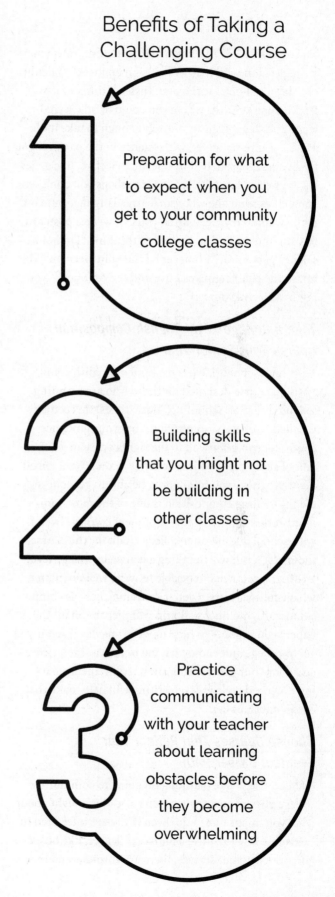

Benefits of Taking a Challenging Course

1 Preparation for what to expect when you get to your community college classes

2 Building skills that you might not be building in other classes

3 Practice communicating with your teacher about learning obstacles before they become overwhelming

The objective isn't to set yourself up for failure; if you struggle a ton with math, don't sign up for AP Calculus one day and hope for the best. Instead, think of it as finding one key area where you could handle a challenge and then pushing yourself enough to take it on. Maybe you've struggled with science in the past, yet you find yourself fascinated by a science elective, like genetics or environmental science. Or perhaps you don't see yourself as someone who can learn a language but you really want to try German so you can write a postcard to your aunt in Berlin. Instead of thinking "I'm not a science person" or "I'll never be fluent in German," sign up for the challenging elective and try your best—you might surprise yourself!

Take a College-Level English Composition Course Your Senior Year

Most high schools have some kind of English composition course designed for those who are planning to attend further schooling. Many times, this course is called "College Composition," but your guidance counselor can point you to the right course in your school's catalog. If your school has a concurrent enrollment program, you might even be able to get college credit—college composition is one of the most commonly offered concurrent enrollment courses. Even if your school doesn't offer college credit for the course, though, it's still worth taking a course in college-level writing; you'll need to be able to write well no matter which college courses you take. Taking college composition in high school will help you prepare for all the papers you're going to have to write one day. Even if you get to college and end up having to take a similar class again for your general education requirements, having practiced college-level writing will help make that course much easier.

Choose Courses That Reflect Your Eventual Career Path

Just because you're planning on going to community college doesn't mean you haven't already thought about what you might like to do. Even if you are interested in fields that don't require a four-year degree, like hospitality or customer service, there are absolutely courses

"My concurrent enrollment college composition course is my favorite to teach. The students all improve so much over the course of the year and you can see it in the quality of their writing. Plus, when they come back to see me after heading to college, all of them tell me how glad they are that they learned how to write a college-level paper BEFORE they got to their first finals week. Clearly, I am biased, but I think college composition is a must-take for every high school student who plans to continue their education."

Kyla, High School English Teacher

you can take in high school that could help you get a leg up later. For instance, Spanish courses are almost universally worthwhile in the United States, since the need for Spanish speakers is high in most fields. If you are hoping to get a hospitality job, such as working at a luxury hotel, knowing a second language like Spanish (or any other language) would be value added, since you could speak to any hotel guests who speak that language. If you know that you might like to go into a field where you'll be dealing with customers a lot, taking classes in public speaking or marketing can help you become comfortable doing so. If you know you want to get your associate degree as a precursor to a job as a firefighter or police officer, then physical education classes could be a good way to start training. Computer coding, graphic design, and personal finance are other electives that tend to be helpful for a wide variety of jobs and life skills. Think about the specific job or type of career you might like to have, then pick classes that help you build the skills that could prove useful later.

Planning for a Vocation or Trade

College isn't for everyone. Maybe you've never heard someone actually say it before, but the truth is that not everyone envisions themselves in a career that requires a degree, nor do all people thrive in a college environment. Plenty of vocations and trades do not require a four-year degree and are pathways to long, successful careers (see Chapter 4 for more information on what options are out there). In fact, because there has historically been such a broad push for students to go to college, both social stigma and a shortage of trained workers mean that many of these fields are now booming, making it easy for motivated high school graduates to put themselves on a path towards a secure (and often well-paid) career. Don't let any kind of stigma about these sorts of jobs keep you from pursuing them if they sound interesting to you. Lawyers and doctors may be necessary and have prestige, but society as we know it would grind to a halt without plumbers, sanitation workers, and commercial truck drivers.

That said, you're not off the hook when it comes to thinking about life after high school just because you plan to go to a vocational school, apprentice to learn a trade, or follow any other path that doesn't involve a college degree. Instead, here are some things you can do to plan for a successful career without a college degree.

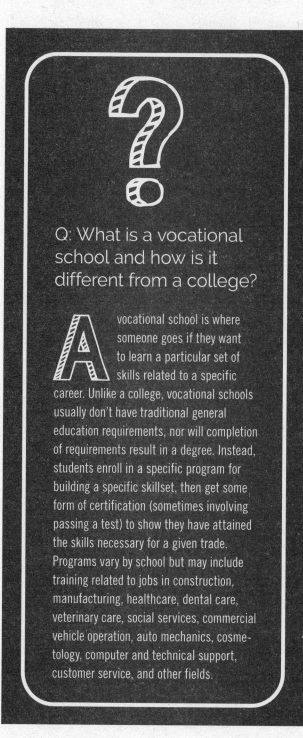

Q: What is a vocational school and how is it different from a college?

A vocational school is where someone goes if they want to learn a particular set of skills related to a specific career. Unlike a college, vocational schools usually don't have traditional general education requirements, nor will completion of requirements result in a degree. Instead, students enroll in a specific program for building a specific skillset, then get some form of certification (sometimes involving passing a test) to show they have attained the skills necessary for a given trade. Programs vary by school but may include training related to jobs in construction, manufacturing, healthcare, dental care, veterinary care, social services, commercial vehicle operation, auto mechanics, cosmetology, computer and technical support, customer service, and other fields.

Take Business Classes

Even if you don't plan on going to school for business, most people who work in trades or vocations will either need to run their own business one day or help manage a business for another. Therefore, taking business classes in high school on topics like personal finance, marketing, and accounting can help you gain a basic understanding of how a business works. With enough planning, you may even be able to write a tentative future business plan that can help lay the foundation for working for yourself after any job training you complete. Imagine, for instance, that you've just completed beauty school and can now work as a makeup artist. Do you want to work for someone else for the rest of your career or would you rather eventually be in business for yourself? Most people would say they'd rather work towards being their own boss and setting their own hours, so business courses in high school can help you think ahead for what would be necessary to do that.

Work Your Electives

Most high schools have a variety of elective courses that map well to various potential career paths. For instance, if you know that you'd like to work in restaurants and perhaps eventually get culinary training to be a chef, taking cooking classes in high school would be an excellent head start. The bigger your high school, the more likely they are to have a robust catalog of potential elective courses to suit any number of needs. Those interested in entering technical fields, like future mechanics and electricians, should see what kind of technology or shop courses are available at their school, while future hairdressers might see if they can take art classes or do courses in things like fashion design. Learning a language (especially Spanish, if you live in the US), taking a class in public speaking, or taking coding, typing, or other computer courses would be useful in just about any field.

Ask Your Guidance Counselor about Job Shadows, Apprenticeships, and Internships

Your guidance counselor isn't just an expert on college planning. They are also usually up to speed on what kind of career programs exist for students who want to enter the workforce right after graduation or for those who would prefer to go to a vocational school or learn a trade. Don't assume that just because you're not interested in a traditional college path, you don't need to talk to your guidance counselor. Instead, tell them what sort of jobs you're considering and ask if there are any types of job shadows (meaning joining someone in the field on a day of work), apprenticeships, or internships that you can do in high school or over the summer. This is a good way to not only get practical experience in a field to see if its right for you but also stand out in the future when you go to apply for jobs. It shows you're serious about the career path you want to pursue.

Consider Any School-to-Career Programs Your School Offers

While this might not be available everywhere, many high schools now offer programs designed to help

"I've seen a lot of memes about how 'high school never taught me how to do my taxes,' but here I am! I teach that! A lot of schools do! Take a personal finance or business class as an elective and you'll likely learn all sorts of things related to managing your money, including how to do your taxes."

Jason, High School Finance Teacher

students get credit for having a job while in high school. Many times, the student will be dismissed from part or all of some school days in order to attend work while getting high school credit for doing so. The advantage of these programs is that students work real jobs, meaning they also get real incomes. That means you're getting more or less paid to earn credit for high school! Most of the time, students will take a business or career course at school alongside the program. Here, they'll learn critical skills necessary for success in the workforce. Ask your guidance counselor if a program like this exists, and if so, consider signing up.

Investigate Concurrent Enrollment Options for Skill Building

You may find that like the concurrent enrollment options available for students headed to college, there are also concurrent enrollment options for students who want to build skills related to trades. For instance, perhaps you would be able to go to a local community college in the afternoon and take a course on welding in hopes of one day completing a welding certification. Like many things, this will depend on what is offered in your specific school district, but it's worth asking your guidance counselor if any programs like this exist.

OH NO, I WANT TO GO TO COLLEGE...BUT I PLANNED NOT TO GO!

So, imagine you just spent most of high school thinking that you didn't want to go to college. Now, it's the second semester of senior year, and it turns out you actually do want to go. Oh no! Are you sunk? Not in the slightest! There are still lots of things you can do.

If, up to this point, you managed to get good (or even just decent) grades without planning for college, you should consider applying as soon as possible. If you apply early enough, you might still be able to get enrolled for the fall. Some schools, particularly public schools in the state in which you live, may also have options for late applicants—check the school's admissions website to see.

Alternatively, particularly if your grades were iffy in high school, you can plan to go to community college and transfer out later. Even if you didn't plan for college in high school, you should be able to get into a community college no matter what. Speak with an advisor there so they can help you focus on knocking out general education requirements that are likely to transfer to a four-year college or university. Then, focus on keeping your community college grades high since your community college GPA will count much more than your high school GPA by that point.

Finally, you can also take a gap year and spend that time building up your skills for college. Maybe you enroll in CLEP courses or use a test prep guide to get the ultimate SAT score so that when applications roll around again, you're a more desirable candidate. Any of these options will work, so don't feel like you're stuck in whatever path you selected as a freshman. Your guidance counselor would be the best person to help you make a gameplan for where you're at.

Your plans for life after high school can take many forms. How you'll make the journey into the real world is an individual matter. Some people take many stops and accumulate various degrees before entering into

> "I didn't take high school very seriously for the first three years because I honestly wasn't planning to go to college. I just didn't like school much, so I figured it wasn't for me. However, when my abuela got sick, I realized how important in-home nurses are. Her nurse, Rhiannon, was such an inspiration that I realized I wanted to do what she did. I talked to my guidance counselor and he helped me make a plan to start off at community college so I could improve my chances of getting into a good nursing program later. I didn't think I could change my mind so late, but I'm glad I finally have a plan to make my dream come true."
>
> Delfina, High School Senior

the workforce. Others know exactly what they want to do and jump right in. And still others hone their craft at a vocational school before entering the real world. Because of all these different paths that life has to offer, it's important to know who you are and what you want—before starting down your own personal path.

Just having a high school diploma is not enough for many occupations. But, the same can be said for having a college degree. Different kinds of work require different kinds of training. Knowing how to operate particular types of equipment, for instance, takes special skills and work experience that you might not learn in college. Employers always want to hire the best-qualified people available, but this does not mean that they always choose those applicants who have the most education. The *type* of education and training you have is just as important as *how much you have*. Right now, you're at the point in your life where you can choose how much and what kind of education and training you want to get.

FINDING YOUR PATH

Even if you have a definite career field in mind, such as working in the beauty industry, there are still several routes you can take to get there, depending on what exactly you want to do, who you want to help, and what skill set you want to pursue. For example, if you know that you are interested in helping people feel good about their skin, you have options: you could manage a retail store that sells cosmetics or skin care and hair products, you could start your own business as an esthetician and offer skin care services to clients, or you could become a dermatologist and treat patients with skin conditions. Even just knowing the general field you want to end up in affords you so many options to choose from; it's just a matter of tailoring your path by considering the type of position you want, how much education you're willing to pursue, what kind of salary you want to make, and other factors related to your lifestyle and goals.

In any case, whether you know exactly what field interests you or you are still figuring that out, you will have to decide if you want to pursue a college education. For those of you interested in some of the benefits of higher education, read on!

Notes

Planning Your Education While in High School

Some people are just born planners. They thrive on organization and routine, finding it easy to create order out of a chaotic schedule or straighten up a messy room. People with this natural predisposition for planning may start high school with their future courses already mapped out, knowing exactly what they want to take, the questions they want to ask their guidance counselor, and how they want to approach their entire high school experience. However, let's face it—most of us aren't those people (and even those people could probably still use a little help, too).

The Short and Sweet Version

Okay, so you're ready to start high school or maybe you already started but you're thinking to yourself, "What's my best plan of attack?" High school can be overwhelming for a lot of reasons that have nothing to do with college and career planning, so when you throw in the expectation that you'll magically have your whole future planned out by the time you graduate? Yeah, it sounds nuts. But planning is planning, not predicting the future with a crystal ball. You're setting yourself up as best as possible for what you can expect to come.

Therefore, planning your education in high school doesn't need to be a scary thing. For one, you should have a guidance counselor (who might be called something different at your school, like an advisor) whose job it is to help you plan your courses throughout high school and guide you in whatever direction you need to accomplish your future goals. Seriously, that's what a guidance counselor is there for, so never underestimate the power of a good relationship with yours!

There are certain steps you should plan to take each year of high school, but if you miss some, most can be made up later. Certain things should be on your radar from day one though, like building positive relationships with the teachers who just "get" you and looking for cool extracurricular activities that challenge you but also bring you joy. Both colleges and employers like well-rounded people who are open to trying new things, so think of high school as an exploration phase for all the things you might like to try.

In high school, try to make it your goal to develop lasting study habits, mature and grow as a responsible member of your community, and discover who you are as a person. You don't have to know for sure what you want to do a decade from now or even a month from now, but it is on you to start thinking about what kind of adult person you want to be. Whether you realize it or not, high school will go by in a flash. Make the most of it so you can step out into the real world full of confidence!

PLANNING FOR YOUR FUTURE

Many of us (maybe even most of us) love to procrastinate on tackling big picture things like planning for the future. That's because humans have this weird tendency to put things off if they seem like they could be overwhelming. However, by reading this book, you're already taking a big step towards thinking about your future. Perhaps you're reading this as a recent 8th grade graduate or as an incoming freshman, with all four years of high school ahead of you. If this is you, you probably want to get a sense of how best to plan your time in high school. Or, perhaps, you're coming to this book later than your freshman year—even then, the tips we lay out here can help you "course correct" during your sophomore or junior year or make the most of the classes you *did* take if you're getting started as a senior or recent graduate. The important thing is to recognize how the work you do (or did) in high school can lay the groundwork for any future education or career plans you might want to pursue. From a planning standpoint, this also means starting early on with figuring out what kind of future you might want to have.

Yes, You *Can* Plan for Success

Perhaps you're the kind of person who sees the words "plan" and "future" and thinks, "Yeah, yeah, I know, I'll get to it." The problem is, people with this attitude (which again, no judgment—it's many of us!) often figure out that what should have already been done either wasn't done well or wasn't done on time. This isn't exactly the best approach if you're trying to plan for something as important as your future after high school. You wouldn't want to wake up the day before your college applications are due and think, "Wow, I wonder if I should have figured out how to write a college essay or taken that third year of Spanish I needed for my school of choice?" Nor would you want to get into the school of your dreams only to find out that it costs four times as much as you had guessed it would, and you never applied to a single grant or scholarship!

You can be certain: there *is* hope for poor planners. A lot of the time, it's just a matter of breaking down planning into its important component parts so you can tackle them one at a time, which is exactly what this book is

"One thing I wish I'd known before I got to high school is that it's okay to make mistakes! Try to turn them into learning opportunities for the future."

Mia, Recent High School Graduate

designed to help you do. For some people, like those with ADHD, this will be much easier said than done, so know that planning is a skill: you can improve at it over time with practice. It's also possible, with practice, for anyone to learn how to break down larger tasks into smaller parts and to develop coping mechanisms that might help with planning, such as using a calendar app to track important deadlines and meetings, creating color-coded to-do lists, or using a whiteboard on a bedroom wall to draw and map out ideas or plans.

Your teen years are a crucial time because they're when you start to better understand yourself and your needs as a person. Pay close attention to which methods and strategies help you feel more successful in other aspects of your life, both in and outside of the classroom—you might find that the 5 extra minutes you spend making your bed in the morning or straightening your desk before you start an essay help you feel more at ease when doing your homework in your bedroom, for instance. Take note of the different little tricks that help you plan better and try to get creative about how to integrate those same methods into other parts of your everyday life.

Here are some things you can do to ease your mind and prepare mentally for high school before the first day of your freshman year:

☐ **Spend some time on your high school's website or social media accounts.** They probably have information on what sort of clubs are available at the school, which teachers teach in which departments, or a calendar of events planned for fall (or at least one that still shows those from last spring, so you can get an idea of what next spring might look like). They may also have pictures on social media of students having a good time at different types of events. This will start to give you a feel for the specific school culture there...and probably get you excited to join that community!

☐ **Take time over the summer to get to know yourself. Think about what kind of foot you want to put forward when you get to high school.** Whether middle school was a dream or a nightmare in your eyes, high school is a chance to write a new chapter in the book of your life. Spend some time imagining the kind of high schooler you want to be and setting personal goals for how to grow in preparation for high school. You might surprise yourself by what you accomplish with the right mindset shift.

☐ **Talk to older siblings and teenagers who are already in high school but take what they say with a grain of salt.** No two people have the exact same experience in high school, so whether your teen neighbor hates high school or your older sister says they were the best years of her life, neither is necessarily "right." Talk to older teens and get a sense of what high school is like these days. Ask them questions—especially any questions you're too scared to ask of parents or other adults—and ask them to give you honest advice for high school. But remember, their advice and experiences are unique to them, and high school will largely be what you make out of it.

☐ **If you already have a class schedule, see if you can find information on your teachers or classes.** Even just seeing a picture of some of your future teachers might make it feel like you already know some familiar faces on day one. Similarly, if the school's website has a map, you might be able to get the lay of the land and figure out where your classes are likely to be. This can take some of the guesswork out of your first day, but you'll also likely have some kind of "orientation" day for first-year students, so don't worry too much if you can't plan ahead on that stuff.

☐ **Plan out an outfit for day one that makes you feel confident.** Clothes aren't everything, but feeling good in your clothes can make an overwhelming day feel less intense. Don't stress yourself out finding the perfect outfit, but try to wear something that brings up feelings of confidence for you...it'll show in how you carry yourself when meeting your teachers and new classmates!

☐ **Try to enjoy your summer and don't stress out about high school!** Sure, do some of the planning we suggest here, but also remember that you'll have a guidance counselor, your parent(s) or guardian(s), your teachers, and plenty of other people around to help you navigate high school. Yes, it's important to plan for your future, but it's important to enjoy being a kid while you still are one, too! Go outside, get messy, and make mild mischief with your friends like kids your age do. That's an important part of your development, too.

☐ **Take time to explore who you are.** You'll have plenty to think about academically once high school starts up, so spend the time you have getting to know yourself. You'll be glad you took the time for self-reflection when planning starts to become more necessary.

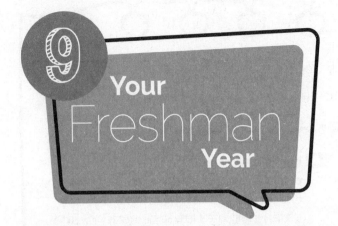

9 Your Freshman Year

Okay, you did it…you figured out the route that gets you from gym class to world history, made a few friends and met all your teachers, and you stumbled upon that one bathroom that's way less busy during lunch. You're starting to get the hang of this high school thing. Now that you have the basics down, it's time to start thinking about how you can use this first year in high school as a foundation for a well-executed college and/or career search later.

Here are some of the things you can do as a freshman (9th or 10th grade, depending on your local school system) to make things easier in the years to come.

☐ **Learn your guidance counselor's name and make it a point to introduce yourself and get to know them a bit.** Your guidance counselor will likely be assigned to you, often based on your last initial, but just because they're randomly assigned doesn't mean your relationship with them should be random. This is an important person for you to get to know early on and someone with whom you should correspond frequently throughout your high school career. If your school does not schedule you an initial meeting with your guidance counselor, ask if you can make one during the first part of your freshman year. Discuss some of your future goals or questions you're considering and ask if there is anything you can do now to help set you up better later. They might have helpful tips about navigating your school to your best potential.

☐ **Request your school profile or planned course of study from your guidance counselor.** Different schools will call it by different names, but you'll likely have some kind of student profile that outlines the classes you are most likely to be placed in over the course of your high school career. Ask to see this planned course of study or, if it doesn't exist, ask your guidance counselor to outline your projected high school course schedule. Which classes will be required, and what choices are available to you? If you wanted to challenge yourself to take more advanced classes, how would that change your projected schedule? Similarly, if you have some reservations about being overbooked in advanced courses, where would you have some wiggle room to take general education courses instead?

☐ **Practice self-advocating early on.** Maybe you know that you have dyslexia, and it helps if you discuss your accommodations with your teachers directly. Or, perhaps, you broke your leg and now you find yourself needing to speak up about a new challenge that has arisen so adults in the school can help you navigate going to school on crutches. Look for opportunities to speak up for yourself, say what you need to succeed, and politely seek out assistance. Start building this habit now as you'll often need to advocate for yourself in the future.

☐ **Become familiar with your high school's graduation requirements as well as general college entrance requirements.** This should help you plan ahead in terms of what courses you want and need to take. This will also help ensure that you aren't surprised by any requirements that pop up in the zero hour during your senior year.

> One thing I wish more of my high school students knew? Teachers talk to each other! Yes, about students! You might think it's only the frustrating things, like 'so and so never stops talking in class,' but more often, a teacher will say something like 'Oh, you have Suzanne? She worked SO hard in my class last year...' and then go on to say how impressed they were with your efforts. I have even gone to bat for former students when other teachers in my department were seeking advice about whether to give them a second chance on a quiz or something. Get to know your teachers and you might just end up with a secret cheerleader in the teacher's lounge.
>
> Oskar, High School Spanish Teacher

☐ **Take your grades seriously.** It's not uncommon for students to think of their freshman year as a "free pass," but in fact, your grades from your freshman year do matter in terms of college and career success. At most schools, your first-year grades will absolutely be part of your GPA. This is not to say that there is no bouncing back if you struggle your freshman year, but you definitely shouldn't think of it as a year that doesn't count. Instead, treat high school like a marathon for which you want to start putting in effort early on so that the final push isn't too hard later.

☐ **Build relationships with your teachers, especially the ones with whom you "vibe."** Having a teacher who you feel comfortable talking to and to whom you can go for advice is incredibly helpful. If you find yourself getting to know a particular teacher or really looking forward to their class, take the time to get to know them a little better or express your appreciation for the impact they make. You might have them for another class, or they might be a surprise advocate if an issue comes up in the future. It never hurts to establish positive relationships with your teachers.

☐ **Start building meaningful friendships.** This one is hopefully easy, but for some, it might be harder; in that case, you'll have to put yourself out there in ways you might not have done in the past. No one can give you a magic handbook for navigating the social dynamics of high school, especially since teen culture and the advice for navigating it is changing all the time. However, one thing is for certain; friends who are loyal, who support you and build you up, who challenge you to be the best version of yourself, and who have your back will always, always be in style. Use high school as a time to build (or keep building) meaningful friendships wherever you find them.

☐ **Work on developing strong study habits that help you be successful.** If you find that certain aspects of studying are harder for you, now is the time to start working on coping mechanisms and strategies to help you overcome those issues. For instance, if you have a hard time sitting for a long time and studying, you might consider using the Pomodoro technique, which involves working hard for 25-minute chunks in between 5-minute breaks. Cultivate good study habits and ask mentors and teachers for help doing so if you're struggling. Practice these habits early on so that they're easy to keep doing for the rest of high school.

☐ **Begin exploring your interests in terms of possible careers.** Your guidance counselor will probably have information on any number of events designed to help students like you start exploring their potential career interests. Try taking advantage of career day opportunities at your school. It's never too early to start looking into career interests; in fact, it's the perfect time!

☐ **Get involved.** Whether its athletics, the arts, or any other extracurricular activities, you'll want to get involved in something by the end of your first year. This is because having more than one year of involvement in an extracurricular activity helps show colleges or employers that you're committed to following through. You won't be at a disadvantage if you decide you don't like it later and want to stop, but use your freshman year as a way to try out some different clubs and activities to see which ones you might like to commit to beyond freshman year.

☐ **Have a mature conversation with your parent(s) or guardian(s) about planning for college expenses.** Even if your family isn't the type to talk about finances often, you need to know what kind of financial support you can expect to have after high school. Determine if your parent(s) or guardian(s) set aside a college fund for you, whether you'll need financial aid to fund your college aspirations, what financial expectations might exist post-graduation (such as if you might be expected to start paying rent while living at home),

and anything else you might need to know to start planning for adulthood before it comes. This might be an awkward conversation and not all parents or guardians will be open to having it, but it's important for you to get this information, so try and approach it with care.

☐ **Look for opportunities for enrichment or volunteering over the summer before your next year of high school.** Whether you attend computer camp or donate time to a domestic violence shelter, you'll be building up your college résumé while also gaining useful life experiences that you can't get in a traditional classroom. Look for summer opportunities that appeal to you and might help you build new skill sets or gain a fresh perspective.

10 Your Sophomore Year

If you attended a junior high and didn't start high school until 10th grade, then your sophomore year may very well be your first year of high school. If this is the case, then the information from the section on your freshman year would also still apply to your sophomore year. For most American students, though, the sophomore year is their second year of high school. It can also be one of the most confusing, as evidenced by the name itself—the word *sophomore* means "wise fool," which is an apt description for how you might feel in 10th grade. You've been around long enough to know what this high school thing is about, but you also may look at the juniors and seniors and feel like they're way ahead of you. These are all normal things for a sophomore to experience, so don't feel bad if this sounds like you!

Your sophomore year is also your last year before the job or college search needs to get more serious. At this point, you can still consider your coursework a foundation for the work you'll do in junior and senior year. If you struggled during freshman year, this is a chance to turn things around before your rigorous junior year. If you did well, now might be the time to seek out new challenges (like advanced courses) and step up your game.

Remember, your guidance counselor is the ideal person to help you figure out what your best steps for sophomore year might be. However, in general, here are some things you can do to make the most of your sophomore year.

Sophomore year is a great time to start figuring out which priorities matter to you and which friendships you want to develop. Make no mistake—junior year will probably be the busiest year of high school for most students, so you want to go in prepared for what to expect. Challenge yourself to mature and grow as a student as much as possible during your sophomore year so that junior year feels like no sweat.

☐ **At the beginning of the year, find out which tests you'll need to take and get them in your calendar.** The PSAT/NMSQT, for instance, should usually be taken in October. By the way, when you take that test, you'll be able to have some information sent to colleges you're already interested in, so you'll probably start to get mail from potential colleges and you can start looking at those materials. When your scores for various tests come in, make appointments to discuss them with your counselor.

☐ **Look out for college fairs and career development activities through your school's guidance office.** Your guidance counselor and others in your district will likely organize several career and college fairs for students over the course of the year. This is a way to "shop around" and look at different possibilities. As a sophomore, you're in a prime position to see all that's out there before getting more serious on narrowing things down later.

☐ **Get involved in new activities outside the classroom and/or continue to develop activities you already started.** Now might even be the time to work for leadership positions in your extracurriculars if you are presented with an opportunity to do so. Use extracurriculars to make new friends, develop non-academic skills, and learn strong teamwork.

☐ **Try to find an adult mentor.** Maybe you have an especially close relationship with your biology teacher, your gymnastics coach, or the school librarian. It's a good idea to find an adult somewhere in the school who you trust and with

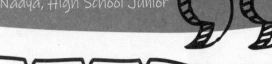

People always told me 'It's not gonna be easy!' and now that I have gone through some of high school, I can see that. What I wish I had known earlier is how personalized you can make it. Science? You got it, join the Science Club! Music? Try out for band or a musical! High school is what you make it. The downside is that you can make it too easy. That makes it so much harder to transition to a more intense college workload. Find that balance in high school.

Nadya, High School Junior

whom you can develop a positive relationship. Not only will this prove useful when it comes time to ask for letters of recommendation later but it will also help you feel more safe and secure in your school if there's someone you can go to for advice or when you need help solving a problem. Most of the adults who work at high schools love teenagers and want to be there for them. It might feel kind of weird to ask someone "Hey, will you be my mentor?" so don't worry about asking them directly. However, if you find that you enjoy talking with a particular adult at your school, take time to keep developing that friendship.

Just remember: It's an adult's responsibility to maintain a professional and respectful relationship with any student they work with, even if they feel like a friend. A mentor should make you feel respected and secure—if an adult ever makes you feel uncomfortable or crosses a boundary, tell another adult you trust.

☐ **If it's easy or convenient to do so, start visiting college campuses.** If there are college campuses nearby that you might like to check out, feel free to start doing so as early as sophomore year. Don't freak yourself out about going on a nationwide tour of potential colleges, but *do* consider visiting a nearby college campus so you can get a feel for what a campus is like in general. Plus, if you decide to go to school close to home, you'll have already visited a few options! If

it is not convenient or affordable to visit colleges, you can also start trying to take "virtual tours" on college websites.

☐ **Start saving now. . .for college, for moving out, for anything.** When you get even a little bit of money as a teenager, it can be tempting to blow it all right away. You don't have to save every single penny you make mowing lawns over the summer, but it's a good idea to start putting away at least some of the money you bring in so you can have it as savings when you graduate high school. If you're able to get a summer job, this can be an even better way to put money away. No one in the history of ever has been disappointed that they saved themselves some money for after high school.

☐ **Keep up the good habits you developed freshman year (or course correct if you developed bad habits).** As a sophomore, it may seem like you've been in high school forever already, but you're not even half done! That means if you're on the right track, you'll want to keep at it, and if you're not, then you still have plenty of time to change things around. A lot of times, you'll have new teachers compared to freshman year, so you'll even have opportunities to make new first impressions as a student. Continue the process of self-reflection and goal setting that helped you freshman year.

11 Your Junior Year

Of all the years of high school, many graduates say that junior year was the most intense. On top of all the job and college prep that tends to happen during this year, you'll also likely be taking your hardest courses of high school. Don't let this scare you! Instead, think of your freshman and sophomore years as a "warm-up" to get you ready for that junior year. If you do, then there will be fewer surprises when you're in the thick of it.

Your junior year is so busy, in fact, that to help you break it down, we have divided the suggestions for this year by season.

Things to Do in the Fall

- ☐ **Make an appointment with your guidance counselor to discuss your progress.** The halfway point of high school is a great time to evaluate your course progress. If you still have some courses that you'll need to take to graduate, finding out now will be a lot more useful than finding out later. This is also a good time to start talking with your counselor about any potential post-graduation plans you're contemplating.

- ☐ **Look at the college information available in your counselor's office and in your school and public libraries.** Now is the time to look at any school that piques your interest and learn as much as you can about it so you can start narrowing down your choices. Check out college websites, brochures, and any other resources you can get your hands on.

- ☐ **Begin considering which colleges you might like to visit and plan accordingly.** Even if the only college you visit is the one nearest to you, you'll want to visit at least one campus, if you can, to start getting a feel for what it's like to be on one.

- ☐ **Start figuring out your priorities for a college or career.** If you can do skills assessments (like the one in Chapter 2), do so; otherwise, begin thinking about what matters to you in a college or in your first post high school job. For instance, if you're college-bound, you'll want to start zeroing in on the type of college you would prefer (two-year or four-year, small or large, research-heavy or liberal arts, public or private, etc.) Notably, this will also help make your

overall college search less overwhelming since you'll be able to eliminate schools that don't match what you're seeking.

- ☐ **Continue visiting college and job fairs.** You may be able to narrow your choices or add a college to your list this way.

- ☐ **When college representatives visit your school, make a point to speak with them.** Even if you aren't sure you want to go to their school, this is good practice for conversing with admissions representatives. Plus, you might surprise yourself by being interested in their school, even if you weren't before you started the conversation.

- ☐ **If you are interested in participating in Division I or II sports in college, start the certification process.** Check with your counselor to make sure you are taking a core curriculum that meets National Collegiate Athletic Association (NCAA) requirements. Register with the NCAA Clearinghouse.

- ☐ **Stay involved with your extracurricular activities throughout the year.** If you're sick of something, don't keep doing it just for the college application. If you like something, though, challenge yourself to be involved for as much of high school as you can, as this will look good on applications. If an opportunity arises for you to pursue a leadership opportunity, such as by being captain of the robotics team or earning the role of first chair violin in orchestra, and you have the time and energy to do so, take it!

Things to Do in the Winter

- [ ] **Make a list of colleges that meet your most important criteria (size, location, distance from home, majors, academic rigor, housing, and cost).** Weigh each of the factors according to their importance to you. You'll eventually want to get it down to 1–3 top choices, 2–5 secondary choices, and a "safety" school (a school where you can be fairly certain that you'll get in no matter what.)

- [ ] **Collect information about college application procedures, entrance requirements, tuition and fees, room and board costs, student activities, course offerings, faculty composition, accreditation, financial aid, and your own impressions of the school for the institutions on your list.** Yeah, it's a lot to compile, so using a spreadsheet or some other form of note-taking is a smart idea. However, even though this seems time-consuming, you'll want to go through the process of determining how much goes into each application now so you can plan better for the application process later. You wouldn't want to spend hours on an application only to find out the deadline passed (and the school didn't have your major anyway).

- [ ] **Register to take the SAT and ACT if you haven't already done so through your school.** Many high schools these days administer the SAT, ACT, or both directly to students. They may even designate special testing schedules to allow students to do this as part of the normal school year. However, if your school does not do this, or if you'd like to retest independently, you will need to register on your own. These tests have dates throughout the year, but seats are limited, so don't wait too long to register.

- [ ] **Have a conversation with your parent(s) or guardian(s) about the schools or careers you're interested in and your post-graduation prospects.** Like the finances conversation we suggested you have during your freshman year, this may be a hard conversation for some to have, so approach the topic with care. That said, it's important to sit down with your parent(s) or guardian(s) and discuss the different options you're considering so they can support you and offer insights on how to make those plans reality. It's especially important to revisit the topic of finances and to see how much they will (or will not) be able to contribute after your graduate high school, if they haven't already made that crystal clear.

- [ ] **Create paper and digital filing systems for the correspondence you'll receive.** Applying to and talking with colleges creates a lot of paperwork. Sometimes, this will be literal paper, so you'll want some kind of paper filing system in place so you can keep correspondence from different schools separate. However, you're just as likely to be getting a tremendous amount of email and digital correspondence, too. Make sure you have a designated place on your computer to save these materials so you can reference them later. A smart way to categorize materials is by having a separate folder for the materials you receive from each school.

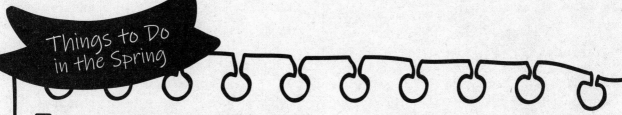

Things to Do in the Spring

- [ ] **Make an appointment with your guidance counselor to review your course selections for senior year and discuss graduation requirements.** Most high schools make it far more difficult to change schedules once a semester or quarter is underway, so it will be a lot easier to make sure all your graduation requirements are covered by the end of senior year if you discuss things with your counselor at the end of your junior year.

- [ ] **Discuss your ACT/SAT scores with your counselor.** Making sure to do this by the end of your junior year means that if you don't like your scores and want to retest, you'll have time to do so.

- [ ] **Begin brainstorming or outlining ideas for a college essay.** You might not know what the exact prompts you'll have to answer in application essays are, but it's a good idea to brainstorm some ideas as a junior so you can work on a "base" essay over the summer. If you have some ideas of what you might like to write about when applications come around, you will be able to build stronger essays based on that prior work. Your English teacher, guidance counselor, and any mentors are good sources for discussing essay ideas. They can also help when it comes time to edit your essays. Of course, they may be busy, so remember that you also know many other skilled people who can help with writing, such as librarians, other teachers, relatives with writing-intensive jobs, and even peers with exceptional English skills.

- [ ] **Start considering which teachers you might like to have write your college recommendations.** Think about asking teachers who know you well. Letters from a coach, an activity leader, or an adult who knows you well outside school (e.g., volunteer work contact) are also valuable as supplemental recommenders. Procrastinators, take note: this is where it comes in handy to have built teacher relationships from Day 1 of freshman year. If you want a glowing recommendation, you need to invest enough energy and time into building and maintaining these relationships.

- [ ] **Inquire about scheduling personal interviews at the colleges that interest you.** This is something that may be able to wait until your senior year, but even if you decide to schedule the interview for later, you'll want to call the schools you're interested in and find out about the interview process. They may have advice for you about the best way to time things.

- [ ] **Look for enriching summer opportunities, such as camps, summer jobs, or internships.** Try and use the summer between your junior and senior year of high school to build crucial work and life experience that can help you look more attractive to prospective colleges.

- [ ] **Figure out how fees and deadlines will affect your college application process.** Some schools charge a very high fee to apply while others don't charge anything at all. Figure out how much sending off your various items will cost you. Remember to factor in not just the fee for the application itself but also the fees that may be associated with sending test score reports to different colleges, printing materials for things like art portfolios, and any other fees that may be necessary to process your application. You'll be able to determine more about this on the admissions website of any school you're interested in.

- [ ] **Start looking for and applying to scholarships and grants if you haven't already.** You will be glad you took the time to seek out and apply to any scholarship or grant you can find. Even if you only get a handful of what you apply to, that's still free money for school!

- [ ] **If you're able to, plan college visits.** The spring of your junior year and the fall of your senior year are the two best times to visit schools that interest you.

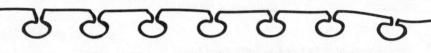

> At our university, we consider the types of classes students have taken. We seek not only academically talented students but also those who are well-rounded. We look for students who are involved in their communities and schools, who hold leadership positions, and who have a balance of activities outside of academics. This gives us a look at that person as a whole.
>
> Bill, Admissions Counselor

Things to Do in the Summer before Senior Year

- [ ] **Send thank you letters to anyone with whom you interviewed for college or a job.** After each college interview, send a thank-you letter to the interviewer. This is also a good practice for any jobs you applied to. Even if you don't end up getting the job or gaining admittance to the college, this is a polite habit that reflects positively on you and may even help keep your name in someone's mind if things change.

- [ ] **Make an effort to speak with students who currently attend or recently attended the schools you're most interested in.** Even if you just reach out to someone on social media, most people will be willing to answer questions about their school. If you know anyone who has attended the colleges in which you are interested, try to take them out for coffee so you can ask them lots of questions.

- [ ] **Familiarize yourself with the Common Application.** This is the college application used at more than 900 schools to help students save time and minimize the amount of paperwork they have to fill out. There's a good chance that at least one of the colleges you're interested in uses the Common Application, and it's fairly similar to any other application you're likely to receive, so it's a good idea to start thinking about it early.

- [ ] **Volunteer in your community.** Service always looks good on college applications. Even if you can't make a huge time commitment, carve out some space for you to get some volunteering under your belt.

- [ ] **Compose rough drafts of your college essays and get feedback on them so you can get them in shape.** Have a teacher or counselor read and discuss them with you. Polish them and prepare final drafts. Proofread your final essays. Then, proofread them again. You don't want to do this part last minute—leave yourself plenty of time to do it right and put your best work forward.

- [ ] **Develop a financial aid application plan.** You'll want to have notes listing the different aid sources you want to seek out, requirements for each application (such as for scholarships), and a timetable for meeting the filing deadlines. More information on preparing for the financial realities of college can be found in Chapter 10.

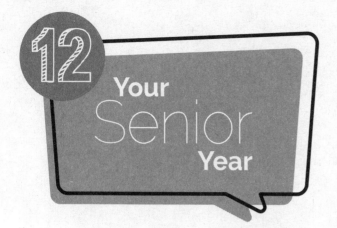

Wow, you did it! You got through your first three years of high school and now you're a senior. If you talk to your family members or any recent high school graduates, you might notice that some of their best memories of high school come from senior year. Between all the senior year traditions, having time to enjoy your now well-developed friendships, and the ease that comes with having more maturity and a better rapport with all the teachers you've gotten to know, senior year can feel pretty great.

Still, though, you're not out of high school yet, so your work isn't over when you get to senior year—there's still a lot to do! As with junior year, we've broken down the tasks into different seasons so you can see what you should be doing and when your senior year.

☐ **Make an appointment to check in with your guidance counselor.** You know the drill by now… at the beginning of each year, it's always a good idea to check in with your guidance counselor and see how you're progressing and if they have any relevant advice for where you're at in the college or job search process. Counselors find out about new resources all the time, so also make sure to keep checking in throughout your senior year.

☐ **Resist senioritis at all costs…keep those grades up!** It's so tempting to start slacking off during senior year, especially if you've done well up to that point. But just like your freshman grades still very much count, your senior grades do as well. Keep pushing hard to make sure your grades reflect well on your abilities.

☐ **Continue to participate in extracurricular and volunteer activities and take on a leadership role if you can.** Even if you aren't team captain, as a senior in an activity, younger students may be looking to you as a role model. Make sure to demonstrate initiative, creativity, commitment, and leadership in each activity in which you participate. You may even be able to take a younger student under your wing and mentor them.

☐ **If you are male or interested in serving in the military, register for selective service on your eighteenth birthday to be eligible for federal and state financial aid.** As of printing, US law only requires males to register for selective service at age 18. Your guidance counselor can give you more information on how to do this if you're unsure this law applies to you.

☐ **Talk to counselors, teachers, parents, and any other trusted mentors about your final list of colleges to apply to.** If you're having trouble narrowing down your list, these people can give you sound advice to help you figure out what school should be your priority.

☐ **Make a calendar showing application deadlines for admission, financial aid, and scholarships.** Even if you're not the type to make a calendar, just do it. You'll be so glad to have all those deadlines in one place, and it will help you prioritize which to work on when. Check resource books, websites, and your guidance office for information on scholarships and grants.

Things to Do in the Fall

☐ **Send online recommendation forms (through Naviance, the Common Application, or however your school asks you to) to the teachers you have chosen.** The earlier they get it, the better, since teachers are very busy. Some related tips:

- Don't be afraid to (politely!) remind them of the due date if it's getting close and they still haven't submitted it. The college you're applying to should have a way of showing who has and has not submitted a recommendation.

- It can be helpful to give your teachers a short list of what you believe you accomplished in their class, a sample of some good work you did, and a few "idea points" about the kind of student you believe you are. Some of these suggestions might possibly be included in their letters about you. You can also request that they highlight some aspect of your school history in their letter, though they don't necessarily have to follow this request.

- Generally, teacher recommendations are supposed to be anonymous, so you will not get to see what your teacher wrote about you. Therefore, it's important to track the submission status of letters of recommendation, since you won't necessarily know when they've submitted it until you see it accepted by the school.

- Thank anyone who writes you a recommendation with a note and perhaps a gift card or another small token of thanks. Teachers don't get paid extra to write your recommendations (which can take a lot of time to compose!), so be sure to show your gratitude.

- Some schools may ask for recommendations from someone who is NOT a teacher, so it's a good idea to have in mind a coach, employer, religious leader, or any other trustworthy adult who can speak to your traits and abilities.

☐ **If you need to retake the ACT or SAT, register to do so.** You don't want to let the deadlines pass, so do it as early as possible.

☐ **Make sure you have requested that standardized test score reports be sent to any school that needs them.** The way you request these score reports and have them sent will likely vary from test to test, so make sure you figure out the protocol on the test's website.

☐ **If you decide to apply early decision to a school, figure out when the deadline is for this application type at that school.** For more information on early decision, see Chapter 7.

☐ **If you're able to, plan college visits.** The spring of your junior year and the fall of your senior year are the two best times to visit schools that interest you.

☐ **Start applying!** At this point, you'll likely need to start getting some of your earlier applications in. One thing: Every time you apply to a school, make sure you save the confirmation of the application.

Things to Do in the Winter

☐ **Keep an eye out for college-preparatory nights, job fairs, career days, or any other opportunity presented for soon-to-be graduates at your school.** Attend whatever college and career events are held at your school or by local organizations. This is especially crucial if you have procrastinated some and didn't start preparing for your future until senior year. Events like these can act as a sort of crash course to help you get on track and make a plan.

☐ **Continue to focus on grades and resist senioritis so you can send good mid-year grade reports to colleges.** Yes, it's incredibly tempting to slack off a little now that you can see things falling into place. Instead of giving into the temptation to coast out the rest of the year, rely on the good study habits you've built up and keep your grades afloat. If you've fallen behind, now is the time to talk to your teachers and maturely request assistance catching up. If you're in this position, remember to demonstrate that you're willing to work to catch up and not just looking for a handout. This shows maturity and may help you get any second chances you need.

☐ **Fill out the Free Application for Federal Student Aid (FAFSA) and, if necessary, the CSS/Financial Aid Profile.** These forms can be obtained from your guidance counselor, or you can find them electronically through **fafsa.gov** and the College Board website. These forms may not be processed before January 1, so don't send them before then, but do get them done as early as you can. More information on filling out these forms can be found in Chapter 10.

☐ **Send any remaining college applications and financial aid forms off before winter break.** Make sure you apply to at least one college that you know you can afford and where you know you're very likely to be accepted. Remember, it's a good idea to make a calendar of application deadlines and to strive to get applications done early whenever possible.

☐ **Meet with your counselor to verify that all forms are in order and have been sent out to colleges.** Ask them if there is anything they recommend for you to do at this point to ensure all applications went off without a hitch.

☐ **Save your email confirmations as proof that the colleges have received all application information, including recommendations and test scores.** Hopefully, you won't need this information, but if you do, you'll be glad you saved it.

Things to Do in the Spring

☐ **Keep an eye out for college-preparatory nights, job fairs, career days, or any other opportunity presented for soon-to-be graduates at your school.** Just like you have been the rest of the year, continue to attend these events and practice your networking skills.

☐ **Watch your email or snail mail between March 1 and April 1 from colleges that do not offer rolling admissions.** If you don't get into your school(s) of choice, try not to freak out too much. There's a reason you sent out more than one application.

☐ **Await notification of financial aid awards between April 1 and May 1.** A lot of times, these are sent alongside an acceptance letter, but they may also be sent separately.

☐ **Compare the financial aid packages from the colleges and universities that have accepted you and don't be afraid to ask your top choice if they can match your best package.** You might be surprised what kind of incentive aid schools are able to give out, and the worst they can tell you is that they can't raise your initial offer.

☐ **Once you know where you're going, try to attend admitted student events or on-campus revisit days to get a feel for student life at your new school.** For instance, if you're going to school out of state, there may be an event for students from your area who are all going. This can give you some built-in connections before you even arrive to campus and make the transition to college life easier.

☐ **Make your final choice and notify all schools of your intent by May 1.** Keep an eye out for a different deadline, but this is generally when students are expected to have made a decision.

☐ **Make sure you or your guidance counselor (depending on the item) send off anything that the school needs to receive by a deadline.** Items on this list include things like nonrefundable tuition deposits, final school transcripts, roommate placement questionnaires, forms for scheduling your orientation, and other necessary forms.

☐ **Tell your teachers who wrote you recommendations where you were accepted and ultimately decided to go.** Thank them again for their support. It's always classy to give a token gift of appreciation, like a gift card. Seriously, never underestimate how much teachers love getting gift cards for things like coffee and lunch.

☐ **If you received a Student Aid Report (SAR) as part of your FAFSA, make sure it gets to your school and retain a copy for your own records.** Usually, students who applied for a Pell Grant through the FAFSA will receive this report.

☐ **Graduate!** You did it! Woohoo! You should be so proud of yourself for what you accomplished! Enjoy these last moments as a high school student and take time to show love and appreciation for the friends, teachers, counselors, coaches, librarians, and literally anyone else who helped make your high school experience worthwhile.

Things to Do in the Summer

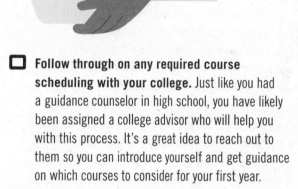

- ☐ **If you need to apply for a Stafford Loan (see Chapter 9), now is the time to do it.** Allow eight weeks for processing.

- ☐ **Make sure you know when and how you'll be attending your college's orientation.** This will vary from school to school and may include specialized options, like pre-orientations centered around camping trips or volunteer opportunities. As soon as your school sends you orientation information, sign up for the option that suits you and make a note of all the important related dates and expectations.

- ☐ **See if you can match with your roommate(s) in advance of your arrival on campus.** Many schools now allow for pre-college roommate matches. Other schools may simply assign you a match based on a survey and will include information on how to contact your new roommate. Even if you're shy, challenge yourself to reach out to your new roommate(s) before you arrive to take some of the jitters out of your first day in the dorm room together.

- ☐ **Follow through on any required course scheduling with your college.** Just like you had a guidance counselor in high school, you have likely been assigned a college advisor who will help you with this process. It's a great idea to reach out to them so you can introduce yourself and get guidance on which courses to consider for your first year.

- ☐ **Get pumped for adulthood!** Congratulations! You are about to begin the greatest adventure—your adult life. Believe in yourself because you've got what it takes!

We've said it before in this chapter and we'll say it again: high school is what you make it. If you need help or are struggling, don't be afraid to reach out, but know that you have the skills in your toolkit to succeed in high school and beyond. It might take some hard work, commitment, and planning, but it really is possible to create the life you want one step at a time.

Ten Study Skills that Lead to Success

1 **Set a regular study schedule.** In college, you are solely responsible for remembering to do your homework. Develop the study patterns in high school that will lead to success in college. Anyone who has ever pulled an all-nighter knows how difficult it is to function in school the next day, so try to tame any procrastination or other bad study habits early.

2 **Save everything.** Develop an organized system for storing your papers and assignments, whether they're physical papers or digital files. It helps if your filing system separates these things and labels them by class name and when you took the class, such as having a folder called "10th Grade Biology." Stay on top of your materials and be sure to save quizzes and tests so you can review them. It is amazing how questions from a test you took earlier in the year can miraculously reappear on your final exam.

3 **Listen.** Teachers give away what will be on the test by repeating themselves because repetition is part of learning. If you pay attention to what the teacher is saying both in class and in any online materials, you will probably notice what is being emphasized over and over again. Furthermore, most teachers are not going to test on anything they didn't make sure to teach directly, usually more than one time. If something tends to repeat itself in your notes and in review sessions, chances are that material will be on the test. However, you probably won't notice that repetition unless you're paying attention, taking notes, and reviewing them to begin with. Note: Pay close attention to teachers' directions, too! So many students lose otherwise easy points by simply not listening closely to directions.

4 **Take notes.** If the teacher has taken the time to prepare a lecture, then what they say is important enough for you to write down. Even if they share materials with you later, such as by posting slides on a digital classroom, you should still write down what stands out to you because the act of writing notes keeps you better engaged in class and makes it more likely that you will remember what you learned. In fact, studies have shown that physically writing notes (rather than typing them) is the best at helping you form memories of your notes. Of course, if typing works better for you and is allowed in your class, that's good, too; however, consider physically writing your notes if you're the type who tends to mentally check out during class. You should also develop a system for reviewing your notes. After each class, rewrite them, review them, or reread them. Try highlighting the important points or making notes in the margins to jog your memory.

5 **Set up a study space free of distractions.** Now more than ever, a teen's life is full of distractions. Unfortunately, if you allow yourself to be distracted while studying, chances are you will perform poorly at school. It's critical that you study and do your homework in a well-lit, distraction-free space. That means no phones, TVs, video games, or social media, to name a few common distractions. If the temptation to binge-watch TikTok is too great, try putting your device in a completely different room.

6 **Create your own "reward system."** Studying is hard work, and it's even harder when it seems like one endless, mundane task. Make your study experience more enjoyable by giving yourself small rewards after completing smaller chunks of your homework. For example, treat yourself to a round of your favorite casual game after you complete your history homework or give yourself a short break to do some yoga after finishing your English essay.

7 **Find a homework strategy that works for you.** Some students find that tackling their hardest homework first makes it easy to get through a bunch of assignments. Students who feel this way find that they're less mentally drained by the end of studying if they take on their hardest tasks. Others, especially those who struggle with what is sometimes called "executive function," meaning the ability to manage tasks and responsibilities in a timely way, would be better served by breaking down all of their tasks into smaller pieces and tackling each one at a time based on which are most urgent. You may find that another system works best for you. The important thing is to note which homework practices work well for you and then develop them into habits.

 Manage your time wisely. Devise a system that works for you to note your short- and long-term assignments, projects, and tests. An old-fashioned paper study planner still works wonders for your time management skills! Be sure to write everything down in this notebook even if your teachers post your assignment online. Having your week planned out all in one place can help you find openings in your schedule and be more productive. Don't forget to schedule breaks, meals, and snacks into your busiest days!

 Attend office hours or schedule meetings with teachers. Chances are you won't understand every single question or homework assignment you encounter. It's incredibly important to recognize what you don't know and seek out help to learn that material. Most teachers have office hours or another set way for you to contact them and get more direct help. Keep in mind that if you email your teacher at 10 p.m. the night before a test, they probably won't have time to help you beforehand. When possible, attend the set office hours your teacher has or ask if there is a time you can come discuss an assignment with which you struggled. As an added bonus, teachers really like to see you taking the initiative and meeting with them during their office hours. Note: If you make a meeting with a teacher, show up! They are setting aside time for you and it's not a good look if you don't follow through on the meeting.

 Form a study group or get a study buddy. Establish a group that will stay on task and ask one another the questions you think the teacher will ask. Compare notes to see if you have all the important facts. Discuss your thoughts or have debates about what came up in your assignments. Talking ideas out can help when you later have to respond to an essay question or take part in a discussion-heavy class assignment like a Socratic seminar.

PREPARING FOR THE FUTURE IF YOU DON'T PLAN TO GO TO COLLEGE

Many materials for teens that talk about career planning, including this one, tend to put a lot of emphasis on treating high school as if you are preparing for college. That's because even if you ultimately do not decide to go to college or if you decide to put it off for a while, solid college preparation will still put you in good shape for any possible future plans you could make. That said, if you feel fairly confident that college is not the right path for you, you can still start thinking about your future prospects while in high school.

If you plan to go to the military, treating high school like "college prep" time will also help you develop the basic skills necessary for any number of military careers. STEM courses (meaning courses that focus on science, technology, engineering, and math) tend to correlate especially well with military skills, but any class can teach you useful skills for service. For instance, a speech class can help you develop confidence when speaking to others, as might be necessary if you become a commanding officer. Perhaps it's obvious, but extra physical education classes could be just what you need to be in tip-top shape when it's time for basic training.

Similarly, if you feel certain that you want to pursue a career path that does not require a college degree, there are often still ways for you to focus those interests in high school. Many schools offer elective classes in things like cooking, fashion, gardening, photography, and numerous other skills that translate to real-world jobs. Think about the kind of things that interest you and the kind of skills that various classes, especially electives, might be able to teach you for the future. Learning Spanish, for instance, is useful in just about any job you can think of. Who knows, maybe the class you take in car maintenance helps solidify your desire to be a mechanic one day, but it might also help you become more comfortable using different types of tools that could come up in any number of future jobs.

One more thing to consider is if your school has any kind of school-to-work classes or programs. A lot of times, there are opportunities for high school students to work in the local community, get paid to do so, and receive school credit at the same time. In fact, some schools even allow juniors and seniors to leave school early to attend work and will help them find job placements. Your guidance counselor will know if programs like this exist.

Another thing to ask your counselor about is what's sometimes called concurrent enrollment, meaning classes that earn you both high school and community college credit. Sometimes, there are even programs to learn certain technical skills (such as welding or coding) as part of a program that earns you an associate degree while you attend high school. You may also be able to get community college credit for various high school courses, allowing you to use those credits if you decide to attend a community college later. In short, high school prep isn't only about college—planning in high school can help you maximize success in any field you might want to pursue.

CLASSES TO TAKE IF YOU'RE GOING TO COLLEGE

As you should know by now, classes you take as early as the 9th grade can still help you get into college. Make sure you meet at least the minimum high school curriculum requirements necessary for college admission. Even if you don't plan to enter college immediately, take the most demanding courses you can handle without overexerting yourself. Talk with your guidance counselor to select the curriculum that best meets your needs and skills.

Generally, admissions counselors do like to see advanced courses, such as AP classes, honors or advanced level classes (what these classes are called depends on your school), and courses for which students simultaneously receive community college credit, like college composition courses that seniors might take. Ask your guidance counselor what your options are for advanced courses and challenge yourself to take an advanced course in at least one subject per year, if you're able. For instance, you don't need to be in AP everything, but if you're a whiz at math, there is no reason you couldn't take AP Calculus instead of a regular calculus course. Focus on one or two subjects to challenge yourself in if the idea of a lot of advanced classes sounds overwhelming.

Getting a Head Start on College Courses

These days, many high schools allow students to take college courses while still in high school so that they can get ahead of the game. As we discussed in Chapter 2, some places call this "concurrent enrollment" while others call it "postsecondary enrollment" or something else entirely. No matter the name of the practice, what it means is that students who take these courses and earn a minimum grade (usually a C) receive both high school and college credit for the courses taken. It's like a two-for-one deal!

Concurrent enrollment is designed to provide an opportunity for qualified high school students to experience more advanced academic work. Participation in such a program is not necessarily intended to replace courses available in high school but rather to enhance the educational opportunities available to students while in high school. For instance, while AP classes may exist for the most advanced students in a subject, concurrent enrollment opportunities may go at a slightly less intense pace than an AP class while still helping students earn college credit. Generally, two common types of concurrent enrollment exist, though your guidance counselor can help clarify which options are specifically available for you:

- **Option A:** Qualified high school juniors and seniors take courses directly at their high school for college credit. The high school may or may not pay for books and fees on the students' behalf and the teacher is usually a high school teacher who has been trained to do concurrent enrollment courses. Generally, the student is expected to receive a certain grade to earn the college credit but will receive high school credit so long as they pass.

- **Option B:** Qualified high school juniors and seniors take courses for high school and college credit directly from college instructors, often by traveling to a local community college. For students enrolled under this option, the local school district usually (but not always!) covers the related costs, provided the student completes the selected courses. If the student fails to complete the requirements, the student and parent are often assessed the costs even if the school initially paid.

Certain pre-established conditions must be met for enrollment, so check with your high school counselor for more information.

Earning Credit Elsewhere

Earning college credits in high school doesn't have to be boring. Participating in an outdoor education program or traveling to a foreign country can actually be really fun ways to earn college credits and valuable life experiences that will enhance your college applications. Admittedly, options like these tend to be pricey, though it's worth inquiring if financial assistance is available for those with need. However, if you can swing it, opportunities like these can be adventurous and joyful ways to earn college credits.

Outward Bound

Outward Bound is a nonprofit educational organization that describes itself as a wilderness adventure school. They offer active learning expeditions to people of all ages and backgrounds. They also generally offer a few different ways to earn college or professional credit for a variety of outdoor learning activities. Programming shifts from year to year, so make sure to check them out online and see what kind of programming is available now.

> I tell pretty much every high school student I meet to take concurrent enrollment classes, especially if they know they want to stick with going to community college, like I did. I was able to get almost an entire semester finished for free during high school, and I learned stuff that ended up being really important when I did start my community college classes, like how to write a college paper effectively.
>
> Atlanta, Community College Student

Study Abroad

Numerous organizations offer study-abroad programs for both high school and college students. Your high school guidance counselor or college advisor may have information on organizations that pair with your school, or you can pursue opportunities through independent study abroad organizations. An advantage of studying abroad while in high school is that you'll earn a competitive edge over other students when applying to colleges. It also gives you an advantage later in life when you are looking for a job because you will have gained valuable knowledge about other cultures and languages. These programs have varying commitments, periods of study, prices, and guidelines, so you will have to do some research to find a program that suits you. If you have questions about a program, ask your guidance counselor to help you vet it.

Studying abroad in high school is sometimes referred to as foreign exchange. In a foreign exchange program, students normally live with a host family in a foreign country, where they attend high school and can participate in school and community activities. Various foreign exchange programs are available, depending on the length of time you wish to live abroad. You can choose to study abroad for a full academic year, one semester, or during the summer. In most cases, credits earned while away will go toward credits you need to graduate from your American high school, but not always, so make sure you know what kind of situation is involved in your chosen program. It is highly recommended that you begin planning early and speak with your school guidance counselor to get written documentation about what you'll need to do to receive credit.

YOUR HIGH SCHOOL EXPERIENCE IS *YOUR* HIGH SCHOOL EXPERIENCE

If you've gotten to the end of this chapter, you've probably picked up on a theme—high school is what you make of it and you are in control of your high school experience. While you are definitely in high school to learn necessary academic subjects for your future, don't forget about the social and emotional parts of your development that high school helps foster. This is your transition from being a kid to being an adult, so you'll likely find yourself changing as a person in ways you couldn't have predicted. These changes are good, though, because they will bring you closer and closer to the person you envision yourself one day being. Embrace the changes and challenges of high school, both in the classroom and outside of it, so you can look back on these years and know you made the most of them.

Notes

Other Options after High School

In the past, people would often join the workforce straight out of high school. These days, in addition to a high school diploma, most jobs require applicants to have additional training, certification, licensure, or a college degree. However, don't let the idea of needing additional training deter you from pursuing a career path that resonates. Just as careers today are more fluid and creative than ever, so are today's options for after high school.

The Short and Sweet Version

There are many paths you can take after high school. For starters, consider community college. Community colleges are much more affordable than four-year institutions and make it easy to complete your general education requirements if you do plan on pursuing a four-year degree. Doing well in your community college courses will also strengthen your qualifications when you go to transfer to a four-year institution. Most community colleges offer helpful student and career services so that you are well-prepared to enter the workforce or continue your education.

Another option is pursuing additional education online either through an entirely online institution or through a four-year institution that offers online courses. Keep in mind that these programs are geared toward working adults or nontraditional students, so if you're looking for a more typical college experience, this probably isn't the option for you. However, if you plan on working part- or full-time, or if you have other medical needs or family obligations, you might benefit from the additional flexibility offered by online courses.

If you don't plan on going to college, there are numerous career paths that don't require a four-year degree. However, keep in mind that most jobs do require some kind of training, certification, or licensing in addition to a high school diploma. In lieu of a traditional four-year college experience, consider attending a technical or vocational college, which can prepare you for a specific career path or even a job at a specific company. No matter what option you pursue, be sure to look into the financial aid options available to you.

Alternatively, you could opt for a trade or apprenticeship. Trades are practical skills that are always in need, so learning a trade will offer you a relatively stable career path. In fact, learning a trade or completing an apprenticeship program can put you in a better financial position than earning a four-year college degree, since you can prepare for a specific career without having to repay years of student loans.

A FOUR-YEAR DEGREE ISN'T ALWAYS THE ANSWER

Why do so many students choose unique post-secondary educational or career paths? The reasons are as varied as the students. Life events can often interfere with plans to attend college. For example, family responsibilities may materialize that make it impossible to delay earning an income for four years. You might first go directly into the workforce and then come back and spend time pursuing higher education. Traditional colleges demand certain conventions, behaviors, and attitudes that just aren't necessarily a good fit for every kind of person. Some people need a lot of physical activity to feel satisfied, while others just aren't interested in another four years of schooling. Still others may find that a disability or illness they live with won't be served well by a traditional college setting.

If any of these reasons apply to you, rest assured that you have many postsecondary options available that will allow you to pursue further education while training for a career. Let's take a look at some of the educational paths you can follow.

COMMUNITY COLLEGES

One of your most affordable and convenient postsecondary education options is your local community college. With their open-door policies (admission is open to individuals with a high school diploma or equivalent), community colleges provide access to affordable higher education for millions of Americans who might otherwise be excluded. What's more, you can usually find a unique and heterogeneous (meaning "not all the same") learning environment at a community college, as classes comprise students of all ages, races, and economic backgrounds. While many community college students enroll full time, a large number attend on a part-time basis so they can fulfill employment and family commitments as they advance their education. Since community colleges offer evening and weekend courses, they can especially benefit those who are working or have children.

> "I often encourage students to look into attending a local community college. Not only is it far more affordable (a real benefit for students whose families are in a tough financial situation), but the community college has great transfer rates into some very good state schools."
>
> Jacqueline, High School Guidance Counselor

Community colleges are also referred to as either technical or junior colleges, and they may either be under public or independent control. What all two-year colleges have in common is that they are regionally accredited postsecondary institutions whose highest credential awarded is the associate degree. Community colleges offer a comprehensive curriculum, which includes transfer, technical, and continuing education programs.

Important Factors in a Community College Education

Students who attend a community college can count on receiving high-quality instruction in a supportive learning community. This setting frees students to pursue their own goals, nurture special talents, explore new fields of learning, and develop the capacity for lifelong learning.

From the student's perspective, these characteristics capture the essence of community colleges:

1 They are community-based institutions that work in close partnership with high schools, community groups, and employers in extending educational programs at convenient times and places.

2 Community colleges are cost effective. Annual tuition and fees at public community colleges average approximately half those at public four-year colleges and less than 15 percent of private four-year institutions. In addition, since most community colleges are generally close to their students' homes, these students can also save a significant amount of money on the room, board, and transportation expenses traditionally associated with a college education, provided they live at home while attending.

3 They provide a caring environment with a broad range of counseling and career services that are intended to assist students in making the most of their education. This gives students the opportunity to successfully transition from community college to the workplace.

4 Many community colleges offer comprehensive programs, including transfer curriculums and career programs. For example, certain liberal arts programs, such as chemistry, psychology, and business management, lead directly to a baccalaureate degree. Career programs prepare students for employment or assist those already employed in upgrading their skills. For those students who need

to strengthen their academic skills, community colleges also offer a wide range of developmental programs in mathematics, languages, and learning skills designed to prepare students for success in their college studies.

Getting to Know Your Two-Year College

The best way to learn about your local community college is to visit in person. During a campus visit, be prepared to ask a lot of questions. Talk to students, faculty members, administrators, and counselors about the college and its programs, particularly those in which you have a special interest. Ask about available certificates and associate degrees. If you plan to transfer to a four-year college, ask about the community college's transfer rate and relationships with specific state schools and universities. Be sure you find out which kinds of student services are offered, such as educational or career guidance.

The Money Factor

The main appeal of community college is its affordability: You can save a lot of money by attending a community college first before heading to a public or private four-year institution. If you aren't sure what you want to do or what talents you have, community colleges allow you the freedom to explore different career interests at a low cost. Additionally, community colleges offer a more affordable way for you to knock out your general education requirements before transferring to a four-year institution, where you can focus on your degree program.

Working and Going to School

In recent years, a steadily growing number of students have chosen to attend community colleges while they fulfill family and employment responsibilities. Many two-year college students maintain full-time or part-time employment while they earn their degrees. To allow these students to balance the demands of home, work, and school, most community colleges offer classes at night and on weekends.

For the full-time student, the usual length of time it takes to obtain an associate degree is two years. However, your length of study will depend on the course load you take. The fewer credits you earn each term, the longer it will take you to earn a degree. To help you complete a degree efficiently, many community colleges now award credit based on examination scores or for equivalent knowledge gained through relevant life experiences. Find out what credit options are available to you at the college you are interested in; you may discover that it will take less time to earn a degree than you initially thought.

Preparation for Transfer

Students who first attend a community college and then transfer to a four-year college or university can certainly do as well academically as the students who entered the four-year institutions as freshmen. In fact, most community college students are bright adults who would be perfectly capable of achieving academic success at a four-year institution but who simply want to save money on two years' worth of tuition. Most community colleges have agreements with nearby four-year institutions to make the transfer of credits easier. If you are thinking of transferring, be sure to meet with a counselor or advisor before choosing your courses. You'll want to map out a course of study with transfer in mind. Make sure you also find out the credit transfer requirements of the four-year institution you might want to attend.

New Career Opportunities

Community colleges realize that many entering students aren't sure which field or career they want to pursue. Community colleges have the resources to help students identify areas of career interest and to set their own occupational goals. In addition, community colleges can connect you with local community leaders. For example, some community colleges have established partnerships with local businesses and industries to provide specialized training programs. Some also provide the academic portion of apprenticeship training, while others offer extensive job shadowing and cooperative education opportunities. In a sense, community colleges can directly prepare you to work for specific employers in your area.

ONLINE LEARNING

Online education has made higher education more accessible (and potentially more affordable) for students. Many state school systems have created online campuses to reach more potential students, not only within their respective states but across the country and the world. These schools often pitch themselves as alternatives to the traditional college experience for working professionals with busy lives. If a university doesn't have a devoted online campus, then they likely have some online course offerings or even degree or certification programs that can be completed entirely online.

"I wasn't able to attend college because some family situations forced me right into the workplace. But even though I was working right after high school, I didn't miss out entirely on a college education. I just completed my online degree, and I really am grateful that online learning was so flexible and fit into my schedule."

Sultan, College Graduate

Because online programs are often aimed at adults with families, careers, and busy schedules, students who are looking for a more traditional college experience may not want to pursue this option. Since there is no physical campus where students attend courses, it can be hard to feel a sense of community, and there may be fewer options for extracurricular activities, like academic and student services, clubs, or organizations. While online institutions are always working to create a unique student experience and tight-knit student body, it can be difficult to replicate the experience of attending classes in person.

The COVID-19 pandemic generally accelerated the trend toward online learning. While there have been growing pains as schools adapt face-to-face coursework for an online platform, more and more university systems now offer flexible or hybrid coursework options to reach more students. An increasing number of students need the flexibility and independence that online learning offers. Whether you attend a fully online institution or take online courses at a traditional college or university, there are a few things you should know about online education compared to face-to-face courses.

How Can I Take Online Courses?

Independent online universities or existing colleges with online course offerings are both ideal options to learn remotely. There are two main categories your online courses can fall into.

CREDIT COURSES: In general, if courses for credit are completed successfully, they can be applied toward a degree. Most colleges and universities today offer some courses in their curriculum online as a way to save money and ensure that learners can get the courses they need. Other universities offer entire programs in online formats, from undergraduate degrees to master's and Ph.D. programs. A student's online major can run the gamut from education, business, and science to professional degrees in psychology, counseling, and even accounting, for example.

NONCREDIT COURSES AND COURSES OFFERED FOR PROFESSIONAL CERTIFICATION: These programs can help you to acquire specialized knowledge in a concentrated, time-efficient manner and stay on top of the latest developments in your field. They provide a flexible way to prepare for a new career or study for professional licensure and certification. Many of these university programs are created in cooperation with professional and trade associations. This means courses teach practical skills that are based on real-life workforce needs, making them immediately applicable in the field. Moreover, many nonprofits and private companies are publishing online material to be used as noncredit learning tools. For instance, Khan Academy and TEDx offer helpful lessons available to the general public on topics ranging from calculus to economics to biology.

> "I had already gotten my bachelor's degree and had a full-time job, but I wanted to switch careers. My state's university system had a fully online campus, and I enrolled in their 6-week certification program in web development. All the coursework was entirely online, and I could do everything at my own pace. I didn't have to quit my job and I never had to drive to a campus or sit in a lecture hall. It was so worth it."
>
> Nicola, College Student

How Online Learning Works

Enrolling in an online course may simply involve completing a registration form, making sure that you have access to a computer and internet connection, and paying the tuition and fees. In this case, your application may be accepted without entrance examinations or proof of prior educational experience. For degree programs, students apply for admission to the university and are accepted based on their transcripts, recommendations, and ability to meet the required standards of a particular program.

Other courses may involve educational prerequisites and access to equipment not found in all geographic locations. Some institutions offer detailed information about individual courses, such as a course outline, upon request. If you simply wish to review course descriptions, you may be able to peruse an institution's course catalog on their website.

Time Requirements

Geared toward adults who are raising families or have more established careers, online schools may offer either synchronous or asynchronous coursework.

Synchronous coursework mirrors the traditional classroom setting with live lectures and discussions. Asynchronous coursework is more flexible as there are no set class times or live lectures. Instead, students can read, watch, or listen to course materials in their own time. Assignments for online courses might consist of discussion board posts, research papers, portfolios, and other coursework with practical applications.

Admission to a Degree Program

If you plan to enter a degree program, consult the academic advising department at the institution of your choice to learn about entrance requirements and application procedures. You may find it necessary to develop a portfolio of your past experiences and accomplishments that resulted in college-level learning as well as academic transcripts showing your educational background.

How Do I Communicate with My Instructor?

You will likely be expected to communicate with your instructor through email and video conferencing software such as Zoom, Google Meet, or Microsoft Teams. Usually, online schools manage courses in a learning management system, like Canvas, Blackboard, D2L, or Google Classroom, where you will submit all your assignments. This is where your instructor will provide feedback on and grade your assignments. If you need help with a concept or aren't sure how to approach an assignment, it's important that you take the initiative and reach out to your instructor using their preferred method of communication—whether by phone, email, or within the learning management system. Because you are not communicating with your instructor in real time, it will take time for your instructor to respond to your questions, comments, or requests for clarification. Be patient and reach out again if you haven't heard back after a day or two (remember that they might not work on evenings or weekends!).

What Else Does Online Learning Offer?

Along with traditional college degrees, you can earn professional certification or continuing education units (CEUs) in a particular field through online learning. Online learning has also been very beneficial for people working full- or part-time, raising children, in the military, or involved in other pursuits that would otherwise not allow them to return to school to further their education and skill acquisition.

College Degrees

You can earn degrees online at the associate, baccalaureate, and graduate levels. Two-year community college students are able to earn baccalaureate degrees by transferring to online learning programs offered by four-year universities. Corporations are forming partnerships with universities to bring college courses to worksites and encourage employees to continue their education. Even those who are incarcerated are increasingly being granted access to online learning opportunities that would not otherwise be available to them.

Online learning is especially popular among people who want to earn their degree part-time while continuing to work full-time. Although on-campus residencies are sometimes required for small parts of certain online learning degree programs, they generally can be completed while employees are on short-term leave or vacation.

Professional Certification

Certificate programs often focus on employment specializations, such as hazardous waste management or web development, and can be helpful to those seeking to advance or change careers. Also, many states mandate continuing education for professionals such as teachers, nursing home administrators, or accountants. Online learning offers a convenient way for many individuals to meet professional certification requirements. Healthcare, engineering, information technology, business, and education are just a few of the many professions that take advantage of online learning to help their professionals maintain certification. Many colleges also offer a sequence of online learning courses in a specific field of a profession. For instance, within the engineering profession, certificate programs in computer-integrated manufacturing, systems engineering, waste management education, and research consortium are offered online. As online education continues to become a more popular option for traditional and nontraditional students alike, the list of program, certification, and course offerings will likely continue to grow as well.

Continuing Education Units

If you choose to take a course on a noncredit basis, you may be able to earn continuing education units. The CEU system is a nationally recognized system to provide a standardized, quantifiable measure for accumulating, transferring, and recognizing participation in continuing education programs. One CEU is defined as 10 contact hours of participation in an organized continuing education experience under responsible sponsorship, capable direction, and qualified instruction.

CAREERS WITHOUT A FOUR-YEAR DEGREE

There are many career paths that don't require you to attend a traditional four-year institution. The graphic in this section lists occupations that don't require a four-year degree and that have a positive job outlook according to the US Department of Labor, Bureau of Labor Statistics. However, for many of the jobs listed, you can find a related degree program. A degree can help you be a more competitive applicant no matter what job you're looking for. For example, you can be a self-taught photographer or web developer, but additional training or education will help you learn important skills and strategies so that you can become even more skilled at your craft and familiar with the standards of your industry. The more experience and training you have, the more likely it is that you will find the job you want.

Even if you don't pursue a four-year degree, keep in mind that most career paths have become more specialized. In addition to a high school diploma, some sort

of additional training, licensing, or certification may be required. If a specific career path really interests you, then don't let a year or two of additional education discourage you from pursuing the job you want. Also, remember that this list doesn't include every option that's out there. New industries emerge all the time. Talk to your guidance counselor or do your own research to find the path that's right for you.

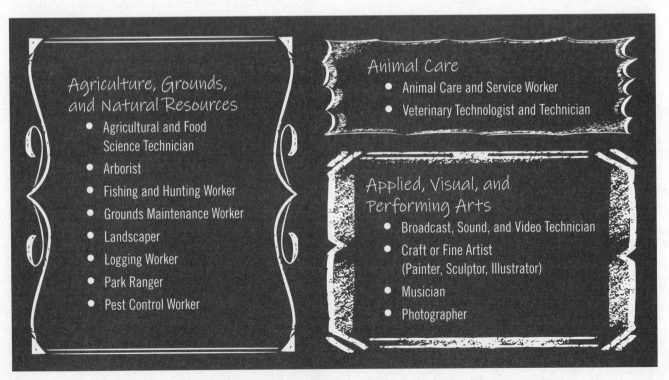

Agriculture, Grounds, and Natural Resources
- Agricultural and Food Science Technician
- Arborist
- Fishing and Hunting Worker
- Grounds Maintenance Worker
- Landscaper
- Logging Worker
- Park Ranger
- Pest Control Worker

Animal Care
- Animal Care and Service Worker
- Veterinary Technologist and Technician

Applied, Visual, and Performing Arts
- Broadcast, Sound, and Video Technician
- Craft or Fine Artist (Painter, Sculptor, Illustrator)
- Musician
- Photographer

Architecture and Engineering

- Aerospace Engineering and Operations Technologist
- Geological and Hydrologic Technician
- Mechanical Engineering Technologist and Technician

Construction and Extraction

- Drywall Installer
- Electrician
- Elevator and Escalator Installer and Repairer
- Flooring Installer and Tile and Stone Setter
- Hazardous Materials Removal Worker
- Ironworker
- Solar Photovoltaic Installer
- Welder
- Wind Turbine Technician

Computer and Information Technology

- Computer Support Specialist
- UI/UX Designer
- Web Designer
- Web Developer

Education

- Teacher's Aide
- Teaching Assistant

Healthcare

- Cardiovascular Technologist and Technician
- Dental Assistant
- Dental Hygienist
- Emergency Medical Technician and Paramedic
- Hearing Aid Specialist
- Home Health Aide
- Licensed Practical or Vocational Nurse
- Massage Therapist
- Medical and Clinical Laboratory Technician
- Medical Assistant
- Medical Billing and Coding Specialist
- Medical Records and Health Information Specialist
- Medical Sonographer
- Radiologist and MRI Technologist
- Nuclear Medicine Technologist
- Nursing Assistant
- Occupational Health and Safety Specialist and Technician
- Occupational Therapy Assistant
- Optician
- Personal Care Aide
- Phlebotomist
- Physical Therapy Assistant
- Psychiatric Technician and Aide
- Radiation Therapist
- Respiratory Therapist
- Ultrasound Technician

Source: US Bureau of Labor Statistics, *Occupational Outlook Handbook*, Sept. 2021. https://www.bls.gov/ooh/

Installation, Maintenance, and Repair

- Aircraft and Avionics Equipment Mechanic and Technician
- Automotive Body and Glass Repairer
- Diesel Service Technician and Mechanic
- General Maintenance and Repair Worker
- Heavy Vehicle and Mobile Equipment Service Technician
- Medical Equipment Repairer
- Small Engine Mechanic

Legal

- Interpreter and Translator
- Paralegal and Legal Assistant

Management

- Hospitality/Lodging Manager
- Food Service Manager

Personal Care and Service

- Childcare Worker
- Cosmetologist
- Hair Stylist
- Flight Attendant
- Fitness Instructor
- Funeral Service Worker
- Gambling Services Worker
- Manicurist and Pedicurist
- Personal Trainer
- Recreation Worker
- Skin Care Specialist

Production

- Baker
- Dental and Ophthalmic Laboratory Technician
- Machinist and Tool and Die Maker
- Painting and Coating Worker
- Stationary Engineer and Boiler Operator
- Welder, Cutter, Solderer, and Brazer
- Woodworker

Protective Service

- Detective
- Fire Inspector
- Firefighter
- Gambling Surveillance Officer
- Police Officer
- Private Detective and Investigator
- Public Safety Telecommunicator and Emergency Dispatcher
- Security Guard

Sales

- Insurance Sales Agent
- Marketing Assistant
- Model

Transportation and Material Moving

- Commercial Pilot
- Delivery Truck Driver
- Hand Laborer and Material Mover
- Heavy and Tractor-Trailer Truck Driver
- Passenger Vehicle Driver
- Water Transportation Worker

VOCATIONAL/CAREER COLLEGES

From the largest employers down to the smallest companies, issues of keeping up with technology and producing goods and services cheaper and faster require a skilled workforce. Therefore, companies are looking for skilled employees who have knowledge in a particular field and are trained to complete specific tasks. In good or bad economic times, you'll always have a distinct advantage if you have a demonstrable skill and can be immediately productive while continuing to learn and improve. If you know how to use technology, work collaboratively, and find creative solutions, you'll always be in demand.

Luckily for you, there is a place where you can acquire all these skills and traits! Career colleges offer opportunities to learn the technical skills required by many of today and tomorrow's top jobs. This is especially true in the areas of computer and information technology, renewable energy, manufacturing and production, healthcare, and hospitality (culinary arts, travel and tourism, and hotel and motel management). Career colleges vary widely in size, from the smallest classrooms to large, sprawling campuses. You can find these schools across the country, and though they may differ in many aspects, they all share the common goal of preparing students for a successful career in the world of work through a focused, intensive curriculum.

America's career colleges are privately owned and operated by for-profit companies. Instead of using tax support to operate, career colleges actually pay taxes. Because career colleges are businesses, they must be responsive to the workforce needs of their communities and prepare students for in-demand jobs. Generally, career colleges prepare you for a specific career. Some will require you to take academic courses such as English or math, but others will relate every class you take to a specific job, such as computer-aided drafting or interior design, while still others focus solely on business or technical fields.

A disadvantage to this kind of education is that if you haven't carefully researched what you want to do, you could waste a lot of time and money. Unlike community colleges, where you can find yourself and try out courses in several areas, these schools don't allow much room for exploring alternative career options. Career colleges are for people who know exactly what field (or even what company) they want to work in. Credits from for-profit colleges are also very unlikely to transfer to a four-year university if you change your mind later.

How do you find the right career college for you? Having a general idea of what you want to do is a good place to start. After you've determined the trade you want to pursue, it would make sense to ask some of the following questions of your chosen career college:

Questions for Career Colleges

- Which company is the biggest employer of your graduates?

- Do your graduates feel that the training you have given them has prepared them to enter the workforce?

- Is your career college accredited? (Though not every career college has to be accredited, it is a sign that the college has gone through a process that ensures quality. It also means that students can qualify for federal grant and loan programs.)

- Does your college meet the standards of professional training organizations? (In health-related professions, for example, these criteria are paramount.)

In addition, seek out recent graduates of the career college and ask them how their experience in the workplace has been. These graduates can tell you what kind of impact the career college has made on their work lives. Research any career college thoroughly to make sure it's legit.

FINANCIAL AID OPTIONS FOR CAREER AND COMMUNITY COLLEGES

The financial aid process is basically the same for students attending a community college, a career college, or a technical institute as it is for students attending a four-year college.

The federal government is still your best source of financial aid. Most community colleges and career and technical schools participate in federal financial aid programs. To get detailed information about federal financial aid programs and how to apply for them, read through Chapter 9: "Financing Your College Plans."

Don't overlook scholarships: Many two-year students could be eligible for scholarships. Remember, scholarships aren't only for the super-geniuses at the top of their classes at the most prestigious universities. You'd be surprised to learn how many community and career colleges offer scholarships, so reach out to the financial aid offices at the schools you plan to attend to see what options are available to you.

Students at two-year institutions should find out how their state of residence can help them pay for tuition. Every state has some level of state financial aid that goes to community college students. The amounts are dependent on which state you live in, and most aid is in the form of grants.

APPRENTICESHIPS AND TRADES

Perhaps you are looking for some sort of alternative postsecondary educational option, but the community college or vocational route is not quite for you. Some students like working with their hands and have the skill, patience, and temperament to become expert mechanics, carpenters, or electronic repair technicians. If you think you'd enjoy a profession like this and feel that college training isn't for you, then you might want to think about a job that requires apprenticeship training.

An apprenticeship is a program formally agreed upon between a worker and an employer where the employee learns a skilled trade through classroom work and on-the-job training. Apprenticeship programs vary in length, pay, and intensity among the various trades. A person completing an apprenticeship program generally becomes a journeyperson (skilled craftsperson) in that trade.

Here are some advantages of an apprenticeship program:

Apprenticeships lead to practical lifetime skills.

After completing an apprenticeship, your skills will open the door to creative, exciting, and challenging jobs.

Skilled workers advance much faster than those who are semi-skilled or whose skills are not broad enough to equip them to assume additional responsibilities in a career.

Once you have completed your apprenticeship, you will have a first-person understanding of the skills and judgment needed to start your own business. This can be extremely helpful knowledge at some point down the line in your career.

How to Begin an Apprenticeship

The road to an apprenticeship has some specific criteria you will want to consider:

☐ Potential apprentices must be at least 16 years old. In fact, federal regulations prohibit anyone under the age of 16 from being considered for an apprenticeship.

☐ You must fill out an application for employ-ment. These applications may be available year-round or only at certain times during the year, depending on the trade in which you're interested.

☐ Some programs require a high school diploma or certain coursework. Other requirements may include passing certain aptitude tests, proof of physical ability to perform the duties of the trade, and possession of a valid driver's license. Make sure that you are aware of all the requirements before you complete your application for an apprenticeship.

Should You Pursue a Trade Instead?

In the past, trades were much more commonplace and were steady sources of income. A person would specialize in one area of need and become an expert in it, serving the community through their expertise. For example, most communities needed a farrier who shoed horses, a farmer who worked the land, and a cobbler who made shoes, and these trades were passed down through families and generations. Today, trades-persons are still important in a variety of contexts, including as electricians, woodworkers, wind turbine technicians, solar photovoltaic installers, massage therapists, plumbers, estheticians, nail technicians, and more.

In the present, tradespeople sometimes carry the stigma of being less educated than those with four-year degrees. However, while this unfair stigma does exist, pursuing a trade can be a clever and business-savvy option for many students. In fact, it is entirely possible to be more financially successful as a tradesperson than as a college graduate, especially given the ris-ing costs of education. Colleges are businesses, and most are very expensive to attend. Putting money into tuition and incurring significant debt from years of student loans can be a financially unsound decision. If you're unsure that you can complete a four-year degree or that a degree can get you one step closer to the kind of job you want, then you might consider exploring a trade instead.

If you're considering an apprenticeship or trade, the best sources of assistance and information are voca-tional or career counselors, local state employment security agencies, field offices of state apprenticeship agencies, and regional offices of the Employment and Training Administration's Office of Apprenticeship (OA). Apprenticeships are usually registered with the OA or a state apprenticeship council. To determine if a certain apprenticeship is legitimate, contact your state's apprenticeship agency or a regional office of the OA, or you can visit the OA's website.

EVERY CAREER IS NECESSARY

While a lot of the messages teenagers get make it seem like four-year universities are the only good postsecondary option, there are actually a lot of ways to learn the skills and trades necessary for lucrative, secure, and rewarding work outside of fields that require a four-year degree. Our society cannot function without some young people every year deciding to pursue these routes—plumbers, sanitation workers, HVAC specialists, bus drivers, and more are all just as necessary to a functioning society as are engineers and teachers. Don't let stigmas or people's impressions of what it means to pursue a particular path stop you from considering a trade that would be a good fit for you. Every career is necessary and society needs people like you who are motivated to do a particular job!

Notes

Considering the Military Option

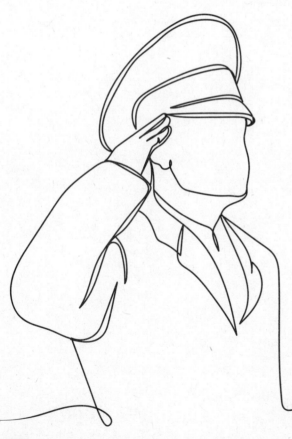

Just like some teenagers know exactly which college they hope to go to after they finish high school, there are others who dream of becoming a Navy SEAL or flying planes for the US Air Force. Still, there are others who may not have initially envisioned enlisting in the armed services (Army, Navy, Air Force, Marines, Coast Guard, and Space Force), but in weighing their options, they determined that it would make sense for them. Like all the college and career paths we discuss in this book, the US military is just one of numerous ways to step into the so-called "real world" after high school. As with any other option, it's important to weigh the myriad factors that you must consider when determining if this path forward is the right one for you.

The Short and Sweet Version

Most of us form our impressions of the US military from TV and movies. However, the real military is much different than Hollywood makes it seem, so it's critical to do your own research rather than basing your enlistment decision on your favorite action movie. Today's military is one of many potential routes to a worthwhile career, including if you decide to make your career in the military beyond your enlistment term. The military life may not be for everyone, but for those to whom it appeals, it can be a secure and invigorating way to make a living.

If you are considering enlistment, the first thing to do is determine if it would be a good fit for you. Each of the different branches has different requirements for those who enlist, so you'll need to make sure that you meet the qualifications. You'll also need to prepare for the ASVAB, which is a series of tests you'll need to take before you can enlist. You can take the ASVAB any time after your sophomore year, and it is good for enlistment for 2 years.

For those who do decide that they'd like to join the military, your next step is to decide which branch would be suitable for you. Many people are tempted to join a given branch because of its reputation or because a family member was part of that branch, but it's an important decision that you shouldn't take lightly! Take as much time as you need to figure out which branch has the benefits and career training that best fit your vision for your future.

Just like with other career paths, it's important to do your research. Learn everything you can about the branch(es) you're interested in before ever talking to a recruiter. It's their job to convince you to join, but you'll want to have your own questions prepared before you go into a meeting. If you do decide to enlist, start preparing for boot camp before you get there so it's not a shock to your system. There's no doubt that with planning and some thoughtful research, the military can be an exciting endeavor for any recent graduate who wants to serve.

DETERMINING IF THE MILITARY IS A GOOD FIT FOR YOU

Every year, thousands of young people make the choice to pursue a military career. For those who make this decision, it may be to pursue their own dreams, build on a family legacy, fulfill a desire to serve their country, or any number of other reasons, many of which involve a lot of purposeful self-reflection. For those who do decide to pursue the military option, the US military is one of the largest employers in the country and offers a variety of stable careers and benefits. Enlistment in the military may also help one pursue different educational and career goals either during or following one's enlistment period, so it can be a springboard to other paths later in life as well.

"In the [military], you can get training in everything from culinary arts to truck driving and all the way to aviation mechanics, military intelligence, and computer networking."

Max, Staff Sergeant in the United States Army

For as many young people who enthusiastically enlist in the military, there are many others who either eventually recognize that this option doesn't align with their life goals or who learn that the requirements of this type of service do not match what they are capable of offering. The important thing to remember is that this is a highly personal decision and there is no right or wrong way to make it so long as you make it for yourself—you are the captain of your own destiny!

Questions to Consider Before Enlistment

- Is the military a good fit for me and the kind of lifestyle I lead or want to lead?

- Have I considered all the changes I'd have to make and responsibilities I may be called to take on as part of a commitment to military service, and am I willing do what it takes to uphold that commitment?

- Do the benefits and training offered by the military suit the goals I have for my life and future?

- If I do decide to enlist, which branch of the military would be best for me?

- Do I meet the qualifications for service that are required for the branch or niche in which I'd like to serve?

- Am I considering enlisting because I truly want to or because I feel pressure from outside sources (like family members or recruiters) to do so?

"The military is really unique. The main unique feature is that you can't just quit it if you don't like it. There are several ways to get out of your contract, but it is still a contract. That's why relying on it exclusively for college money or job skills isn't the best motivation to join. When you're out lying on the ground in the pitch-black dark of a training area and the rain turns to wet snow, you have to have your heart in it, not just your mind."

David, Marine and Army Chaplain

Particularly, given that you may be called upon to serve in combat, deciding whether to join the military can feel daunting for those who are undecided. To sort your thoughts, it may be helpful to make a list of the pros and cons you can identify before you ever set foot in the recruiter's office. Whether your list of pros is long—with such items as money for college, job security, opportunity to travel, technical training, and good pay—or if your list of cons seems to outweigh the pros, you will be better able to discuss options with a guidance counselor, your family, your friends, or anyone else you trust to help you fully weigh your options before speaking with a military recruiter. That way, you can feel confident that you know which questions you want to ask to make the most of your time speaking with the recruiter.

"In my seventeen years in the military, in two branches, I have had a few broken promises from recruiters and commanders. For instance, when I went to boot camp, my recruiter calculated that I would show up for my first day of college with about $2,900 in the bank. I was making about $1,000 a month as an E-1, and there wasn't anything to spend it on in boot camp. Well, during my last month or so of training, we had to buy uniforms and even cleaning supplies. I showed up for college with around $1,000. Things are probably different now, but with the current drawdown there are less freebies in the military. It's more like it was for me back in the 90s."

David, Marine and Army Chaplain

If you find that you are leaning towards wanting to join the military, your first course of action is to collect your reasons to join and put them in order of importance to you. Then, think about how you may be pressed to explain why you are qualified to pursue the particular branch that interests you. You must be prepared to potentially answer tough questions just like you might in a job interview.

By the same token, be sure to ask tough questions to the recruiters. They mean well, but they are also on their own mission to get qualified recruits, so you must make sure to get enough details to make an informed decision. Ask questions about money, about whether you will be able to transfer to a new unit if you are unhappy, about work/life balance, and about anything else that matters to you. You need to make sure that you have the full picture of what to expect when making the commitment so that if and when you do, you can do so with confidence.

CHOOSING WHICH BRANCH TO JOIN

If you are seriously considering joining the military, you probably have checked out at least two of the branches. However, you should make it a point to check them all out, even if it means just going online or requesting literature and reviewing it. As a word of caution, brochures and websites do not tell the complete story, and it's very difficult to base your decision either for or against a military branch on the contents of a web page or brochure alone. Put your research skills to work and read up on each branch of the military, their requirements for joining, what training looks like for new recruits, the kinds of career paths they offer, and anything else that will help you determine which branch you are best suited to.

For instance, you might find that one branch offers you more opportunities to see the world, or another makes it easy to enter the career path you're interested in after service. Try and read testimonials or find people who have recently been in the branches you're considering and get their perspective on what the culture and environment is like. Don't just make the decision based on what you've heard in the past about each branch; instead, take time to learn what everyday life in each branch might look like for you.

In many ways, the process of choosing the right branch of the military will mirror the process you used to determine if joining the military was right for you.

Here are some factors you can look at when trying to decide which branch is right for you:

- **LENGTH OF ENLISTMENT:** Some branches may require a longer term of enlistment to gain the same benefits that you could receive from another branch with a shorter term of enlistment.

- **ADVANCED PAY GRADE:** You may be entitled to an advanced rank in some branches based on certain enlistment options.

- **LENGTH AND TYPE OF TRAINING:** How long will your training take? Usually the longer the training, the more in-depth and useful it is. You'll also want to consider how useful the training will be once you've left the military.

- **ENLISTMENT BONUSES:** Be careful when using an enlistment bonus as the only factor in deciding which branch to choose. However, if it comes down to a tie between two branches and only one offers a bonus, it's not a bad reason to choose that branch.

- **ADDITIONAL PAY AND ALLOWANCES:** You may be entitled to additional pay that only one particular branch can offer. For instance, if you join the Navy, you may be entitled to Sea Pay and Submarine Pay, something not available if you join the Air Force.

- **ABILITY TO PURSUE HIGHER EDUCATION:** While all the military branches offer educational benefits, you must consider when you'll be able to take advantage of these benefits. If your job requires 12-hour shifts and has you out in the field a lot, when will you be able to attend classes?

- **EXISTING QUALIFICATIONS:** Do you have an existing skill set that could be useful to one particular branch? For instance, maybe you have already been working towards a pilot's license while in high school or you're fluent in a second language. If you have a specialized skill that may be valuable to a certain branch, this is something to consider.

- **SKILL BUILDING:** What sort of skills does each branch help you build? What sort of skills do you want to learn? Consider things outside of just job qualifications. For instance, if it has always been your dream to learn to sail one day, the US Coast Guard might be an option—all recruits learn that skill during basic training.

> Determine what you want to accomplish in the next 5 years and what you are willing to give up. If you don't want to travel far from home or want to complete college, then the reserves and National Guard would be better for you. If you have no idea what you want to do with your life yet, then active duty is a good choice. You will have a guaranteed place to live, dental and medical, food, and job security. More importantly, you will have time to determine how you want to develop.
>
> Carla, Staff Sergeant in the Army National Guard

"During the hardest phase of training (90% attrition rate), I overcame the debilitating desire to quit by telling myself, 'I'm not going to quit right now while I'm struggling, I'm going to wait until this hard portion is over and quit after.' I succeeded in never quitting."

Rudy, Major Sergeant and Pararescueman in the US Air Force

"You must have determination and will to be a woman in the military. It is a male-dominated space and by nature competitive. You will have to be comfortable advocating for yourself and making your voice heard in a personal and professional space. I am a second-generation female soldier. My mother retired as a 1SG and we both shared the experience of being the only female in the room at times. I would like to say to young women entering the service that you do not have to erase or tame your personality to fit in. Despite the military's rigid nature, it is full of myriad personalities and has more than enough space for you."

Carla, Staff Sergeant in the Army National Guard

Once you have considered these factors, and perhaps some of your own, you should be able to decide which branch is right for you. If you still haven't been able to select one branch over another, though, consider the following:

- Ask your recruiter if you can speak to someone who has recently joined.

- If you live near a base, you may be able to get a tour of its facilities.

- Visit internet forums that cater to military members and ask a lot of questions.

- Talk to friends and family members who are currently serving in the military.

- Consider talking to people who left the military for some reason or another. It's important to hear what factors may have played into their decision to leave.

- Talk to people who have been out of the military for some time to gain insights on how things might have evolved since their service to address (or not address) issues that are important to you.

- While it's good to find information that confirms your choice, don't shy away from reading criticism about a branch or the military in general. Even if you're enthused about enlisting, try and weigh all the details you can from as many perspectives as you can find. Seek information from a variety of sources with different relationships to military service. To feel confident that your decision is coming from a fully informed place, seek both critical and positive feedback.

THE ASVAB

If you choose to continue with processing for enlistment, your next step will probably be to take the Armed Services Vocational Aptitude Battery (ASVAB). The ASVAB, a multiple-aptitude battery of tests designed for use with students in their junior or senior year in high school or in a postsecondary school as well as those seeking military enlistment, was developed to yield results useful to both students and the military. The military uses the results to determine the qualifications of candidates for enlistment and to help place them in military occupational programs. Schools use ASVAB test results to assist their students in developing future educational and career plans.

Frequently Asked Questions about the ASVAB

The idea of another test may seem intimidating, but preparing for the ASVAB is actually quite straightforward. Furthermore, there are plenty of materials out there to help you prepare, including Peterson's ASVAB test prep materials. That said, here are some answers to questions you probably have.

What is the Armed Services Vocational Aptitude Battery (ASVAB)?

The ASVAB, sponsored by the Department of Defense, is a multi-aptitude test battery consisting of nine short individual tests covering Word Knowledge, Paragraph Comprehension, Arithmetic Reasoning, Mathematics Knowledge, General Science, Auto and Shop Information, Mechanical Comprehension, Electronics Information, and Assembling Objects. Your ASVAB results provide scores for each individual test, as well as three academic composite scores—Verbal, Math, and Academic Ability—and two career-exploration composite scores.

What is the AFQT? Is it different than the ASVAB?

The acronym AFQT stands for the Armed Forces Qualification Test. When you take the ASVAB, your scores from four of the components of the test (Mathematics Knowledge, Arithmetic Reasoning, Paragraph Comprehension, and Word Knowledge) will be calculated to represent your score on the AFQT, which will help determine if you are eligible to serve in the Army, Marine Corps, Navy, or Air Force. Therefore, simply by taking the ASVAB, you will have already taken the AFQT.

Should I take the ASVAB even if I'm not planning to enlist?

As a high school student nearing graduation, you are faced with important career choices. Should you go on to college or a technical or vocational school? Would it be better to enter the job market? Should you consider a military career? Even if you ultimately do not decide to pursue the military career path, ASVAB scores are measures of aptitude that can help you understand what your strengths are. Your composite scores measure your aptitude for higher academic learning and can also give you useful ideas for career exploration.

When and where is the ASVAB given?

ASVAB is administered on paper annually or semiannually at more than 14,000 high schools and postsecondary schools in the United States. Military recruiters can also help you identify alternative testing locations near you. Note that certain alternative test sites, known as a Military Entrance Processing Station (MEPS), have computer-based tests. If you end up taking a computer-based test at a MEPS, you will not be able to return to questions if you skip them.

ASVAB is also used in the regular military enlistment program, so MEPS sites around the country are also where thousands of young people who are interested in enlisting in the military but who did not take the ASVAB while in school are examined and processed.

Can I take the test more than once and, if so, how often?

Following your initial test, you will have to wait a month before you can take the test again. If you wanted to test a third time, you would have to wait another month following the initial retest. If somehow you still want to take the test again after these initial three tries, you will have to wait six months following the third test.

How long do my scores stay current?

You have up to two years from your date of testing to enlist. After that, you would need to take the ASVAB again.

Is there a charge or fee to take the ASVAB?

The ASVAB is administered at no cost to the school or to the student.

How long does it take to complete the ASVAB?

ASVAB testing takes approximately three hours.

If I wish to take the ASVAB but my school doesn't offer it, what should I do?

See your guidance counselor. In some cases, arrangements may be made for you to take it at another high school. Alternatively, you may also contact a local military recruiter to help schedule you at a nearby alternate location like a MEPS.

How do I find out what my scores mean and how to use them?

Your scores will be provided to you on a report called the ASVAB Student Results Sheet. Along with your scores, you should receive a copy of *Exploring Careers: The ASVAB Workbook*, which contains information that will help you understand your ASVAB results and show you how to use them for career exploration. Test results are returned to participating schools or available online within thirty days.

What is a passing score on the ASVAB?

No one "passes" or "fails" the ASVAB. The ASVAB enables you to compare your scores to those of other students at your grade level.

If I take the ASVAB, am I obligated to join the military?

No. Taking the ASVAB does not obligate you to join the military in any way. You are free to use your test results in whatever manner you wish. You may use the ASVAB results for up to two years for military enlistment if you are a junior, senior, or postsecondary school student. The military services encourage all young people to finish high school before joining.

If I am planning to go to college, should I take the ASVAB?

Yes. ASVAB results provide you with information that can help you determine your capacity for advanced academic education. You can also use your ASVAB results, along with other personal information, to identify areas for career exploration.

Basic Training in the military is a place where you need to laugh at everything but smile at nothing. You can do it, though, because harder stuff will come later. I'll be real: In my technical training, I had multiple drowning (shallow water blackout) incidents . . . now, when I'm faced with terrible circumstances [as a Pararescueman], I like to think 'well, at least I can breathe.'

Rudy, Master Sergeant and
Pararescueman in the US Air Force

Should I take the ASVAB if I plan to become a commissioned officer?

Yes. Taking the ASVAB is a valuable experience for any student who aspires to become a military officer. The aptitude information you receive could assist you in career planning.

Should I take the ASVAB if I am considering entering the Reserve or National Guard?

Yes. These military organizations also use the ASVAB for enlistment purposes.

What should I do if a service recruiter contacts me?

You may be contacted by a service recruiter before you graduate. If you want to learn about the many opportunities available through military service, arrange for a follow-up meeting. However, you are under no obligation to enlist in the military as a result of taking the ASVAB.

Is any special preparation necessary before taking the ASVAB?

Yes. A certain amount of preparation is required for taking any examination. Your test scores reflect not only your ability but also the time and effort spent preparing for the test. The armed services use ASVAB to help determine a person's qualification for enlistment and to help indicate the vocational areas for which the person is best suited. Achieving your maximum score will increase your vocational opportunities, so take practice tests to prepare.

BASIC TRAINING: WHAT HAVE I GOTTEN MYSELF INTO?

The main objective of Basic Training is to transform civilians into well-disciplined military personnel in a matter of weeks. Performing such a monumental task takes a lot of hard work, both mentally and physically. For most people, Basic Training ends with a parade on graduation day. For others, though, it ends somewhere short of graduation. It is those "horror stories" that make Basic Training one of the biggest fears, or anxiety inducers, for those considering military enlistment.

Unlike the Hollywood versions of boot camp you may have seen, today's military dictates that all recruits should be treated with dignity and respect without being subjected to verbal and physical abuse. It's not that enlistees aren't yelled at (because they are), but the vulgarity and demeaning verbal attacks once associated with the US military are no longer the norm. From time to time, incidents involving instructors who contradict the military's policies do arise. Remember, though, that the US military's policies are intended to protect recruits from this type of behavior. Should issues arise, it is within your rights as a recruit to bring these issues to higher military authorities so they can be investigated. Instructors who are found to have abused their power are generally subjected to discipline.

If you are still uncertain of which branch you'd like to join, don't allow the type of Basic Training you'll receive to be your only deciding factor. If, for example, the Marine Corps meets all your needs and is clearly your first choice, don't select the Air Force because its Basic Training seems easier. Conversely, if the Air Force

> A lot of kids are worried about Marine boot camp. They've seen movies or heard stories. Boot camp is not set up to make you fail. It's challenging, but that's the purpose of it. You're learning that no matter what life throws at you, you will be able to improvise, adapt, and overcome.
>
> Ian, Infantry Sergeant in the
> United States Marine Corps

is clearly your first choice, do not select the Marine Corps because it has the "toughest" Basic Training and you want to prove that you're up to the challenge. Basic Training is simply a period of skill development and a transition from civilian life to military life. It covers a relatively short period of time compared to the entire length of your enlistment.

Preparing for Basic Training

No matter what you may have heard or read elsewhere, there are no secrets to getting through Basic Training; only common sense and preparation will get you through. The following graphic offers some dos and don'ts that should help you survive Basic Training for any of the branches of service.

Tips to Prepare for Basic Training

Don't

- Skip preparing yourself physically because you assume that Basic Training will whip you into shape.
- Leave home with open tickets, summonses, warrants, or other unhandled legal issues.
- Get yourself into heavy debt or accrue a lot of long-term expenses.
- Bring prohibited items with you to Basic Training.
- Make drastic alterations to your appearance including haircuts, dyeing your hair, getting new tattoos or piercings, or any other type of physical alteration of your outward presentation.

Instead, you should:

- Start an exercise program and begin preparing your body for training as soon as you decide to enlist.
- Treat your body well by getting restful sleep, maintaining a sensible relationship to food, and taking care of your health. If you smoke, consider quitting before you get there.
- Stay out of trouble and attend to any legal matters, such as traffic fines.
- Ensure that all your financial obligations are in order and will be attended to while you're away, as needed.
- Bring all the items required of you and leave prohibited items at home.
- Understand what the expectations will be for your appearance when you get to training and come prepared for any haircut or other standard grooming you may receive.

Two Perspectives on a Military Career

"Like any job, the military has its ups and downs. You may work for days, weeks, or even months without a break. You may find yourself taking orders from someone who is unjust or even abusing their authority. You may discover that it's been weeks without a good meal if you are on deployment. You may get punished for someone else's mistakes. You may see your friends die, and you may take the life of someone else. Is it worth it?

Although this question is answered differently by those who have served, it is important to understand why people serve. Because of the military, I went to college on the Post 9/11 GI-Bill and graduated with a bachelor's and master's degree. While in college, I received a stipend for housing and books. When I buy a home with a VA loan, I won't need to put money down. Every year, I get free registration for the most expensive vehicle I own. I have a free lifetime fishing and hunting license in my state. I often get discounts at stores and restaurants. I also have free unlimited access to every state park.

During my time in the Navy, I went to many different countries and states and made some long-lasting friends as well. Honestly, the military was not for me, and I do not encourage people to join, nor do I discourage them from joining. All I do is tell them what my experience was in the military and tell them what I got because of it. For me, it was worth it, despite not enjoying it. I was in for five years, and they felt like the longest years of my life. However, I would not be where I am today without the military and that is the truth."

Cody, Third Class Petty Officer in the US Navy

When I graduated college, I considered going to law school but received a cold call from a recruiter wanting to talk about opportunities to serve in the Navy. Ultimately, I thought that if I didn't give it a try, I would always wonder what would have happened if I had. I was commissioned a few months later and was off on an adventure so rewarding that now I can't imagine having done anything else. I retired after a very fulfilling career.

Some of the pros of a military career include the opportunity to be part of something bigger than yourself, to challenge yourself, to be a leader, to get an education, to travel around the world and meet people from around the world and every walk of life, to expand your horizons. The major cons include the potential to be away from your family and friends and living in tight quarters for considerable lengths of time. You make a commitment to serve your country and your fellow man (which I see as a big pro!), but if you don't want to play by the rules and don't like taking orders, it is most probably not the career for you.

One thing I'd say to other women or anyone else considering a military career is that it's an opportunity to do things you only ever dreamed of. To fly on and off an aircraft carrier, to be a nuclear engineer, to go to sea on a ship, in a submarine, to have command of any of the above—the opportunities are endless! I found it very rewarding, but you have to be comfortable with who you are and not try to be something that you're not. You are a professional, a sailor, a whatever you volunteered to do—just like everyone else who volunteered to serve their country. Strive to be your best at everything you do and that will bring respect.

Nell, US Navy Veteran

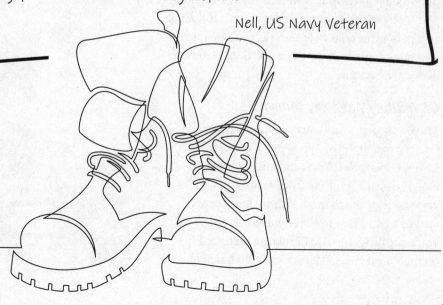

PAYING FOR COLLEGE THROUGH THE ARMED SERVICES

You can take any of the following paths into the armed services—all of which provide opportunities for financial assistance for college.

Enlisted Personnel

All six branches of the armed services (Army, Air Force, Navy, Marine Corps, Space Force, and Coast Guard) offer college-credit courses on base. Enlisted personnel can also take college courses at civilian colleges while on active duty.

ROTC

Thousands of college students participate in Reserve Officers' Training Corps (ROTC). Two-, three-, and four-year ROTC scholarships are available to outstanding students. You can try ROTC at no obligation for two years, or, if you have a four-year scholarship, for one year. Normally, all ROTC classes, uniforms, and books are free. ROTC graduates are required to serve in the military for a set period, either full-time on active duty or part-time in the Reserve or National Guard. Qualifying graduates can delay their service to go to graduate or professional school first.

US Service Academies

The United States has five service academies. Openings at the US service academies are few, so it pays to get information as early as your freshman or sophomore year of high school. Every student is on a full scholarship, but free does not mean easy—these intense programs train graduates to meet the demands of leadership and success.

US Military Academy (Army)

The US Military Academy, often informally referred to simply as "West Point," is located in West Point, New York, and offers a broad-based academic program with majors in various fields of study. The admission process for West Point is almost as rigorous as its academic program. Applicants are evaluated on their academic performance in high school, SAT or ACT scores, demonstrated leadership potential, physical aptitude, and medical qualifications. In addition, as part of the application process, those seeking admission to the US Military Academy must receive a congressional nomination for entry or a service-connected nomination. Service-connected nominations can come from military personnel who have served continuously on active duty for at least eight years. After graduating from the academy, officers must serve five years of active duty and three years in a Reserve Component, for a total of eight years of service. At the US Military Academy, extensive training and leadership experience go hand in hand with academics.

US Naval Academy (Navy and Marines)

The US Naval Academy, often informally referred to simply as "Annapolis," is a unique blend of tradition and state-of-the-art technology. Located in Annapolis, Maryland, the Naval Academy emphasizes math, science, and engineering but offers a full academic curriculum of study. Classroom work is supported by practical experience in leadership and professional operations. Annapolis has special learning facilities to support its programs; among these are a learning resource center, a planetarium, wind tunnels, a radio station, a propulsion lab, a nuclear reactor, an oceanographic research vessel, towing tanks, and a flight

> Talk to as many people as you can who are serving in the military (all branches, officer and enlisted) or who have served to get their perspective and to learn more about what opportunities are out there. Have a list of questions to ask them. Understand from the recruiter what the commitment is for your particular desired field—it varies depending on schooling/training involved, i.e. flight training, nuclear training, law school, med school, etc.
>
> Nina, US Navy Veteran

simulator. Annapolis follows the same rigorous admission process that West Point follows and, in addition to completing a preliminary application, all applicants must include a congressional or service-connected nomination, complete a physical fitness assessment, and undergo a medical examination. If admitted, you'll become a "midshipman" at the Naval Academy.

US Air Force Academy
(Air Force and Space Force)

The US Air Force Academy, located north of Colorado Springs, Colorado, prepares and motivates cadets for careers as Air Force officers. All cadets complete a core academic curriculum, which includes classes in the humanities, social sciences, engineering, basic sciences, and physical education. Cadets then specialize in one of thirty-one majors offered by the Academy. Admission into the Air Force Academy mirrors the requirements of other US service academies and should be started as early as your junior year in high school. The Air Force Academy is also one of the primary sources of recruits for the Space Force, which was newly created in 2019.

Merchant Marine Academy

The US Merchant Marine Academy is located in Kings Point, New York, and offers classes in marine transportation, marine engineering, maritime operations and technology, and logistics and intermodal transportation, to name a few. The academic year runs eleven months, from July to June, and is divided into trimesters, or three academic terms of thirteen weeks each. The admission process for the US Merchant Marine Academy is similar to that of the other service academies; you will need to submit an application, an essay, high school transcripts, SAT or ACT scores, three letters of recommendation, and a congressional letter of nomination. A medical exam and candidate fitness assessment are also required. In addition, during the application process, a candidate must list a tentative major, which does not have to be affirmed until the second trimester.

Coast Guard Academy

The US Coast Guard Academy is located in New London, Connecticut, and is the smallest of the five US service academies. The Coast Guard Academy offers a four-year Bachelor of Science degree program and offers thirteen programs of study. This broad-based education includes a thorough grounding in the professional skills necessary for the Coast Guard's work. Admission into the Coast Guard Academy is similar to that of other US service academies, but a congressional nomination is not required. Admittance is based solely on personal merit.

The Reserves and the National Guard

Perhaps you may not want to apply to a service academy and you're not looking to enlist in active duty either, but the idea of military service is still appealing. If this is the case, you're in luck, since every branch of the US military has a reserve force. Usually, the basic training for the reserve force is the same, but when you graduate, you report to a reserve unit near wherever you choose to live.

Serving in the Reserves

The reserve commitment is generally two days per month and two weeks per year. The two days generally happen on a weekend and the two weeks during a summer break. The reserves are a big commitment because as a member you must maintain a civilian job or civilian school schedule while still attending your required military days. One should consider whether this seems feasible or overly exhausting before making the decision to enlist in a reserve force.

The financial benefits of joining the reserves are not as good as enlisting in Active Duty (Active Duty members can retire after twenty years of full-time service and receive free healthcare and about half their salary for the rest of their life). However, there are still significant financial benefits for reserve members. For instance, reserve members who do twenty years of part-time service receive free healthcare and approximately half their salary after they turn 60 years of age.

Serving in the National Guard

If you plan on living in the same state for a long time, you may want to join the National Guard, which is a reserve component of the armed forces. It is harder to move around the country in the National Guard than it is in the reserves, but the National Guard is certainly a good choice because you can still pursue education and a career full-time.

Financing Higher Education During and After Service in the Armed Forces

Here are some ways that the US military provides options to help you get financial aid for postsecondary education.

The Active Duty Montgomery GI Bill

The Active Duty Montgomery GI Bill (ADMGIB) provides up to thirty-six months of education benefits to eligible veterans for college, business, technical or vocational courses, correspondence courses, apprenticeship/job training, and flight training. You may be an eligible veteran if you get an Honorable Discharge; you have a high school diploma, GED, or, in some cases, 12 hours of college credit; and you meet the necessary requirements related to military service. You must have elected to participate in the ADMGIB, which involves giving up $100 of your pay per month for the first twelve months of military service. The monthly benefit paid to you is based on the type of training you take, length of your service, your category, and whether the Department of Defense put extra money in your college fund (called "kicker"). You usually have ten years to use your ADMGIB benefits, but the time limit can vary.

The Selected Reserve Montgomery GI Bill

The Selected Reserve Montgomery GI Bill (SRM-GIB) may be available to you if you are a member of the Selected Reserve. The Selected Reserve includes the Army Reserve, Navy Reserve, Air Force Reserve, Marine Corps Reserve, Coast Guard Reserve, and the Army National Guard and Air National Guard. You may use this education assistance program for degree programs, certificate or correspondence courses, cooperative training, independent study programs, apprenticeships/on-the-job training, and vocational flight training programs. Remedial, refresher, and deficiency training are also available under certain circumstances. Eligibility for this program is determined by the Selected Reserve components. The US Department of Veterans Affairs (VA) makes the payments for this program. You may be entitled to receive up to thirty-six months of education benefits. Your eligibility typically ends on the day you leave the Selected Reserve.

Tuition Assistance

All branches of the military pay up to 75 percent of tuition for full-time, active-duty enlistees who take courses at community colleges or by distance learning during their tours of duty. Details vary by service.

The Community College of the Air Force

Enlisted Air Force personnel can convert their technical training and military experience into academic credit, earning an associate degree, an occupational instructor's certificate, or a trade school certificate. Participants receive an official transcript from this fully accredited program.

Educational Loan-Repayment Program

The armed forces can help repay government-insured and other approved loans. Each of the services is free to offer such programs, but individual policies differ.

Other Forms of Tuition Assistance

Each branch of the military offers its own education incentives. To find out more, check with a local recruiting office.

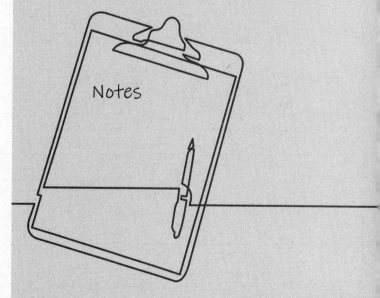

Notes

PART

3

Continuing Your Education
with College

CHAPTER 6

The College Search

Now that you've had a chance to dive deep into examining your interests, talents, wants, needs, and passions, it's time to start investigating colleges. At this point, you might have an idea of what you want to do when you graduate college, but it's okay if you're still undecided. Of course, if you're undecided, you'll want to make sure to attend a school with a wide variety of options for fields of study. Otherwise, if you feel fairly certain of what you might like to study, you'll want to look for schools that have programs to help you prepare for your future accordingly.

The Short and Sweet Version

Once you know that you want to go to college, there's the whole pesky matter of figuring out where you want to apply. It can be a whole thing because there are so many choices out there, so it's really important to buckle down, do some introspection, and figure out what's most important to you. You're the one who will have to spend four years there (unless you transfer, which you can totally do!), so you have to make sure the college you pick suits you.

This is the kind of situation where it's good to bring in outside help, especially your guidance counselor and your family. If you're trying to go to the same school as a friend, that's not necessarily a bad idea, but you definitely want to make sure the school is a great fit for both of you. Ultimately, the most important factor in the decision-making process is whether a college is somewhere you can thrive academically and socially or not. Figure out what's important to you and then make your list of schools to apply to accordingly.

Campus visits are an incredible way to narrow down your list since they give you a sense of what it's really like to be on campus. Most campus visits will involve an interview of some sort, the purpose of which is to help the school understand who you are and how you'd fit in with their academic community. By the way, if you don't have the resources to visit campus or do an in-person interview, don't stress; instead, contact the admissions office at the school you're interested in to see what options exist for virtual tours or digital interviews.

There are tons of different options out there, including highly competitive colleges like the Ivy Leagues, schools that historically served particular populations, and schools that are perfect for those with specific needs, such as Gallaudet University, which is for the deaf and hard of hearing. Take the time to really see what's out there, narrow it down to a handful of top and secondary choices, then do your research to make sure you're finding the perfect place to expand your horizons.

CONSULT YOUR BEST RESOURCES

Applying to college may certainly feel like a daunting task. With over 4000 four-year colleges and universities to choose from, you may not even know where to begin! But that's okay because, whether you know it or not, you have a support network that can help you find the colleges that are right for you. Here are some great resources and people to talk to about narrowing down your college choices before you start applying.

Your Guidance Counselor

Your guidance counselor (sometimes called a college counselor or advisor) is your greatest asset in the college search process. They have access to a vast repository of information, from college bulletins to financial aid resources. Your guidance counselor knows how graduates from your high school have performed at colleges across the country. They also understand software programs and application systems such as Naviance, The Common Application, and your state college application. In short, one of your guidance counselor's main jobs is to help guide you through high school and onto

your future prospects, so they are your go-to source for information on your college search. Furthermore, because they have access to your transcripts and work with your teachers, they'll be able to help guide you toward schools that might be a good fit for you.

Your guidance counselor's knowledge doesn't end with understanding the ins and outs of college applications. In fact, one of a guidance counselor's greatest attributes is that they can bring more first-hand knowledge to your doorstep. They facilitate visits from college admission representatives from across the United States and even help organize local college fairs, where a vast array of colleges come together to present information about different postsecondary options. If there is not a job or college fair at your school, there may be one at another school in your district or nearby—your guidance counselor is the person who would know!

Since your guidance counselor is such a treasure trove of helpful knowledge, it would make sense that you build a meaningful relationship with them starting as early as possible in your high school career. In fact, a good piece of advice is to go out of your way during your freshman year to introduce yourself to your guidance counselor and give them a sense of what your long-term goals might be so they can start helping you early on. The more your guidance counselor sees you and learns about you, the easier it is for them to help you. What's more, your guidance counselor will probably be writing some

sort of recommendation or at least compiling comments from your teachers or other adults on your high school campus, and the things that they'll write about you in this letter will be sent to many of your colleges. So, make sure you stop by the guidance office often, whether it's to talk about your progress as a student or just to check in and say "hi." Remember, your school has hired these guidance counselors specifically to help students like you along this process, so take advantage of this tremendous resource.

Your Teachers

Consider your teachers resources, too. Your teachers probably understand the way you learn and think better than most because they see you in a classroom setting day in and day out. Therefore, they can be great resources to talk to about what type of postsecondary educational experience you may be interested in. Ask their opinion on your preliminary college list and see if it matches up with schools that their previous students—ones who are like you—have attended. You could also ask them for feedback on your strengths as a student, which can help you brainstorm potential career paths that might suit your goals. For instance, if your English teacher points out that you are an excellent public speaker, that might get you thinking about a career in politics or business.

Sometimes, teachers will have specific knowledge about particular colleges or programs. Perhaps they attended a summer workshop or teacher development program at a college or university, so they will have gotten a feel for what that school's academic culture is like. Perhaps they attended undergrad at the same school you want to attend and can give you some insights into what it's like to go there. Teachers often have professional colleagues who attended or worked at various colleges, so they may be able to put you in touch with someone who can help you learn more about a school, particularly if you're interested in attending somewhere close to home.

In addition to being helpful in providing advice about prospective colleges, your teachers play another extremely important role in your college application process. Almost every college asks for some form of teacher recommendation. This means that at least one

"Use the summer after your junior year to get a head start on the college application process. Don't wait until Thanksgiving of your senior year to begin figuring out which schools you want to apply to. The bulk of your college application work can be completed in the summer, which will make for a much less hectic start to your senior year."

Roberta, Counselor at a Private University

(but in most cases two) of your teachers will be writing to tell colleges about you as a student. For this reason, it's very important to build at least a few strong teacher relationships. Just like with your college counselor, the better that teachers know you, the more relevant and detailed their recommendations will be!

Your Family

Your family can be an integral part of the college-selection process, regardless of whether they are helping finance your education or not. They have opinions and valuable advice, so listen to them carefully, but remember that you are also your own person and you shouldn't make a decision this big based purely on what your family wants. Try to absorb all their information and advice, then reflect and see if it applies to you. Does it fit with who you are and what you want? What works and what doesn't work for you? Is some of what they say dated or old-fashioned? How long ago were their experiences, and how relevant are they today? Take in the information, thank them for their concern, compare what they have said with the information you are gathering, and discard what doesn't fit. Ultimately, this is your decision to make for yourself, but don't discount the wisdom that your family can offer.

College Fairs

Don't forget to go to college fairs! They are free and usually sponsored by your local guidance counselors' association and the National Association for College Admission Counseling (NACAC). Admission officers from community colleges, vocational/career schools, and four-year colleges and universities attend college fairs all over the country each year. This is a great time and place to get your questions about various institutions answered by professionals who work for those schools.

Admission officers may also visit your high school directly. In general, college admission counselors come to a school to build personal relationships with and gain a better understanding of specific high schools. For you, this means an opportunity to establish a connection with someone who works at the admission office of a particular school (and may even be the reader of your college application). Try to attend any of these personal information sessions from colleges that may interest you. Make it a point to introduce yourself and commit that admission counselor's name to memory as well, which may prove useful later in the process.

Website Searches

College and university websites are also good places to research the schools that interest you. You'll want to try to answer a few key questions. What academic offerings, athletic programs, extracurricular opportunities, and kind of campus life does the college offer? What does the campus look like? The school website presents clues about what student life is like at those schools, but keep in mind that these sites are still essentially promotional pieces for the college. You are the consumer, and they are the business trying to sell you an education at their institution. To get a full picture, then, you may also want to go to social media pages or internet forums for students at the school and get a sense of how they talk about the school culture there. Similarly, if you visit the campus, don't

be afraid to ask current students for their thoughts on what it's like to go to school there. These interactions will give you a lot more information than a website alone could.

Read the student newspaper. Visit college-sponsored forums or bulletin boards. Look at the different clubs offered at the school or check out pictures from recent events. Go to the department for the major you are investigating and see what kinds of professors work in that department and what their research fields are. Look at the course bulletin to see what courses are required and which electives are offered. In short, use the college's website to paint a portrait of what the school as a whole offers to students who decide to go there.

Print Guides

Sometimes, it helps to pick up a book and peruse the pages. There are many college guides that you should be able to find in your guidance office or at your local bookstore or library. You can find Peterson's guides to both four-year and two-year colleges with essential information on thousands of schools, including in-depth college descriptions that offer details on everything at the school—from tuition and financial aid to degrees offered to life on campus—and much more.

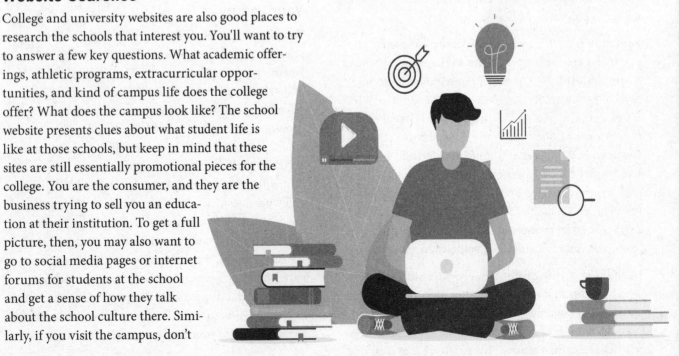

FIGURING OUT WHAT YOU WANT IN A COLLEGE

There are so many different factors that influence what you're looking for in a school. Before you even jump into searching, it might be helpful to do some brainstorming to help you determine what matters to you. Use this table and the space provided to think through the questions presented or do your own brainstorming in a journal, if you prefer. In any case, use the prompts below to think about what's most important to you in a college or university.

What Am I Looking for When Searching for a College?

Location and Lifestyle

- Do I want to be close to home or move across the country?
- Do I want to save money on in-state tuition or pay more to move out of state?
- Do I want to go to a school where everyone lives in the dorms or would I prefer to go somewhere where most students live off-campus?
- Do I want to be on an urban campus in a bustling city or would I prefer to be somewhere in the suburbs or even rural?
- What sort of weather patterns are tolerable for my health or lifestyle?
- Do I want to be on a small, compact campus where I can walk everywhere or am I fine with a sprawling campus that might involve driving from location to location?
- Are people like me accepted and welcomed on this campus?

Educational Offerings

- Do the schools I'm looking at include the major(s) I'm most interested in pursuing?
- Do the schools I'm looking at include the degree type I would like to pursue, such as a bachelor's degree?
- How big is the course catalog—will I have a lot of variety in the classes I can take or only a little?
- How big are classes usually and are they taught by professors or teaching assistants?
- What is the faculty-to-student ratio?
- What sort of reputation do professors at this school have?
- Are there options for studying abroad, online learning, passing course equivalencies, or anything else that might better fit my education style?
- If I need special learning accommodations, what resources exist on campus for me?

Cost

- What sort of financial aid exists for students in my economic situation?
- How costly will related expenses like rent, transportation, and local cost of living be?
- What will my total annual budget need to be if I live and go to school in this location, and is it feasible?
- How much will I have to spend on annual travel to and from home if my school is far from my family?

What Am I Looking for When Searching for a College?

Campus Offerings

- Does the school offer extracurriculars, clubs, or athletics that match interests I'd like to continue pursuing?

- Does the campus appear to have good facilities for things like dining, events, student healthcare, fitness and wellness, and other things that will be important to me as a resident of a campus community?

- Is there a writing center or other resources to help students academically?

- What sort of assistance programs exist for students who fall on hard times?

School Reputation

- Does the school have a favorable reputation that will look good to future prospective employers?

- How is the school ranked or reviewed compared to other comparable schools?

- Is the school accredited, meaning the US Department of Education can certify that it meets minimum education standards?

- Has there been any significant negative press about the school that might affect its reputation?

- What do former students or employees say about the school in public forums?

Social Life

- Are there fraternities and sororities on campus, and if so, how big of a role does Greek life play in the social climate of the school?

- Do students who attend the school seem to enjoy it?

- Where do students eat— do they dine together in a dining hall or do they tend to cook alone?

- What sort of school traditions or community events exist to help students form meaningful connections with another?

- What are some of the important policies that affect students' social lives on campus?

Admissions Process

- How competitive is the school and are my grades and achievements in line with the expectations of admission?

- Do I have the time, energy, and resources (like application fees) to complete this application or is this school not worth it to me when I weigh all the factors?

Different people will give you different advice on how many schools to consider. As a rule of thumb, you should have 1–3 top choice schools and about 4–6 secondary choice schools. You may also want to consider having a "safety" school or two, which is a school you apply to knowing you are almost guaranteed to get in. That way, if things don't go as planned and you don't get in anywhere else, you know you'll have at least somewhere to go. If you don't get into a top choice school, you may also consider attending community college for awhile to improve your GPA and knock out some general education requirements, then try to transfer to your school of choice later.

CAMPUS VISITS

While you can get a lot of information about colleges from guides, online searches, official websites, and school newspapers, the best way to really get a feel for a particular college is to visit the campus. The "prime time" to experience the college environment is during the spring of your junior year or the fall of your senior year. Although you may have more time to visit colleges during the summer, you might be better served while school is in session (in the spring or fall). That way, you can see the campus when it is alive and bustling with activity, rather than when it is in "summer mode." Visits can take many forms, ranging from short afternoon tours to overnight visits where you stay in the dorm with a current student. Talk to the admissions offices of the schools you are interested in to see what kinds of programs might exist for visiting students.

Campus visits are ideal but understandably, for a variety of reasons, many students find themselves unable to visit multiple campuses. If your schedule or budget does not allow for campus visits, don't despair! A great alternative is to take a "virtual tour" of the campus, often offered on a college's website. This way, you'll be able to "see" the college without physically being there. In addition, you should make sure to get in touch with current or recently graduated students from that college who live locally. They can give you the most authentic description of a student's experiences on campus. The admission offices at the schools you're interested in may be able to put you in touch with local alumni associations or arrange for you to virtually speak with a current student as well. Again, the key is to speak with the admission office at each of the schools that interest you and see what sort of resources they have for helping students get a feel for campus if they can't visit in person.

> "I went into my college visits thinking this one school was my top choice. The thing is, when I got there, the students didn't seem very friendly, the class I visited seemed super boring, and the weather on campus was a disaster. Nothing about being there made me excited about college like I thought it would. However, at this other school, I fell in love with the beautiful local landscape, was impressed with all the facilities I saw, and thought the students all seemed warm, kind, and genuinely happy to be there. That school had a totally different vibe that just worked way better for me... I ended up accepting their offer as soon as my dad and I got home!"
>
> Jaylon, High School Senior

I'm a campus tour guide at my college, and I love helping prospective students get a feel for campus life. Here are some great questions to ask a tour guide like me during your college visit!

1. What's the best academic experience you've had?

2. What did you do last Saturday night? Was it a pretty typical evening?

3. If you could change something about the college, what would it be?

4. Why did you choose to come to this college? Where else were you accepted?

5. What is the surrounding community like?

Martin, College Sophomore

 If you have decided that you are able to visit a campus, here is a list of steps to take when planning that visit:

☐ Read campus literature, such as student newspapers or school websites, prior to the visit.

☐ Contact the admission office of the college you want to visit. Find out what times and dates campus tours and admission information sessions are offered, and, if necessary, schedule your interview for the date that you will be on campus.

☐ Ask if there are any classes that you can observe while on campus. Not all colleges offer this, but if your prospective school does, it would be wise to sit in on a class in a discipline that you could see yourself pursuing.

☐ If you are an athlete, email the coach for your sport to schedule an on-campus meeting.

☐ If you already have a specialized area of academic interest, reach out to a professor or faculty member from that field to schedule an in-person meeting while you are on campus.

☐ See if you can spend a night in the dorm. It's worth asking, especially if you have an older friend or contact who is attending the school you are visiting, but usually this experience is reserved for admitted students.

☐ If you are particularly interested in a certain club or extracurricular activity, like the college radio station or the theater group, see if you can arrange to speak with someone involved.

☐ If you visit a college during the school year, be sure to obtain permission from your college counselor to miss school.

Once you have planned your visit, you can start getting excited about being on campus! Here are some things to do during your campus visit:

- ☐ Take a campus tour to get a helpful overview of the school.

- ☐ Talk to current students that you see while visiting. Asking questions about their experiences can give you valuable information about the school.

- ☐ Visit the student center, bookstore, library, dining halls, and other social locations on campus. This can give you an idea of the school's student culture and social life.

- ☐ See a typical dorm room, even if you cannot spend the night there.

- ☐ Check out the athletics or arts facilities that may interest you.

- ☐ Visit with any coaches or professors with whom you have pre-arranged meetings.

- ☐ Make sure that you politely ask for the email address of your tour guide, admission officers, or any friendly students you meet on campus. If you have questions later on, you can circle back to them!

> When helping my daughter with the college search process, the key was to pace things out so that every college visit doesn't take place in the fall of your child's senior year, which is pretty late. Some kids want to start looking at schools in 9th grade; my daughter didn't feel ready until the spring of her junior year. As a parent, don't be afraid to ask questions to help your child figure out exactly what they want to do and the kind of school they will feel most comfortable at. It's a big decision. Some parents hire a college consultant to help with the whole admissions process. My daughter and I looked in several college guidebooks and on various websites. Then, when she had selected a few schools in the same geographical area, we planned a road trip. That was the most important part of the process. At one school, my daughter determined halfway through the tour that the school was definitely not right for her. At another school, she knew it was a perfect fit—and she actually ended up at that school!
>
> Lourdes, Mother of a College Sophomore

THE ADMISSIONS INTERVIEW

Before you arrive on campus for your visit, it would make sense to try to schedule an interview. Interviews are not required by all schools, but your campus visit is a good opportunity to try to speak with someone or obtain an interview. If interviews are not offered at the college you are visiting, try to attend an "information session" or college tour. The admission website for your school should have information on scheduling and availability and you can always call to ask if they don't. Most likely, you'll need to sign up for something like this in advance of your visit, as it's unlikely they'll be able to schedule you last minute once you're on campus.

Remember, you're looking for a school that will be the "best fit" for you, so use both your visit and interview to help you determine if that school is somewhere that you can envision building your future. Think of it like "trying on" the school to see if the fit works. Interviews (required or requested) can also happen in your local community, oftentimes with traveling admission personnel or people who are part of the alumni network for the college, so don't panic if you are not able to snag an interview on campus. Contact individual admission offices to request an interview or keep an eye out for an email that the school may send your way about interview requests.

The purpose of an interview is to give the interviewer a more in-depth understanding of who you are, both academically and personally, beyond the information contained in your file. In the interview, you're a real-life person talking to another real-life person, not just another set of data points on a piece of paper. That means it's your time to paint a fuller picture of who you are so the school can better understand how you'd fit into their academic community.

Remember, an interview is a two-way street. It is most productive when both participants interview each other. Be assured of who you are and what you want from a college and find out what you need to know from them. If you go into an interview just to impress the other person, you may not come away with a clear understanding of whether that school is actually suitable for your needs. You are interviewing them as much as they are

"I'm in my college's alumni network and sometimes do interviews with prospective students on behalf of them now that I live in a different state. I love meeting all the different students and giving my feedback to the admissions office. Mostly, they want to know what character traits stood out, if the student seems mature and capable of handling the workload at the school, and any insights I might have on whether they'd be a good match for the school's overall culture. But really, I spend most of the interview encouraging students to ask me questions, too. They need to know if the school is a good place for them just as much as the school needs to know if they're a good match!"

Ilsa, Liberal Arts College Alumna

interviewing you, so be prepared to ask real questions, especially if you are speaking with an alum who is more likely to give you straightforward answers about social life at the school than an admission officer might.

An interview will never make or break your admission decision, so at a minimum, it is good practice talking about yourself with a professional adult. To prepare, you should gather some background information about the school you are interviewing with so you are able to sound knowledgeable and well-versed. Here, you'll find a list of questions to help you collect vital, need-to-know information. If a question can be easily answered on the college's website, try to avoid asking it at your interview. Rather, use that information as a knowledge base from which you can ask more insightful questions and learn more interesting or nuanced details about the school from your interviewer.

Questions to Consider Asking During an Admissions Interview

- How many students apply each year and how many of them are accepted?
- What is the school's procedure for offering credit for Advanced Placement (AP) high school courses or other course equivalencies, like CLEP?
- As a freshman, will I be taught by professors, teaching assistants, or a combination of both?
- What is the student-to-instructor ratio and what is the average class size?
- What resources exist on campus to help students if they fall behind academically?
- If you have any kind of developmental, physical, or learning disability, you'll want to ask: What kind of resources exist on campus for someone in my situation and how would I go about getting those accommodations?
- When is it necessary to declare a major?
- Is it possible to have a double major or to declare a major and a minor?
- How does the advising system work?
- Does this college offer study abroad, cooperative programs, or academic honors programs?
- What is the likelihood, due to overcrowding, of getting closed out of the courses I need?
- Is there a career center and how effective are job placement services at this school?
- What teaching methods are used in my area of interest?
- How many students graduate in four years in my area of interest?

- What are the demographics of the student body and how socioeconomically diverse is it?
- What percentage of students live in dormitories vs. off-campus housing?
- What precautions are taken on campus and in the dorms to keep students safe and secure?
- What sort of medical and mental health facilities exist on campus to serve students' needs?
- Are there problems with drug and alcohol abuse on campus, and if so, how does the college address them?
- How central are sports and arts to student life and which extracurriculars are most popular on campus?
- What percentage of the student body belongs to a sorority/fraternity?
- Are students involved in the decision-making process at the college and do they sit on major committees?
- What percentage of students receive financial aid based on need?
- If a family demonstrates financial need on the FAFSA (and CSS Profile, if applicable), what percentage of the established need is generally awarded?

Tips to Help You Do Well in Your Admission Interview

- Speak clearly and maintain eye contact with people you meet.
- Act confident—even if you don't feel confident, pretend like you do because your interviewer won't know the difference!
- Be honest, direct, and polite.
- Be prepared to answer questions about yourself.
- Do a mock interview with someone in advance to prepare.
- Don't be shy about explaining your background and why you are interested in the school.
- Convey your interest in getting involved in campus life and don't be afraid to mention specific ways you'd like to do so.
- Be positive and energetic.
- Don't feel as though you must talk the whole time or carry the conversation yourself. It's okay to take a moment to think of an answer or give the interviewer space to respond to you as well.
- Try to relax and enjoy just having a conversation.
- Thank those you meet during the interview and send thank you notes when appropriate.

One useful way to prepare for your admissions interview is to do a mock interview. Your guidance counselor may have a way to set this up with one of your teachers or someone at your school, or you can simply have a parent, friend, or sibling read the questions for you at random to give you practice answering on the spot. If there is someone you know who is good at roleplaying, you can get them to act serious to help you practice dealing with nerves if your interviewer doesn't come off friendly. You can never practice too many times—even doing so in the mirror with yourself as the mock interviewer counts! Doing so will help you have fewer jitters the day of the real deal. Here, we've compiled just a few of the many different types of questions that could come up.

Practice Questions for a Mock Admission Interview

- What's your favorite book and why?

- Describe the best teacher you've had and what made them a good teacher.

- How do you like to spend your free time?

- Tell me a little bit about your family and home life.

- Which of your traits would you say is most important to your personal identity and why?

- How did your life or worldview shift because of the COVID-19 pandemic or any other big event you experienced as a child or teenager?

- What's your favorite class you've ever taken and why?

- What kinds of things did you do last summer? What do you plan to do this coming summer?

- Can you think of a defining moment of your life so far? What did you learn about yourself in that moment?

- What unique contributions could you offer to our school community?

- Why are you interested in our school?

- What recent news events have piqued your interest?

- How have you given back to your local community?

- What's your biggest strength and your biggest weakness?

- Tell me about a specific time you overcame a challenge and what you learned from it.

- Where do you see yourself after college?

- What is something you wish more people knew about you?

You don't need to know exactly what will be asked. Instead, practice giving thoughtful responses when put on the spot. At the end of your interview, your interviewer will generally ask if you have any questions for them as well. Don't be caught off-guard by this. Instead, make sure you have already thought of some questions beforehand.

A Few Questions about Campus Culture for Admissions Interviewers

— — — — — — — —

- What are some fun campus traditions or annual events?

- Are there any particularly memorable classes or professors that students should try to take before graduation?

- What is campus culture like and how tight-knit is the campus community?

- What one thing most distinguishes this college from others?

- With which other colleges do you see the greatest number of overlapping applications? Which colleges are considered most similar and comparable to this one?

- A few questions work particularly well for alumni interviewers specifically:

  ○ What was your favorite college memory?

  ○ What did you like most about campus?

  ○ What were the pros and cons of going to school there?

  ○ If you could go back and do it over, what's something you wish you had known from day one?

  ○ Can you describe the social culture on campus and the general vibe of this place?

  ○ What's something only a former student could tell me?

Notes

Tips for Your Admissions Interview and/or Visit

- **PREPARE IN ADVANCE.** Schedule an interview time beforehand, and once you have a date and time scheduled, reach out to the admissions office regarding any professors you want to meet or whose classes you want to observe.

- **WRITE DOWN QUESTIONS BEFOREHAND.** Be sure to peruse the school's website so that you're not asking questions to which you can easily find the answers.

- **BE ON TIME. BETTER YET, BE FIVE MINUTES EARLY.** If you're going to be late for any reason, call and let them know. You're probably not the only student with an interview or tour scheduled that day.

- **BE WARM AND RESPECTFUL TO EVERYONE YOU MEET.** This includes the admissions receptionist, student panelists, your tour guide, the person who hands you your cafeteria meal, EVERYONE. Honor the community you might be joining.

- **SILENCE YOUR CELL PHONE.** Like, fully silenced, not just on vibrate. Turn it off if you must. You don't want your embarrassing ringtone to go off in the middle of an interview. Ask the people accompanying you to silence their cell phones as well.

- **BE POLITE.** If the interviewer extends their hand, be sure to give them a firm handshake. Sit up straight, and don't chew gum, yawn, swear, slouch, or otherwise look disinterested.

- **BE AUTHENTIC.** It's important to be real (but not too real) in your interview. You don't want to make it seem like everything is rainbows and sunshine always, but if you need to discuss hard topics, you also don't want to dwell too much on the negative. Strike a balance and present an authentic but hopeful version of yourself. Similarly, don't just give an answer because you think that's what they want to hear—be genuine.

- **SHOW THEM WHO YOU ARE IN PERSON.** You're not here to just reiterate everything in your brag sheet or admissions materials. Instead, focus on providing details and insights that they can't glean from your application.

- **REMEMBER THAT THE INTERVIEW IS JUST ONE PIECE OF THE PUZZLE.** The interview itself won't make or break you, but it can complement the other pieces of your application. Make sure that you prepare in advance so you're ready for the big day, but don't stress too much if things don't go perfectly.

SHOULD YOU TRY FOR A HIGHLY COMPETITIVE SCHOOL?

Competitive schools tend to have the best reputations, but getting into them can be like a full-time job. Students hoping to get into these types of schools usually have to start planning before they're even in high school. While that sort of commitment is worth it for some, it might not be the best use of energy for many others. In this section, we'll outline some things to consider if you're hoping to gain admission to a highly competitive institution.

The Ivy League

Determining whether to apply to one of the eight Ivy League schools (Harvard University, Yale University, Columbia University, Brown University, Princeton University, University of Pennsylvania, Dartmouth College, Cornell University) is something you should think long and hard about. While the Ivy League is associated with a great deal of prestige and success, it is also notoriously difficult to gain admission to these schools. Furthermore, because so many students tend to shoot their shot at these schools, your admission application will have to compete against that many more potential students.

It's true that it can't hurt to toss your application into the ring if you can afford the application fee (or have it waived, for students with financial need) and you can spare the time you'll spend writing the essays. This is especially true if you are a very high-performing low-income student, as these schools tend to have programs that make tuition low-cost or free for those with financial need. But if you want to figure out if you'd be a legitimate candidate for acceptance at one of these top-tier schools, you should understand the type of student that they look for and how you compare.

Given the statistics presented here, it's worth examining for yourself if you have the grades and scores to be competitive with these schools. If it seems like you're pretty far off the mark and there is no way to turn that around before admissions season, you might want to consider at least choosing some safety schools in case you don't get in at the Ivy of your choice.

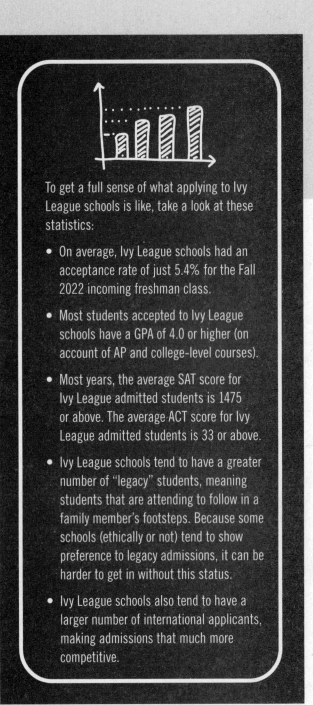

To get a full sense of what applying to Ivy League schools is like, take a look at these statistics:

- On average, Ivy League schools had an acceptance rate of just 5.4% for the Fall 2022 incoming freshman class.

- Most students accepted to Ivy League schools have a GPA of 4.0 or higher (on account of AP and college-level courses).

- Most years, the average SAT score for Ivy League admitted students is 1475 or above. The average ACT score for Ivy League admitted students is 33 or above.

- Ivy League schools tend to have a greater number of "legacy" students, meaning students that are attending to follow in a family member's footsteps. Because some schools (ethically or not) tend to show preference to legacy admissions, it can be harder to get in without this status.

- Ivy League schools also tend to have a larger number of international applicants, making admissions that much more competitive.

Competition Outside of the Ivy League

Of course, the eight Ivy League institutions aren't the only competitive schools in the country. Schools like the Massachusetts Institute of Technology (MIT), Stanford University, and the University of Chicago are all not technically in the Ivy League, but they are competitive enough that any advice that applies to the Ivy Leagues would apply to them as well. Other colleges, like the Julliard School, the Berklee College of Music, or the United States Naval Academy are highly competitive for people with niche career interests. As with the Ivy Leagues, our advice for gaining admission to schools like these is the same: Figure out early on what the statistics are for admission and how likely your prospects are. Talk with your guidance counselor about setting goals to make sure you stand out when the time comes, and be realistic with yourself about whether you are interested in the school because it is right for you or because it is a "big name." You might find that you can get everything you're looking for at a less competitive but still prestigious institution.

Improving Your Prospects for Admission to Competitive Schools

Being accepted at a highly competitive school is a process that starts early, often in middle school but definitely by 9th grade. If gaining admission to such a school is important to you, discuss this with your guidance counselor early on so that they can help you take the steps necessary to achieve this goal. Ivy League and other competitive university hopefuls should select demanding courses and maintain top grades in those courses throughout all four years of high school. They should also get involved in extracurricular activities, community service, and student leadership and try to take on leadership roles in extracurriculars when possible, such as going out for team captain. Of course, if you're trying to get into a highly competitive school, you'll also want to do as well as possible on your standardized tests.

Attending a Historically Black College or University (HBCU)

Another option to explore is attending a historically Black college or university (HBCU), such as Howard University, Spelman College, or Morehouse College, among others. The decision to go to an HBCU is, like any college decision, a highly personal one that will depend on a lot of intersecting and individualized factors. While these colleges were originally founded to provide Black Americans access to a quality education, anyone of any race may apply to and attend an HBCU. Suffice it to say that as with most things in your college search process, it's a good idea to talk to your family, any adult mentors you trust, and any current students you might know at HBCUs to get a sense of whether one of these institutions might be the right college path for you to take.

As students at these institutions will tell you, though reasons for attending vary from person to person, there are numerous potential benefits to choosing an HBCU. For one, HBCUs generally have lower tuition fees than other higher education institutions. According to the United Negro College Fund (UNCF), the average total cost of attendance at HBCUs is about 26 percent lower than at other nonprofit

US colleges. Similarly, to support their goal of making quality education available to more of the population, HBCUs tend to offer comprehensive forms of financial assistance to help cover the total cost of education—not just tuition. By providing quality education at an affordable cost, these schools are actively contributing to closing the racial wealth gap. HBCUs especially continue to encourage growth in STEM subjects; since the early 2000s, 24 percent of Black STEM graduates in the US have earned their degree from an HBCU.

Another potential benefit is that for some students, attending a school with a different demographic makeup than other institutions (where white students tend to be in the majority) helps shift their perspective in a way that makes them feel secure and better connected to a diverse society. As with single-gender education, some HBCU students feel that this type of environment diminishes the amount of stereotyping they have to deal with or "code-switching" they might have to do to fit into other spaces, allowing them to focus more energy on learning.

Additionally, HBCUs also serve a proportionately larger number of first-generation college students, meaning students who are the first in their family to ever go to college. First-generation students might therefore find that an HBCU is uniquely equipped to support them and creates an environment where they feel more at ease. For these and many other reasons, it's worth keeping HBCUs on your radar.

Source: United Negro College Fund, Inc.

Attending a Historically Single-Gender College or University

Attending a college aimed primarily at men or women used to be much more commonplace than it is today. One of many reasons that single-gender education has become less commonplace could have to do with the fact that questions about gender proliferate in our modern world, so the use value of single-gender education may seem diminished for some. It's worth noting that with few exceptions, most colleges aimed at a single gender do still allow application and admission from people of all gender identities. It's just that they historically have aimed their education at fulfilling the needs of either men or women and tend to have student populations that reflect that.

At this point, there are more women's colleges remaining than men's colleges; in fact, Wabash College, Hampden-Sydney College, and Morehouse College, which is an HBCU, are the only three men's colleges that remain as

of printing. Notable women's colleges still in operation include Smith College, Barnard College, Spelman College (which is also an HBCU), and Bryn Mawr College. Those who like this type of education say that the benefits include dealing with less gender-related stereotyping in the classroom, greater support for the needs of a particular population (such as robust women's health services at women's colleges), and a relaxed environment that helps students feel at ease with one another. Of course, others would say that they prefer mixed-gender education because they believe it helps close gender equality gaps and promote understanding among people of different experiences. There's no right or wrong answer to the question of whether to attend a historically men's or women's institution so long as you make the decision based on what works best for you. For some, the environment of a women's or men's college may be exactly what they need to thrive.

THE BOTTOM LINE: CHOOSE WHAT'S RIGHT FOR YOU

When you get down to the nitty gritty, the most important part of your college search is making sure it's YOUR college search: not that of your parent(s), guardian(s), guidance counselor, or peers. You can't make the decision because your best friend is going there, because you like the city, because you have heard the name of the college before, or for any other reason that doesn't have to do with you personally and the education you want to get. Sure, those can all factor in, but at the end of the day, you need to be thorough and figure out which college checks the most boxes on your personal list. Once you've figured out your favorites (we recommend having at least three top choices and five other options), then you'll be ready to jump into the application process. You got this!

Applying to College

Now that you've finalized a list of colleges you want to apply to (and completed three busy years of high school!), it's time to actually apply. Applying to colleges is a multi-step process that involves a lot of moving parts. Your application is your opportunity to bring together many different aspects of who you are as a student and person, so read on to get started!

The Short and Sweet Version

Lots of teens get overwhelmed when they even start to think about everything that goes into the college admission process, but the truth is, it's actually pretty straightforward when you break it down into its parts. For instance, the Common Application makes it easy to create one or two base essays and then build on them for individual schools who use it.

This chapter will help you put together the important pieces of the puzzle so you can make sense of it all. The bottom line is that things vary from school to school, so once you've searched for schools and determined which are your top choices, you'll want to look into the specifics of their individual admissions processes and organize yourself to get things together by their respective deadlines.

It sounds like a lot, but again, you aren't alone in this. This book can help, and you also have your parent(s) or guardian(s), guidance counselors, and others to support you as you sort through your options. We'll tackle questions like "Should I apply early decision or not?" and "Which teachers are the best to ask for letters of recommendation?"

This is a super exciting time in your life, and it's normal to be anxious, nervous, or overwhelmed—it's a big decision and a long process! But it's also the first step to the future you've mapped out for yourself. Just start early, get yourself in order and your essays and other documents prepared, make sure you know the deadlines you need to know, and try to enjoy the ride!

YOUR COLLEGE APPLICATION

Before you dive in, it is helpful to know what exactly the college application process entails. The process varies from school to school, so you will need to check with each individual institution you are interested in to make sure that you are giving each what they require. Generally, you can find out what a school requires by visiting the "admission" section of their website.

Pieces of the College Application

The list below gives you a good overview of what most colleges ask from you. Remember that not all colleges will ask for every one of these pieces of information.

- **Biographical Information:** Name, address, email address, phone number, family info, etc.

- **Transcript:** The grades you have earned from 9th grade on, including summer school, community college courses you may have taken, etc. If you took any high school classes before you actually started high school, such as an advanced math or language course in 8th grade, you will also get credit for those classes (most likely on your high school transcript, but not always—check with your school counselor).

- **Standardized Test Scores** (SAT, ACT, TOEFL, AP scores, etc.).

- **Brag Sheet/Student Résumé:** A list of everything you have done after school, outside of school, on the weekends, and in the summer: clubs, community service, jobs, internships, other activities, sports, summer experiences, honors and awards earned, and hobbies and interests. Information on the time commitment for each should be included.

- **Teacher Recommendations:** Be sure to ask the teachers who know you best! In most cases, you will need two.

- **Personal Interview:** Be prepared and do your homework before the interview. Know why you want to attend that school. Bring questions and be sure to write a thank-you note to your interviewer afterwards. (Note: Personal interviews by an admission officer or alumni are not always offered.)

- **Personal Statement:** Most schools will ask for at least a personal statement, but some schools may ask for additional writings that can include short answers, paragraph answers, essays, etc.

- **Supplemental Recommendation:** Usually not from another teacher. You may think of requesting a supplemental recommendation from a mentor, employer, religious leader, coach, or someone else unrelated to you who knows you well outside of the classroom.

- **Graded School Paper or Project:** As part of your application, you may be asked to submit a copy of an assignment you completed. Consider using an assignment or project where you received a good grade or positive teacher comments and where you demonstrated strong writing abilities, critical thinking skills, or something else you're proud of.

- **Prepared Music or Art Portfolio:** This is only if your college requests one. Also, be prepared to audition for dance, drama, or music if your college offers or requires auditions. If you cannot attend in person, some schools will allow video or online submissions. Check with your institution for requirements, dates, and locations for auditions and portfolio submissions.

- **Application Fee:** Don't forget to include the application fee for each of your schools or else all the time and effort you've put in to applying will go to waste! If you are worried about application fees making it difficult to apply to schools, talk to your guidance counselor—there may be opportunities to have the fees waived if you can demonstrate financial need.

Your Résumé or "Brag Sheet"

In addition to all of your college essay writing, which we'll discuss a little later in this chapter, many colleges will need you to provide information regarding everything that you have done in your high school career outside of the classroom. Most colleges have a chart or inputs that you can complete to list every activity you have done outside of school since the summer after 8th grade. Don't forget, in the eyes of colleges, high school begins as soon as you graduate from 8th grade, so the summer after 8th grade "counts."

A brag sheet will generally consist of the following:

1. Name of activity—club, extracurricular, athletics, etc.

2. Years/grades you have participated in the activity

3. Hours per week/weeks per year of involvement

4. Description of activity—details about it, leadership roles you may have had, honors/awards within activity

Here, we have given you an example of a "brag sheet." This is simply a student résumé that can be formatted using tables in a word processor like Google Docs or Microsoft Word or in a spreadsheet like Google Sheets or Microsoft Excel. Even though you will complete something like this online in your Common Application or on each school's independent form, it is helpful to have a "master" version to refer to as you begin your college application. A document like this could also be useful to send to the people writing your recommendation letters, to (possibly) share with interviewers, or even to use as a reference point when prioritizing your time and content choices for your college essay responses.

The brag sheet offers a place for you to include all your activities, events, work, community service, summer experiences, and awards received outside of the classroom. This information shows colleges how you spend your free time. Each column is important to understand. The trickiest is knowing the hours per week and weeks per year. Use your best guesstimate of how much time you have dedicated to the activity so that your reader understands your time commitment.

Sample Brag Sheet

Anahita Karzai

Date of Birth: 11-12-2003

Extracurricular/ Club/Organization	School Years	Hours	Positions/Honors/Description
International Rescue Committee	9–12	175 hours total 50–74 hours/year 10 hours/year required	Support Afghan clients by translating English to Farsi and by tutoring children in English. Help clients adjust to life in the US and complete immigration paperwork.
Muslim Student Association	9–11	1 hour/week 36 weeks/year	Gathered signatures and recruited faculty advisor to establish the Muslim Student Association, an organization for promoting awareness and understanding of Islam through activities, discussion groups, and fundraisers. Elected President in grades 9–11.
Anime Club	9–10	2 hours/week 36 weeks/year	Club for watching and discussing anime, holding trivia events, and learning more about Japanese culture.
Soccer	9–11	6 hours/week 36 weeks/year	JV (9); Varsity (10, 11 summer)
Summer Experiences			
Soccer	9–11 (summer)	20 hours/week 12 weeks/year	Soccer camp; practice and games; 3 away tournaments
Tutoring	12	4 hours/week 12 weeks/year	Paid position tutoring 7th grader in math.
Awards			
National Honor Society	10–11		Honor society that requires 3.0 GPA on a 4.0 scale, community service and volunteer experience, leadership experience, and exemplary character.
Soccer	9–11		Most valuable player (10)
Honor Roll	9–11		Recognized for outstanding academic achievement every quarter from grade 9–11

It is a good idea to begin a notebook or computer document to keep track of all your involvement as you go along so you don't forget things when it comes time to fill out this chart. Be sure to include the following sections:

- Extracurricular Activities—Organizations/Clubs/Athletics
- Sports—You can have a subsection for sports or include them in order by most involvement (in school years and hours) to least involvement and/or in reverse chronological order.
- Community Service
- Employment
- Awards and Honors
- Summer Activities

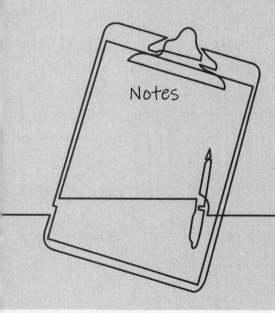

some students' test scores are lower than you would think. Alternatively, exceptionally high test scores may help you get a leg up if you struggled elsewhere (like your GPA). Think of them as one small part of a bigger admissions equation.

- **EXTRACURRICULAR ACTIVITIES:** Colleges look for depth of involvement (variety and how long you participated), initiative (leadership), and creativity demonstrated in activities, service, or work. If one of your recommenders was also a coach or sponsor for an extracurricular, they can help speak to these things as part of their recommendation.

- **RECOMMENDATIONS:** Most colleges require a recommendation from your high school guidance counselor. Some ask for references from teachers or other adults.

- **COLLEGE INTERVIEW:** Most colleges with highly selective procedures require an interview.

HOW YOU'RE EVALUATED

Now that you have an idea of what's included in your application, you'll need to understand what admission committees want from you as you assemble all the pieces of your application.

- **ACADEMIC RECORD:** Admission representatives look at the breadth (how many), diversity (which ones), and difficulty (how challenging) of the courses on your transcript. They also pay careful attention to the grades you are getting in these classes. Some schools even show your class rank on your transcript or somehow indicate your academic standing compared to others in your school. The transcript is widely regarded as the single most important piece of your application because it shows the kind of student you are and what you have done throughout your high school career.

- **STANDARDIZED TEST SCORES:** Colleges that look at test scores examine them in terms of ranges. If your scores aren't high but you did well academically in high school, you shouldn't be discouraged. Admission does not rest on a set formula. Even at the most competitive schools,

When I applied to colleges, I was so busy with my job and honors classes that I didn't have many extracurriculars on my brag sheet. But I still got into 4 of the 5 colleges I applied to. Make sure you apply to a variety of schools and don't be afraid to let your experience and qualifications speak for themselves.

Sergio, First-Year College Student

YOUR ADMISSIONS OPTIONS

Before you begin completing your applications to four-year colleges and universities, you will want to figure out which admission option you want for each school. What this means is determining whether you want to apply early action, early decision, deferred admission, or regular admission—or if your school offers rolling or open admission.

Four-year institutions generally offer the following admission options:

- **EARLY DECISION:** A student declares a first-choice college, requests that the college decide on acceptance early (between November and January) and agrees to enroll if accepted. Students with a strong high school record who are sure they want to attend a certain school may want to consider early decision admission. Early decision is a legally binding agreement between you and the college. If the college accepts you, you pay a deposit within a short period of time and sign an

> "I visited lots of schools in Pennsylvania, but the minute I walked on the campus of Gettysburg College, I knew I wanted to come here. I liked the way the campus was set up. It was small, and everything was together. The student-teacher ratio was low, and it had a good political science program. It had everything that I wanted. Because I was so positive that I wanted to attend Gettysburg, I decided to commit to apply early decision."
>
> Greg, College Junior

agreement stating that you will not apply to other colleges. To keep students from backing out, some colleges mandate that applicants' high school counselors cannot send transcripts to other institutions.

- **EARLY ACTION:** This is similar to early decision, but if a student is accepted, they must wait until the regular admission deadline to decide whether to attend. Individual schools determine whether to offer early decision or early action, and you decide if you want to apply in that way based on their early selection criteria.

- **REGULAR ADMISSION:** This is the most common option offered to students. A deadline is set for when all applications must be received, and all notifications are sent out at the same time.

- **ROLLING ADMISSION:** The college or university accepts students who meet the academic requirements on a first-come, first-served basis until its freshman class is full. No strict application deadline is specified. Applications are reviewed, and decisions are made immediately (usually within two to three weeks). This method is commonly used at large state universities, so students should apply early for the best chance of acceptance.

- **OPEN ADMISSION:** Virtually all high school graduates are admitted, regardless of academic qualifications.

- **DEFERRED ADMISSION:** An accepted student is allowed to postpone enrollment for a year. (See "The Gap-Year Option" at the end of this chapter.)

If you're going to a two-year college, these options also apply to you. Two-year colleges usually have an "open-door" admission policy, which means that high school graduates may enroll as long as space is available. Sometimes, vocational/career colleges are somewhat selective, and competition for admission may be fairly intense for programs that are highly specialized.

When Is Early Decision the Right Decision?

Early decision is an excellent idea that comes with a warning. It's not a good idea unless you have done a thorough college search and know without a shred of doubt that this is the college for you. Don't go for early decision unless you've spent time on the campus and in classes and dorms, and you have a true sense of the academic and social climate of that college. You need to feel absolutely positive that you're making the right choice for you before applying in this way.

Early decision can get sticky if you change your mind. Parents of students who have signed agreements and then want to apply elsewhere get angry at high school counselors, saying they've taken away their rights to choose different colleges. They try to force them to send out transcripts even though their children have committed to one college. To guard against this scenario, colleges ask parents and students to sign a statement signifying their understanding that early decision is a binding plan. Some high schools now have their own form for students and parents to sign acknowledging that they understand the nature of an early decision agreement.

"I was an early decision applicant and it was so great because my school offered superb financial incentives for early decision applicants that helped make attending so much more accessible. Plus, I stopped worrying about the application process at all after November of my senior year, since I already knew I was going to my top choice—I had been there for a pre-college program, so there was no doubt in my mind!"

Tianna, College Senior

That said, early decision can be a positive choice if you have done a thorough search and know absolutely for certain what your top choice school is. Due to a limited number of available spots for incoming students, small or private schools that prefer early decision applicants may even offer financial or other incentives to apply this way. There also tend to be fewer applicants in the early decision pool, so it can help you stand out at highly competitive institutions. However, these should not be the only reasons you apply early decision. Instead, do so only if it makes sense as a way to solidify your commitment to a school you already know is a perfect fit for you.

Financial Arguments against Early Decision

Another common argument against early decision is that if an institution has you locked in, it has no incentive to offer you the best financial package. The consensus seems to be that if you're looking to compare financial aid packages, don't apply for early decision.

Others argue, however, that the best financial aid offers are usually made to attractive applicants. In general, if a student receives an early decision offer, they fall into that category and so would get the best financial aid regardless. That doesn't mean that colleges aren't out there using financial incentives to get students to enroll. A strong candidate who applies to six or eight schools and gets admitted to all of them will look at how much money each college is willing to put up before making a decision.

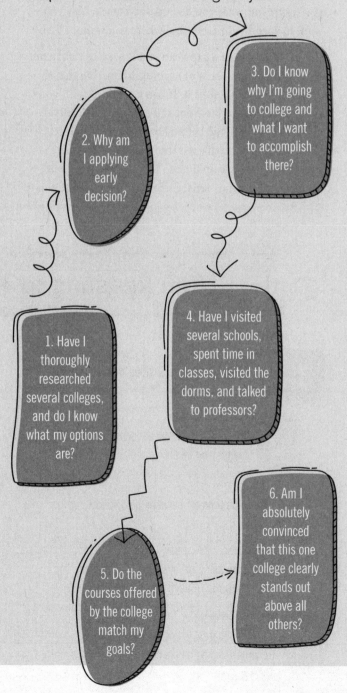

Before You Decide to Apply Early Decision

If you're thinking about applying for early decision at a college, ask yourself these questions first. You'll be glad you did.

2. Why am I applying early decision?

3. Do I know why I'm going to college and what I want to accomplish there?

1. Have I thoroughly researched several colleges, and do I know what my options are?

4. Have I visited several schools, spent time in classes, visited the dorms, and talked to professors?

5. Do the courses offered by the college match my goals?

6. Am I absolutely convinced that this one college clearly stands out above all others?

THE GAP-YEAR OPTION

If you aren't ready to go straight to college from high school, need another year to "prove yourself," or simply want a break from a traditional academic environment, you may want to try a gap year. The gap year has been steadily gaining popularity and acceptance by students, parents, guidance counselors, and colleges alike. Taking a gap year can be an empowering experience that helps you figure out what you do and don't enjoy, how you want to spend your time, and where you want to live.

If you want to take a gap year, you'll need to figure out what you want to learn or accomplish during that time and how you can afford it. If you have lived with your parents during high school and are hoping to spend another year at home before heading off to college, then you'll need to discuss this option with them to make sure they are on board. They might agree but under certain conditions, such as they may want you to

"Taking a gap year gave me the time I needed to discover more about what I wanted to pursue in college and possibly professionally. Having a 'breather' after high school also gave me time to recharge my batteries so I could be more energetic when I began my college experience. My gap year definitely helped me avoid academic burnout, just in time!"

Benjamin, Gap Year Student

Ten Reasons to Take a Gap Year

1 Experience an easier transition from college to the work world.

2 Determine your college focus to avoid changing majors and incurring additional costs.

3 Take some time off between high school and college.

4 Increase your level of self-confidence and maturity through real-world experience.

5 Gain practical skills and work experience (résumé-building before college or seeking a job).

6 Follow up on interests and enhance prospective studies.

7 Choose and create your life for a year.

8 Find your passion or determine what is not of interest to you.

9 Save up money for college.

10 Take time now because it's harder to find when you're older!

get a part- or full-time job, pay rent, or pay a specified amount per month for utilities or groceries. Regardless, remember that once you graduate high school, you are generally considered an adult, so you'll likely encounter adult responsibilities.

How Does the Gap Year Work?

Most students interested in a gap year apply to colleges in their senior year and then request a year's deferral once accepted. Aside from state universities that may not offer the option of a deferred year, colleges are usually willing to defer a student because they realize that an extra year of maturity and life experience often translates into an overall better student. Other students wait to apply to college until halfway through their gap year when they have a better idea of where they want to go and what they want to study.

What Is a Successful Gap-Year Experience?

A successful gap-year experience is any combination of experiences that allow you to learn more about yourself and figure out what you want to do. Some students take a gap year intending to live at home and save as much money as they can before college. Other students participate in a variety of volunteer and work experiences to figure out what they enjoy. Students who can afford to travel may jet set across the globe to get out of their comfort zone and search for enriching cultural experiences. There's no right way to spend a gap year, but it's up to you to figure out how you want to spend your time between high school and college. It will go by faster than you expect, so make sure that you have a plan in place for what you want to do and when you want to do it.

How to Plan the Best Gap Year

A variety of resources are available to assist students and parents in planning a fulfilling gap year. If you want and can afford a more structured experience, then you can always look for a gap-year program. Working with a gap-year consultant can save research time and help you weed out potentially poor program options. The Gap Year Association website (**www.gapyearassociation.org**) has a lot of valuable information and

resources, including a list of gap-year consultants and counselors who can help you make the most of your gap year. Additional information on other gap-year possibilities can be found at **usagapyearfairs.org/programs.**

"A gap year abroad allowed me a firsthand opportunity to immerse myself into another culture, learn a new language, and to experience life outside of my hometown bubble. I was not ready to go right into college and still needed some time to mature a bit and live away from home without the academic pressures of traditional college. The gap year proved to be a great way to accomplish that and to make lifetime memories that have changed me forever."

Sasha, Recently Completed Gap Year

"In the latter years of high school, my time as a student became ineffective. After being in school all day for 13 years, I was burnt out. I needed a break. Just because I got to pick what I wanted to study in college didn't mean I was willing to continue being a student for another four years before I could actually 'do something.' I researched national service programs, and when I found the City Year program, I was immediately drawn to the mission and the structure. It would be regimented, much like the schedule I was used to, and I would be able to help at-risk students graduate on track and on time. I was given the opportunity to move across the country and was given a support system once I got there. I developed my professional skills in public speaking, conflict management, facilitation, event planning, results-driven data analysis, project management, and youth development. I worked on a team with my peers, school faculty members, and individuals in the community I serve—partnering to accomplish amazing things. I significantly expanded my professional network, getting to work with stakeholders and professionals in multiple fields.

Perhaps most formative was the time I spent with my students. They challenged and re-motivated me to pursue my own dreams. They made me confident, and they changed my life.

I am serving a second year as a Team Leader with City Year because of the change I saw in myself. I hope to pass that gift on to as many future AmeriCorps members as I can. I don't regret my decision for a second."

Jordan, Gap Year Student

ADMISSION PROCEDURES

Once you've figured out which schools you want to apply to (whether early or regular decision), it's time to start the application process. College applications can be submitted after you have completed your junior year of high school and once the application is available (usually by the end of the summer). Colleges strongly recommend that students apply by January of their senior year to be considered for acceptance, scholarships, financial aid, and housing. College requirements may vary, so always read and comply with specific requirements.

Your first task in applying is to fill out the biographical information on your application. The Common Application is used by more than 900 colleges (and counting); see if any of your schools are a part of this system. Various state colleges or other university systems tend to also group their schools together into one application form. Other colleges have individual applications available on their websites. Regardless of which system the schools you are applying to follow, you will be asked to fill out simple biographical information as part of the application.

WRITING THE APPLICATION ESSAY

Because you're discussing your best subject (yourself!), the questions and prompts for college application essays can be interesting and fun to write about. However, you may find that it is harder than you anticipated to write about yourself; it can be intimidating and challenging to tout your accomplishments or reflect on past experiences. While the college application essay is important for showcasing who you are, remember that it's just one part of the application. Some students also worry that they're not good writers, but like any skill, writing takes practice. With time and effort, you can always improve your writing skills. In this section, we'll walk through some strategies for how to plan, draft, and edit college application essays.

Self-Reflection Activity: Questions to Answer

Before you even look at the questions that colleges ask, consider making a document by hand or on your computer where you answer the following questions about yourself. This activity will help you "get to know yourself better," and oftentimes, by answering these questions, you can figure out how to start your essay or identify examples and experiences from your life that you can include elsewhere in your application.

• What is your favorite childhood memory? (It doesn't matter whether you remember it personally or if it has been told to you for many years.)

• What hobbies do you enjoy outside of school?

• What games do you like to play or what do you do in your free time?

• What special talents do you have?

• What is your favorite family tradition?

• How would your best friend(s) or closest family member describe you? What adjectives or verbs would they choose? Don't be afraid to ask your friends or close family members this question to collect their reflections of you.

• What is the best book you have read? Why?

• What is your favorite subject in school?

• Who is your favorite teacher from any grade and why?

• What struggles in your life have you overcome?

• Who is your personal hero or role model?

• What activity, which person, what food, etc., brings you happiness?

• How would you describe your family, and what memorable experiences have you shared together?

• What achievements or accomplishments, academic or personal, are you most proud of?

• What are some "defining moments" in your life—i.e., experiences, conversations, moments that changed, challenged, or enlightened you in some way?

• What is your community or neighborhood like, and how do you see yourself or your role in it?

• Looking back on your life so far, what is one experience that looks different now than it did when it happened?

Notes

The Essay Questions

Once you have completed your self-analysis by exploring these questions, look at the colleges' essay questions. The good news is that these questions are meant to guide you and are relatively open-ended, so they leave much to your imagination and creativity. Other colleges have similar open-ended questions or allow you to make up your own question and answer it. Some ask you simply to write a personal statement. The Common Application questions provide a good base from which to start formulating your ideas.

Here are the actual instructions from the 2022–2023 Common Application (from **commonapp.org**):

> "The essay demonstrates your ability to write clearly and concisely on a selected topic and helps you distinguish yourself in your own voice. What do you want the readers of your application to know about you apart from courses, grades, and test scores? Choose the option that best helps you answer that question and write an essay of no more than 650 words, using the prompt to inspire and structure your response. Remember: 650 words is your limit, not your goal. Use the full range if you need it, but don't feel obligated to do so. (The application won't accept a response shorter than 250 words.)"

This graphic illustrates the seven questions or prompts used for the 2022–2023 application cycle.

1 Some students have a background, identity, interest, or talent that is so meaningful they believe their application would be incomplete without it. If this sounds like you, then please share your story.

2 The lessons we take from obstacles we encounter can be fundamental to later success. Recount a time when you faced a challenge, setback, or failure. How did it affect you, and what did you learn from the experience?

3 Reflect on a time when you questioned or challenged a belief or idea. What prompted your thinking? What was the outcome?

4 Reflect on something that someone has done for you that has made you happy or thankful in a surprising way. How has this gratitude affected or motivated you?

5 Discuss an accomplishment, event, or realization that sparked a period of personal growth and a new understanding of yourself or others.

6 Describe a topic, idea, or concept you find so engaging that it makes you lose all track of time. Why does it captivate you? What or who do you turn to when you want to learn more?

7 Share an essay on any topic of your choice. It can be one you've already written, one that responds to a different prompt, or one of your own design.

These topics, whether straightforward or more creative in nature, can be answered through personal experience and reflection. Here's the thing: You can really write about whatever you want to as long as it loosely answers the prompt in a cohesive and structured way while providing insight into who you are as a person and college applicant. When approaching the question, you can decide what you want to share about yourself and determine which prompt fits best. Then, you can fine-tune your draft to respond to the particulars of the prompt more effectively.

Now, imagine a college admission officer with thirty to forty applications to read every day. Next, imagine that your application is the fortieth and final read of the day. Your reader is a bit tired and bleary-eyed and might not be focused enough to recognize the many hours you have put into this application. How will you capture their attention?

While everyone will have their own idea of what your college application essay should look like, one approach is to develop a central argument that reinforces your qualifications, strengths, and achievement as an applicant. In the pages that follow, we'll outline some advice for how to write your application essay if you take this approach.

What Should I Write About?

You may feel overwhelmed by all the different topics you could write about for the essay. If that's you, sometimes it's easier to pick a prompt first so that it narrows down your options and helps you pinpoint an idea. Remember that the prompts are often deliberately vague because admissions committees consider a range of applicants with completely different life experiences. Don't try to write your life story in one page; choose an experience, conversation, or idea that offers the reader a sense of who you are. Sometimes, it can be helpful to think about how you want the admissions committee to view you as an applicant. Pick a few key words or phrases that you want them to see in you: fast learner, compassionate, driven, honest, hard worker, etc. Then, think back to a time where you demonstrated one or more of these qualities.

Some people might advise you to stay away from cliché topics, like how being on the basketball team taught you determination and hard work. Consider how many people apply to college every year. It's inevitable that certain topics come up again and again, especially from high school students with limited life experience. Don't let this discourage you from discussing a common topic that matters to you, but be aware that you might need to approach it creatively.

To make your topic come to life, do your best to tell the story well—use vivid description that makes the reader feel like they're on the basketball court with you. Also, reconsider the takeaways of your story—is the story really about hard work and determination? Is there a more specific lesson you learned that more accurately demonstrates what you will be like as a college student? For example, maybe a difficult basketball season taught you the value of reflecting on your performance and searching for strategies and resources for how to improve yourself.

> I had a hard time coming up with ideas for what to write in my college essay. But as I brainstormed ideas for the different prompts, I realized the same theme kept coming up. I wanted to show how I'm always up for a challenge and how I learn from failure so I can do better. So, I wrote about how I got a 2 on my AP Spanish exam my junior year. Failing the AP exam was a huge blow to my confidence, but I was able to collect myself and enroll in other classes that would challenge me for senior year.
>
> Leanne, High School Senior

Regardless, do justice to your experience by writing it well and showing how it made you into the person you are today.

When choosing what to write about in your personal statement, remember that it's up to you what you do or do not include. Some students feel pressured to disclose information that sets them apart, like a disability, traumatic experience, financial hardship, or something else. In fact, the very first prompt on The Common Application invites you to share some aspect of your story that you find especially important for the admissions committee to know about you. Please know that you are never obligated to disclose sensitive or private information about yourself in your personal statement. You only need to write what you are comfortable with.

If you do choose to write about a difficult experience, give yourself time and space to discuss the experience authentically while also providing a balanced evaluation of your personal character. Don't feel obligated to write a happy ending to the story; at the same time, the admissions committee will expect the story to be included for a reason, primarily to speak to your skills or attributes as an applicant or, if necessary, to explain some kind of misstep in your academic performance. Make sure the goal of your statement reads clearly.

Similarly, while a lot of applicants might write about their experiences volunteering with marginalized or disenfranchised groups, remember to never use other people as props to make yourself look good. For example, let's say you volunteer with an organization that helps resettle refugees in your city. When you write about the individuals you work with, you should treat them with empathy, respect, dignity, and kindness. Imagine somebody writing about you in their college admissions essay. How would you want to be portrayed? If you're telling someone's story or writing about deeply personal details of their life, consider using a pseudonym to give them privacy. Don't harp on their hardships, talk about how sorry you feel for them, or express gratitude for how your own life is better or easier. Instead, focus on what you actually did to help and what you learned from that experience.

How did you grow as a person from helping people fill out immigration paperwork or distributing donations and supplies to families? Remember, someone else's life circumstances are not an opportunity for you to be a hero or savior.

Remember that your essay is supposed to be about you, not a topic you think the admissions committee wants to read about. Keep the essay focused on your character, strengths, and experiences. This isn't the time to rehash your activities or your coursework. The personal statement is also not a manifesto. Avoid writing about controversial topics, especially those that are political or religious in nature. You don't know who will be reading your essay, and offending a reader is not especially helpful when they can influence whether you're admitted. Instead, focus on what you've learned and what you've achieved and emphasize how you would make an exceptional asset to any student body.

How Do I Start?

With a personal statement, it can be helpful to outline your ideas first before you start writing. Remember that 250 words is about equivalent to one double-spaced page of writing, so the maximum length of your essay is close to two and a half double-spaced pages. Start with your responses to the self-reflection questions earlier in this chapter. What experiences or topics are unique to you? Which ideas might captivate your reader's attention? Think about which ideas you're most excited to write about. How can you use those ideas to highlight your strengths? Pick two or three ideas that you like best, then cross-reference those subjects with the given Common Application prompts. Do the ideas you've marked fit any of the questions? If so, that's where you can start.

When you start outlining, plan on an essay that's 3–4 paragraphs long: an introduction paragraph, 1–2 body paragraphs, and a conclusion paragraph. There's some flexibility with your body paragraphs, depending on how much you want to write, but keep the word count in mind as you draft. Here's what each of these sections of your personal statement should accomplish:

- **Introduction:** Your introduction should begin with a compelling anecdote or idea that establishes a theme for the rest of your essay. A theme will make your essay more cohesive by linking your experiences together, which will ultimately make your personal statement more memorable. The goal here is not necessarily to shock but rather to surprise or intrigue the reader so that they want to continue reading about you. The introductory paragraph is important for not only getting the reader's attention but also setting the stage for you to highlight your greatest accomplishments and achievements. The introduction should explicitly illustrate how your qualifications and expertise have prepared you for the program or major of your choice. If you're not sure what program you want to pursue, that's okay. Identify a future goal or career path you are interested in pursuing, but remember that you're not necessarily committed to that path if and when you're admitted.

- **Body Paragraphs:** These paragraphs should reinforce the theme you've established while emphasizing your strongest qualifications and most impressive achievements. Remember, as part of your application, the college admissions committee will also have your transcript, test scores, and other information about you. Use the body paragraphs of your essay to describe experiences that can't be gleaned or understood from looking at your transcript. This is your chance to help the reader get to know you better. For example, think about a problem you helped solve or an obstacle you overcame. Then, clearly describe what you did to handle or resolve the situation. Finally, inform the reader of the outcome of the situation and how it illustrates your strengths or how you learned from the situation.

- **Conclusion:** This is your opportunity to summarize some of the key takeaways from your essay while also connecting back to the theme you established in the introduction. Reiterate your interest in a particular program and make your final appeal for your admission to college and to the program of your choice.

Your first draft of writing is never, ever your last. In fact, revisions can go on and on until you are ready to upload or input them as part of your application and push the "submit" button. Make sure that every word of your final essay counts. Use active verbs rather than linking verbs. Be sure that your voice is heard and comes through clearly in your writing. Don't use a bunch of big words unnecessarily to sound smarter. Read your essay aloud into your bathroom mirror, and check to see if it really sounds natural and genuinely like you. Be yourself, not the person you think the admissions committee wants you to be.

Word of Warning: Plagiarism

Remember that your college application essay is supposed to highlight your unique personality, skills, and character traits. While it might be tempting to cut corners during the college application process, don't use any essay from this book, or one written by anyone else, and claim it as your own. First off, you are the most qualified person to write an essay on the topic of you.

Don't try to write your life story in one page; choose an experience, conversation, or idea that offers the reader a sense of who you are.

Tips for Writing Your College Application Essay

- Make sure your first sentence offers a hook or opening that grabs the reader's attention.

- When telling a story, immerse the reader in the details through vivid description. Use your five senses when you write, showing your reader how things look, taste, smell, sound, and feel.

- Proofread, proofread, and proofread again so that you catch any and all mistakes. That said, if an error slips through, don't stress too much; it happens to the best of us.

- Read your essay out loud to yourself before submitting it. This will not only help you identify areas that are hard to read or understand but also indicate errors or typos. It can also help you revise so that the words flow together more smoothly.

- Prepare your essays in a word processing document before transferring them to The Common Application or other online application. This will make it easier to edit and spell check before pasting it into the online version. Be sure to save the word document often or use cloud computing to automatically save copies of your work.

- If you're submitting through the Common Application, don't include the actual name of any colleges in your writing unless it is in a supplement that is exclusively for that college. This means no names of colleges should be included in your main essay.

- Save your drafts until you are done. Sometimes, you might want to use something you wrote in an earlier draft.

- When writing your personal essay, seek help from a trusted adult: your guidance counselor, a teacher, parent, guardian, sibling, or an older friend who has applied to college.

- Take your time. College essay writing is a process that is not meant to be completed in one weekend. Thoughtful planning, drafting, revising, editing, and proofreading will ensure that when your essay is finally done, it's done! Spend time writing something that you are proud of and that genuinely reflects who you are.

- Remember that your essay is just one part of your application.

No one else will be able to write about your qualifications and character in the way that you can. This is your chance to advocate for yourself and to show prospective colleges why you would be a great asset to their student body.

Additionally, remember that plagiarism is a serious offense and can jeopardize everything you have worked for. You will likely be asked to electronically sign a waiver for your colleges indicating that the work contained in your application is solely your own. Colleges can verify that your work belongs to you by using simple internet search tools and programs to identify sentence strings that might not look like your own. Don't throw it all away by plagiarizing an application essay. Remember, also, that if you can find an essay on the internet, that means others can, too, including your reader. You might not even be the first person to submit the plagiarized essay, which would be a dead giveaway, as readers have probably seen certain plagiarized essays submitted again and again. It's not worth the risk—do your own work!

See the sample personal essay we've included here. This essay is 605 words and would work as a response to The Common Application's prompt that states "Discuss an accomplishment, event, or realization that sparked a period of personal growth and a new understanding of yourself or others."

Sample Personal Essay

When I stepped into the cool, air-conditioned library, I felt my heart race in anticipation of an event I would remember for as long as I lived. With a book on Mars tucked into my backpack, I waited patiently to meet Sally Ride, the first American woman to go to space. She talked about what it was like to be an astronaut, how challenging it was to be a woman in a field dominated by men, and what it was like to see the earth from space. That day, I learned about something called the overview effect: Astronauts who have been to space return to earth in awe of the beauty of life and with a newfound appreciation for the planet they call home. When Sally Ride recalled her stellar view of the "big blue marble" that suddenly felt so small, I knew I wanted to do everything in my power to take care of the only planet I will ever know. I've been volunteering with environmental organizations to promote local sustainability efforts and educating others on how to reduce their carbon footprint, and as a college student, I plan on pursuing a degree in Environmental Science to learn more about advocating for climate change policies and initiatives.

For the past two years, I've been volunteering for the Greenway Foundation, which focuses on revitalizing the South Platte River and teaching high school students about the importance of preservation and conservation efforts. As a Greenway River Ranger, I teach summer camp participants about strategies for keeping the river clean, preserving the ecosystem, and protecting wildlife. Since I started volunteering, I've educated more than 300 students on how to protect local plant life and wildlife along the South Platte River. From this experience, I've learned how important it is to respect the environment and to "leave no trace" whenever I interact with nature and wildlife. These are principles I will continue to abide by for the rest of my life, as a college student and beyond.

As a student at Blake High School, I started and am now president of the Sustainability Club. We meet after school on Thursday afternoons and discuss our school's environmental impact as well as strategies for reducing waste on campus. Last semester, we voted to start a community garden because our school is located in a food desert. We also crowdfunded enough money to purchase several composting bins to reduce food waste while also improving the soil quality in our community garden. Starting a garden has allowed students to experience what it's like to cultivate plants while supplying nutritious fruits and vegetables to the people in our community. While these changes might seem small, I've learned the power and importance of everyone doing their part. I know I am just one person in one city, but I'm teaching my community the power of people working together to create a better world for future generations.

Almost three years to the day since I shook her hand at the library, I learned that Sally Ride had died. She was just one person, but she was able to be an inspiration and a role model for so many people. In my work volunteering for the Greenway Foundation and as president of the Sustainability Club at Blake High School, I've learned how one person's actions, both positive and negative, can impact the world we live in. Someday, I hope that I can use my Environmental Science degree in such a way that people will look back on what I've accomplished and see me as someone who made a positive impact on the world, without leaving a trace.

> "Essays are so important to the college application. Students often assume grades are the end-all and be-all or that an SAT score alone will get them in. For most selective schools, that's just one piece of the pie. Many schools in the upper 20 percent of competitive schools consider the essay more heavily. Essays show whether the student is a thinker, is creative, and is analytical. They're looking for the type of personality that shines rather than one that can simply spit out names and dates. When everyone has high SATs in a pool of applicants, the essay is what makes one student stand out over another."
>
> Salmane, Admissions Counselor

QUESTIONS AND ANSWERS ABOUT YOUR COLLEGE APPLICATION ESSAY

Q: How do I write about myself without sounding too conceited or braggy?

A Remember: your personal statement is not the place to hold back and show too much restraint. It is okay to celebrate your accomplishments as long as you provide evidence and proof of what you've been able to achieve. It is also nice to reflect and appreciate the talent or life experience you have cultivated. Essentially, in your personal statement, you have some degree of "bragging rights." Use them.

Q: What are some ideas of topics or content that could go in the "Additional Information" section of the Common Application?

A There are two fields where you can supply additional information that you want to share with the admissions committee but that wasn't relevant anywhere else in the application. First, there is an opportunity for you to talk about how COVID-19 or natural disasters have impacted your health and well-being. Consider sharing more information here if you or your family were affected by the COVID-19 pandemic and how that has impacted your academic performance, your financial situation, or your health and what accommodations you might need. Remember, you don't have to include information if you don't want to, but this section of the application might help you to explain specific concerns with your qualifications or clarify accommodations you'll need from the college if you're accepted.

The second prompt is essentially asking the same question, but with consideration for other circumstances that are not related to COVID-19 or natural disasters. Here, you can address things like a concerning grade that might be out of sync with your transcript in general; an explanation for why you might have moved levels in a course (for example, down from AP to a standard course); a break in your education, such as a gap year or time off due to illness or a family issue; or some "good news" that you haven't noted yet, such as an award, honor, additional activity, or unique talent. Additionally, you can include any other explanation that you feel you need to share with your reader to offer information that you believe is important in clarifying who you are or for "making your case." One tip: When explaining your circumstances, try not to do so in a blaming or overly critical way, no matter how unjust the situation may have felt at the time or still feels. Even if it's not the kind of thing for which you need to take personal responsibility, you definitely wouldn't want to say something like "my stupid teacher wouldn't change my grade even though I was sick" when you *could* say something like "Unfortunately, I have not yet been able to get a grade adjustment despite the fact I had a note from the hospital." Tone is important for these sorts of things and you don't want to come off as immature or unprofessional.

Q: How strict are the word limits on applications?

 For the personal essay, your response must be at least 250 words, but no longer than 650 words. For those colleges or universities that are not part of the Common Application, you should always check to be sure you're complying with their particular application's word limits. A good rule of thumb is to use as much of your word count as you can without going over or being repetitive and wordy.

Q: What is the best way to ensure I don't have typos or mistakes in my essays?

 Do all your application writing in a word-processing document where you can edit and spell-check. Practice reading your essay aloud to be sure you have caught any awkward phrasing or typos. For example, the computer cannot tell the difference between whether you should use *from* or *form* and, therefore, it may not catch those words as mistakes when they are. If you have time, see if your teacher or guidance counselor can read through your essay, but remember that they might be busy handling the same request from many other students as well. If they do seem too busy to help, remember all the brain power around you: parents, guardians, older siblings, relatives who work in writing fields, school librarians, tutors, coaches, and friends who excel at language arts are all good sources of assistance. If you're lucky enough to go to a school that has a writing center, they would be able to help you as well. When you're sure you have made all the necessary corrections, copy and paste your final version into The Common Application or other online application form.

Q: What about additional or supplemental materials I need to submit for my program?

When you add schools to your My Colleges tab on The Common App dashboard, you'll see each school's requirements and deadlines. If relevant, there will be additional instructions for how to submit a portfolio or schedule an audition. Check with each school individually if you are unsure of the requirements and how to submit your materials.

Q: How do I know when my essay is finished?

 First, pay attention to the content by asking yourself the following questions:

☐ Does your personal statement begin with a hook that grabs your reader's attention? Does your introduction establish a central theme for your personal statement?

☐ Do the body paragraphs provide more detail and insight into your accomplishments and achievements?

☐ Are the experiences you include relevant to the theme you've established? Does your conclusion reinforce the central theme and look forward to your future?

If you've answered *yes* to all these questions, then you can focus more on the writing style and grammar:

☐ Does your essay fit within the word limits?

☐ Do your voice and personality come through in your writing?

☐ Is your tone consistent and professional?

☐ Have you checked the grammar and spelling?

☐ Have you proofread your essay and read it out loud?

☐ Have you looked at the structure backwards (from last paragraph to first) as well as forwards to make sure everything links together as a logical train of thought?

If you've answered *yes* to all these questions, then it seems that you are ready to hit "submit." Woohoo, now it's time to celebrate!

LETTERS OF RECOMMENDATION

Most schools will require you to submit two letters of recommendation from teachers who know you well in addition to a letter of recommendation from your guidance counselor. If you have a teacher who knows you well as a student but can also speak to your extracurriculars, like for instance if they sponsored your Recycling Club or coached you in Knowledge Bowl, all the better. Letters of recommendation are important because they allow the people who know you best to personally attest to your character, your skills, and your academic performance.

Guidance Counselor Recommendations

Nearly all colleges require a letter of recommendation from the applicant's high school guidance counselor. Some counselors give students an essay question that

they feel will give them the background they need to structure a recommendation. Other counselors canvass a wide array of individuals who know a student to gather a broader picture of the student in various settings. No one approach is better than the other. Find out which approach is used at your school. You'll probably get this information as a handout at one of those evening guidance programs or in a classroom presentation by your school's guidance department. If you're still not sure that you know what is expected of you, ask your guidance counselor what is due and by what date. Make sure that you complete the materials on time and that you set aside enough of your time to do them justice. Remember, this is why you want to have taken the time to develop a good relationship with your guidance counselor.

Teacher Recommendations

In addition to the recommendation from your counselor, colleges may request additional recommendations from your teachers. Known as formal recommendations, these are sent directly to the colleges by your subject teachers or compiled by your guidance counselor and sent through a system such as Naviance. Most colleges require at least one formal recommendation in addition to the counselor's recommendation. However, many competitive institutions require two academic recommendations. Follow a school's directions regarding the exact number. A good rule of thumb is to have recommendations from teachers from your junior year or the first semester of your senior year because colleges want to hear from your most current teachers. Be sure to have your recommendations come from two different subject areas.

Approach your recommendation writers personally to request that they write for you. If they agree, provide them with a copy of some excellent graded work you may have held onto from their class (if possible) as well as a "student blurb." A student blurb is a bulleted list that you put together about yourself with personal reflections of what you learned in your teacher's class, how you see yourself as a student, and any other important personal or academic information you think will be helpful to your teacher in crafting a letter of

> "When I write a recommendation for a student, I go all out to try and give an honest but glowing review of who they are. This is much easier to do if I know the student well, for sure, but they don't have to have gotten an A in my class for me to speak well about them. If I know you worked the hardest you've ever worked in your life to get a C+, I can also speak to that spot on your transcript they may be wondering about and say 'Hey, actually, this kid showed a lot of personal responsibility and tenacity working hard to come back from a rough start to the year.' Sometimes it's most important to pick a teacher who knows you and has seen you struggle and overcome because they can really say what makes you shine."
>
> Minerva, High School English Teacher

recommendation. These highlights will help teachers write a more descriptive recommendation for you.

How do you decide whom to ask? The following are some questions to help you select your writers:

- How well does the teacher know you?

- Has the teacher taught you for more than one course? A teacher who taught you over a two- to three-year period has seen your talents and skills develop. A teacher who may have been your coach or club advisor knows you in a different light outside of class, which can also be helpful.

- Does your intended major indicate that a recommendation is required or recommended from a particular subject-area instructor? For example, if you have already decided to apply as an engineering major, it might be required that you obtain a recommendation from a math or science teacher.

- Has the teacher seen a side of your character that others didn't get to see, maybe because you overcame a struggle with their help or sought their advice during a rough year? If they know you well enough to speak about you from multiple perspectives, this can make you stand out.

Other Recommendation Writers

Some schools require or allow for a supplemental recommendation. Consider getting recommendations from an employer, your religious cleric, or someone who has supervised you directly in a work, volunteering, or extracurricular context.

Thank You Notes

Don't forget to thank anyone who writes your recommendation. Your guidance counselor, teachers, and other trusted adults took time out of their busy schedules to advocate for you. Showing them gratitude in return is the right thing to do. When you eventually select your college, be sure to go back to your recommenders and let them know what choice you made and thank them again for the supportive role they played in this decision.

> When I was working on my college applications, I asked my tennis coach and my biology teacher to write recommendation letters for me. Because I planned to apply to medical school someday, I knew it would be great to have a recommendation from someone who could vouch for my commitment to my physical health and someone who could speak to my academic qualifications.
>
> Margaret, Medical School Graduate

CHAPTER 8

College Entrance Exams

Standardized tests are necessary steps on the path to a college education. You've probably heard older siblings or students buzzing about the various college entrance exams—like the PSAT/NMSQT, the SAT, and the ACT—and wondered what they might entail. Each test is different, with its own requirements and scoring system, which can make it kind of mystifying to figure out what doing well would even look like. These standardized tests are certainly a big deal for most (but not all) colleges and can be crucial to your future academic plans. However, you don't need to panic when you hear your friends freaking out about them. Preparing for the tests takes a lot of planning and time, but if you're reading this chapter, you're already doing that—congrats, you're ahead of the game!

The Short and Sweet Version

Standardized tests. Yeah, we know it's not the most exciting topic, and there's a good chance you feel some combination of anxiety, boredom, and stress just thinking about them. But honestly, the cool thing about standardized tests is that they're just that: standardized. That means no surprises. You can figure out what to expect in advance, and there are ways to prepare. See, doesn't that already sound less intense?

In a lot of places, you'll take some of these tests through your school, but you'll need to find out from your guidance counselor which ones you need and which ones you may have to take (or retake) outside of school. Other tests are optional, so you won't even need to think about them unless you're interested in attending certain schools or pursuing certain fields.

The important thing is to figure out what the format is and what topics are covered for the specific year you're taking an exam because things change from exam to exam and can vary from state to state, too. On top of that, the specific exams are always changing, so while we outline most of what you need to know about them here, it's always important to check the websites for the tests you plan to take. That's how you'll get up-to-date information.

Break up study time and prioritize so you can focus on the subjects in which you need more practice. But don't cram! In fact, your best moves before a big exam are to get a good night's sleep and make sure you have a healthy breakfast in the morning. With a little test prep planning and some diligence, you can go into your exam feeling like a confident super genius—which is proven to help you test better, by the way.

WHAT TO KNOW ABOUT STANDARDIZED TESTS

It can be helpful to approach these tests with a few things in mind. First and foremost, these are not intelligence tests; they do assess your general reasoning abilities but also gauge the knowledge and skills you're expected to have acquired in high school. Furthermore, they are doing so in quantitative (meaning countable) ways, not qualitative (meaning uncountable) ways. In other words, the test may be able to tell schools if you can identify the purpose of a reading passage, but not if you are a diligent reader, for instance. For better or worse, take your test scores with a grain of salt; they only measure one facet of the overall picture of who you are as a student.

One good next step after reading this chapter would be checking out the College Board's website. We recommend contacting your guidance counselor, who can offer advice on which test might be best for you and can point you to more information on the format and guidelines for each test. That way, you can make sure that you have the most up-to-date information even if something has changed since the printing of this book.

PSAT/NMSQT®, SAT®, AND ACT®

The major standardized tests students take in high school for college admission are the PSAT/NMSQT, SAT, and ACT. Colleges across the country use scores on these tests to get a sense of a student's readiness to move onto higher education. Therefore, these tests have become notorious because of how important they can be. While it may seem like there's a "magic number" you want to aim for with your scoring, both the scoring mechanisms of the tests and the ranges of scores that schools accept can fluctuate from year to year. That doesn't give you a precise number to aim for, but it does set a range. You can figure out about how many questions you're aiming for per section, and you can see the lowest and average scores accepted by your school of choice. Regardless of your situation, then, that means that you need to do some research and prep work.

Should You Take a College Entrance Test?

You might be thinking, "Wait, but things have changed; these tests don't mean what they used to," and you'd be right. A significant number of US colleges and universities have dropped their testing requirements for admissions. That means their applications are test-optional, but that doesn't mean they ignore scores. Even though ACT or SAT scores may not be required by every school you're applying to, that doesn't mean that such data can't boost the appeal of your application and make you more competitive. In fact, with changes to the testing formats (digital testing) and new policies for administration and scoring (superscoring and section retakes), there's really very little risk in taking either of the tests and seeing how you perform. On your application, a competitive score can do a lot for you: cover deficits in your grades or GPA and get you access to merit-based scholarships and funding. If nothing else, having a score can expand your application options and give you a better sense of whether you're college-ready or have some gaps to fill.

All that doesn't mean there aren't reasons to avoid the tests. Perhaps the testing dates don't align with your schedule or paying for the tests might be a financial burden with money being better spent on admissions application fees or saved for tuition. Whether you take one of the tests or not ultimately depends on the schools to which you're applying and if a decent score can make your application stand out from others.

The PSAT/NMSQT®, PSAT™ 10, and PSAT™ 8/9

The Preliminary SAT/National Merit Scholarship Qualifying Test (PSAT/NMSQT), PSAT 10, and PSAT 8/9 are simply "practice tests" for the SAT. The numbers "10" and "8/9" reflect the grade(s) in which students take the test and offer additional practice before the SAT. The PSAT/NMSQT, available in both the fall of sophomore year and junior year, is used as a qualifying measure for the National Merit Scholarship Program and in designating students for the National Hispanic Scholar Recognition Program—both of which offer significant financial aid opportunities. Digital versions of the tests will be offered starting in fall 2023.

The PSAT/NMSQT, the PSAT 10, and the PSAT 8/9 questions test skills and knowledge in these areas:

Reading

Questions are multiple choice and based on passages that may address topics such as literature, social science, the history of the United States, or scientific concepts. They will investigate your abilities on matters like:

- How authors use evidence to support their claims
- How graphics and other informational evidence provide support for an author's claims
- The meaning of a word or phrase in its context within the passage
- How to examine a hypothesis, make sense of data, and consider the implications of the data in terms of the hypothesis
- How to draw inferences and conclusions from a given passage

Writing & Language

Questions are multiple choice and based on reading passages that contain weaknesses and mistakes that students will need to address. There will be a combination of argumentative, expository, and narrative (story-based) passages. Some passages may be accompanied by graphs, charts, or other visual information. There is no essay component required. Questions in this section will investigate your abilities on matters like:

- Identifying clear and direct expression of ideas
- Recognizing strong and weak development of a passage's main idea(s) using thesis statements, supporting details, and evidence
- Recognizing logical organization and the sequence of an argument
- Using language effectively, including sophisticated use of style, tone, word choice, sentence structure, and flow
- Using standard conventions of English grammar, usage, punctuation, mechanics, and capitalization

Math

Most questions are multiple choice while others are student-produced responses (grid-ins); only one part allows students to use a calculator. Questions in the math section are divided into four topics:

- Heart of Algebra—Questions in this section mostly focus on linear equations and systems.
- Problem Solving and Data Analysis—Questions in this section mostly focus on how you analyze data to pull out important information.
- Passport to Advanced Math—Questions in this section offer more complex equations.
- Additional Topics in Math—While only a small portion of the test, a handful of questions will address college prep math topics like trigonometry and advanced algebra.

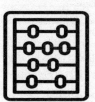

The SAT®

The 2016 version of the SAT is typically taken in a student's junior year and requires 3 hours of testing time. It has two primary sections.

Evidence-Based Reading and Writing

- 100 Minutes (Reading Test—65 Minutes + Writing and Language Test—35 Minutes)
- Points Received: 200–800
- 96 Multiple-Choice Questions
- Questions in this section will investigate your abilities on matters like the following:
  - Command of Evidence
  - Expression of Ideas
  - Words in Context
  - Standard English Conventions

Math

- 80 minutes (Math Test–Calculator— 55 Minutes + Math Test–No Calculator— 25 Minutes)
- Points Received: 200–800
- 58 Multiple-choice and produced-response questions
  - Includes algebra, problem solving, data analysis, advanced math, and additional topics
  - Grid-in sections require you to compute the answer and then fill in the number on your answer sheet

---

The SAT undergoes changes every few years. As recently as 2021, the optional essay component of the test was eliminated. For 2024, the College Board has bigger changes planned. The knowledge and skills tested will remain the same, but the format will change in significant ways with a move to all digital testing. Testing will still occur in school or at a testing center, but the shift in testing format will be accompanied by other changes:

- Testing time of 2 hours
- Adaptive questions that change in difficulty based on student performance
- Shorter reading passages
- Ability to use a calculator on all math questions
- Expedited scoring reports (available in a few days rather than weeks)

Regardless of when you take the test, it's always important to make sure you have the most up-to-date testing information and understand your options. Consult your guidance counselor or the College Board website to learn about the current testing format and see if you qualify for testing accommodations or fee waivers.

SAT Scoring

When you take the SAT, your overall score will be a composite of two scores: a score between 200–800 for Evidence-Based Reading and Writing (ERW) and a score between 200–800 for Math. Those composite scores are the result of taking raw scores of correct answers (incorrect answers are not penalized) and applying a specific formula to yield the score on a scale of 200–800. In 2021, the average composite score on the SAT was a 1060, with an average of 533 for the ERW section and an average of 528 for Math. Different sources will have different ideas of what constitutes a good score; however, the answer to that question largely depends on which schools you are applying to and how much they weight things like test scores. That said, given this average, it's safe to assume that students who score above the average of 1060 have decent prospects at many schools, and anyone who scores a 1250 or more is in approximately the top 20% of test takers.

Source: College Board, *2021 Total Group SAT Suite of Assessments Annual Report*, collegeboard.org, accessed April 2, 2022, https://reports. collegeboard.org/pdf/2021-total-group-sat-suite-assessments-annual- report.pdf.

The ACT®

The ACT is a standardized college entrance examination that measures knowledge and skills in English, mathematics, reading, and science reasoning as well as the application of these skills to future academic tasks. The ACT consists of multiple-choice sections in four disciplines and an optional writing section.

English

- 75 Questions—45 Minutes
- Measures standard written English and rhetorical skills

Mathematics

- 60 Questions—60 Minutes
- Measures aptitude in math subjects that are generally taken between 9th and 12th grade (pre-algebra through trigonometry)

Reading

- 40 Questions—35 Minutes
- Measures reading comprehension

Science

- 40 Questions—35 Minutes
- Measures interpretation, analysis, evaluation, reasoning, and problem solving in the context of the natural sciences

Writing (Optional)

- 1 Prompt—40 Minutes
- Measures high school writing skills

ACT Scoring

Each section of the ACT is scored from 1 to 36. The raw score of the number of questions answered correctly is translated to a scaled score that varies based on the difficulty of the test. For instance, 58 correct answers out of 60 in the math section could translate to a 34 on one version of the test and a 35 on another. Students are not penalized for incorrect responses. The 40-minute optional writing test is scored separately on a different scale. The individual section scores are averaged to yield a composite score. Both section scores and the composite can be used to make admissions decisions. In recent years, the ACT has started automatically reporting superscores to colleges. A superscore averages the best section scores across multiple test attempts. Unfortunately, not all schools accept superscoring, so the ACT will provide at least one full composite score along with any superscore.

Possible Future ACT Changes

To meet the shifting needs of students and provide more accessible and accurate evaluation tools, standardized tests do occasionally change. Sometimes it's a new format. Other times, it might be changes to administration methods. As of this printing, the ACT has not announced changes to the test or its format. In 2020, they had planned to start offering single section retesting. Implementation was delayed due to the COVID-19 pandemic. However, the possibility of such a shift is still likely. The change would mean that after taking the ACT for the first time, if a student felt they underperformed on specific sections of the test, the student would be able to retake just the sections they wanted to score higher in without having to retake the full test. This would then impact the student's superscore, changing what is reported by the ACT. Such changes to testing administration could be combined with a switch to a digital format, similar to the SAT.

"The best way I found to prepare was to take the practice tests to get to know the questions. At first, I'd set the kitchen timer and practice while ignoring the time, just to see what I could do. Then I made sure that I could answer all the questions in the right amount of time. Practice makes perfect!"

Luisa, Student

WHEN SHOULD I TAKE THE SAT® OR THE ACT®?

Ideally, you should take the SAT or the ACT during the spring of your junior year, if not earlier. Registration dates are available on a nearly monthly basis throughout the year. This gives you ample opportunities to retake a test if you're not satisfied with your scores. Keep in mind that spots for testing dates are limited and can be competitive; you should strive to register early. Note, though, that institutions generally consider the better score when determining admission and placement; however, policies do vary. The important thing is to determine the deadlines to register for each test you'll be taking in a given year and to note the dates during which you can test. If it helps, make yourself a calendar with the dates for all the different tests you'll need to take.

WHAT OTHER TESTS SHOULD I KNOW ABOUT?

Here are some additional standardized tests you may also want to think about taking if they apply to you or the schools you want to attend.

The TOEFL® Internet-Based Test (iBT)

The Test of English as a Foreign Language Internet-Based Test (TOEFL iBT) is designed to help assess a student's grasp of English if it is not the student's first language. Performance on the TOEFL may help provide nuance for scores on the verbal sections of the SAT. The test consists of four integrated sections: speaking, listening, reading, and writing. This is because the TOEFL iBT emphasizes integrated skills, meaning it is designed to determine how well a student can use English in practical settings, such as in the classroom and in social interactions. The paper-based versions of the TOEFL will continue to be administered in certain countries until the internet-based version is fully administered by Educational Testing Service (ETS), but most places administer the test digitally. As with any other test you take, make sure to visit the website to see if there are any updates or changes to the testing format since the printing of this book.

The Advanced Placement® (AP) Program

The AP program allows high school students to try college-level work while building valuable skills and study habits in the process.

AP courses explore their subject matter more comprehensively and usually at a faster pace than in other high school classes, so it's important to consider this if you are contemplating taking one. A qualifying score on an AP test—which varies from college to college—can earn you college credit or advanced placement in advance of starting your college courses. Getting qualifying scores on enough exams can even earn you a full year's credit and sophomore standing at many institutions. At present, nearly 40 AP courses are offered in a variety of subject areas ranging from the arts to the sciences. Not every AP course is offered at every high school, so speak to your guidance counselor to find out about AP opportunities at your school and any policies that may affect AP enrollment, such as limits on the number of AP courses the school will allow you to take at once. Once you're in an AP course, your teachers will help you prepare for the AP test, though there are also outside resources available to help students prepare for any AP exam. AP tests usually take place at the end of the school year (the majority of tests are in May). You can find out more on the AP website: **apcentral.collegeboard.org.**

College-Level Examination Program (CLEP)

The CLEP enables students to earn college credit for subjects that they already know well enough to "test out" of the basic education requirements. It doesn't matter if the subject was learned in school, through independent study, or through experiences outside the classroom; in fact, there are many resources out there to help students with CLEP exams. If you're motivated and have the time or resources to practice for a CLEP exam, you may be able to skip some general education courses, so long as you attend a college that accepts CLEP credits. At least 2,900 colleges and universities in the US award credit for qualifying scores on one or more of the 34 CLEP exams. The exams, which are approximately 90 minutes in length, include primarily multiple-choice questions and are administered at participating colleges and universities. More information about CLEP can be found on the College Board website.

Armed Services Vocational Aptitude Battery (ASVAB)

The ASVAB, which we discuss in more depth in Chapter 5, is a career exploration program consisting of a multi-aptitude test battery that helps students explore their interests, abilities, and personal preferences. While it is required for service in the military, you do not need to have plans to join the military to take it, and it can give you useful insights into what sort of career paths might suit your skills and talents. Students can use ASVAB scores for military enlistment up to two years after they take the test. A student can take the ASVAB in 10th, 11th, or 12th grade, so long as they remember that the two-year limit might make it impossible to use their sophomore scores. Ask your guidance counselor or your local recruiting office for more information.

GED® Tests

The Tests of General Education Development, or GED tests, are standardized tests that measure skills required of high school graduates in the United States and Canada. The ultimate goal in passing these exams is to attain a certificate that is equivalent to a high school diploma. Specifically, those who have dropped out of high school for any reason but who wish to prove that they have completed the equivalent education can complete a GED to do just that. Employers who require proof of high school graduation will accept the GED just as they would a diploma.

Knowing that you can take the GED test, however, is not a legitimate or smart reason for dropping out of school. In fact, it is more difficult to get into the military with only a GED, and some employees have difficulty getting promoted without a high school diploma even if the GED can get them hired in the first place. You should not use the GED as an alternative to a high school education unless your circumstances change in a way that requires you to do so. Life happens, so the GED is there if you need it, but don't think of it as an easy way out of a high school diploma.

The GED test has four sections:

Mathematical Reasoning

- 115 Minutes
- Covers basic math, geometry, basic algebra, and graphs and functions
- Includes sections with and without a calculator; test takers are allowed to bring their own TI-30XS calculator or use the onscreen calculator as permitted
- A combination of multiple-choice questions and other question types

Reasoning through Language Arts

- 150 Minutes
- Broken into 3 sections
- Covers three primary test topics:
  - Reading for Meaning
  - Identifying and Creating Arguments
  - Grammar and Language
- A combination of multiple-choice questions, a written essay, and other question types

Social Studies

- 70 Minutes
- Covers three primary test topics:
  - Reading for Meaning in Social Studies
  - Analyzing Historical Events and Arguments in Social Studies
  - Using Numbers and Graphs in Social Studies
- Includes sections with and without a calculator; test takers are allowed to bring their own TI-30XS calculator or use the onscreen calculator as permitted
- A combination of multiple-choice questions and other question types

Science

- 90 Minutes
- Covers three primary test topics:
  - Reading for Meaning in Science
  - Designing and Interpreting Science Experiments
  - Using Numbers and Graphs in Science
- Includes sections with and without a calculator; test takers are allowed to bring their own TI-30XS calculator or use the onscreen calculator in the sections that allow
- A combination of multiple-choice questions and other question types

Source: GED Testing Service, "Test Subjects," accessed April 2, 2022, ged.com/about_test/test_subjects/.

Just like with all tests, make sure to visit the GED website to find out if anything has changed since this book went to print, as procedures do evolve over time. It's also important to see if there are any specific rules that apply to your state and to check what the fees are where you live, since they vary by state.

For practice tests and subject review for preparing for the GED, check out Peterson's *Master the™ GED® Test*.

WHAT CAN I DO TO PREPARE FOR THESE TESTS?

First, know what to expect! Get familiar with how the tests are structured, how much time is allowed for each section, and the directions for each type of question. Make sure you've visited the test's website so that you understand the specific requirements and format for that year.

A variety of products, from books to online courses to videos, are available to help you prepare for most standardized tests. Find the materials that best suit the way you want to learn. As for which products to buy, you have two major categories from which to choose—those created by the testing companies and those created by a third party. The benefit of using resources provided by the testing company is that they will mirror exactly what the test is like; however, the downside is that there is usually a limited number of resources (like practice tests) available directly from the testing company. Third parties, on the other hand, may offer a greater volume of practice resources and have usually done a significant amount of research to make sure their tests are as close to the real thing as possible. The best approach is to talk to someone you know who has taken the exam and find out which product or products they would recommend.

Students who have the resources do report significant increases in scores after participating in coaching programs or designated standardized test preparation courses. These types of environments tend to be more structured, and signing up for a test-prep class can be beneficial if you don't think you will be able to motivate yourself significantly enough to study on your own. However, not everyone has the time or money to do so. As such, self-guided practice resources can still be a significant help. The benefit of buying these resources is that you can write in them and take notes directly on the page. That said, if you don't have the money to purchase your own, resources like this are often available at the library.

Test Prep Resources

You can prepare for standardized tests in a variety of ways—find a method that fits your schedule and your budget. But you should definitely prepare. Far too many students walk into these tests cold, either because they find standardized tests frightening or they just haven't made the time to study. Sometimes, it's because they do pretty well in their classes and assume they'll be fine on the test, but in this case, they're seriously underestimating the benefit of having learned the ropes in advance.

The key to understanding these tests is to recognize that these exams are standardized. That means they focus primarily on the same concept every time they are administered. They must, or else it would be impossible to compare the scores of people who took the tests on different dates. The numbers or words may change, but the underlying content in these tests doesn't. That means that people who have a working understanding of what the tests are looking for have a huge advantage over those who don't.

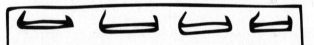

"I used to grade standardized tests for a side job and most of the grading for verbal stuff is done on a rubric, meaning we are always evaluating the same certain key aspects of the writing like language usage, development of ideas, and overall clarity. Practicing for a standardized test helps familiarize you with that 'rubric' even if you don't know the specific factors graders are evaluating."

Robyn, High School English Teacher

So how do you prepare? At the very least, you should review relevant material, such as math formulas and commonly used vocabulary words, and know the directions for each question type or test section. You should take at least one practice test and review your mistakes so you hopefully don't make them again on test day.

Six Steps for Using Practice Materials

Here are some tips for how to prepare for a standardized exam using practice materials.

TAKE A DIAGNOSTIC PRACTICE TEST. This can be one specifically marked as a "diagnostic" test or a "pre-test" in your practice materials or it can simply be the first standard practice test you take. Take this first test before you've studied much at all to see where you stand.

ANALYZE THE RESULTS TO DIAGNOSE THE AREAS YOU NEED TO WORK ON MOST. Most practice materials have some kind of breakdown of which sections correspond with which questions, but you may also just have to make inferences based on your score. For instance, if you take a practice PSAT and your verbal score is way lower than your math score, you can assume you need to spend more time practicing reading than you do solving equations.

PLAN YOUR STUDY TIME ACCORDINGLY. Let's say you plan to spend two hours a week studying for your test. If you know that you need to work the most on reading, you might choose to spend one hour on reading and divide the other hour up among your other subjects. Or perhaps you did about the same in both verbal and math, so you'll devote an hour to improving each. The point is to figure out which subjects to focus on first (the ones with which you need the most practice) and then to spend less (but still some!) time on the others.

TAKE ANOTHER PRACTICE TEST. Once you've devoted some time to practicing, take another practice test. You'll be able to see the difference in your score between now and the first time you tested yourself. If it improved, you'll know you're on the right path and should keep doing what you're doing. If it didn't (or if it got worse, oh no!), that tells you that you probably need to devote more time to studying or you need to structure your study time differently.

REPEAT THE PROCESS UNTIL YOU FEEL GOOD ABOUT THE TEST. Don't overwork yourself—no one needs to take 20 practice tests! A good rule of thumb is to keep taking practice tests until you feel really confident in the test. This will help your brain develop "muscle memory" for the types of questions you'll encounter. This is also why starting early can help. You'll have more time between practice tests, so it feels less like cramming.

GO INTO YOUR TEST DAY CONFIDENT! To enhance your performance, get plenty of rest the night before the test, make sure you're hydrated, and eat a hearty breakfast that morning. On test day, you can stress far less because you'll know that you did what you needed to do to prepare yourself for success. The best part? That confident feeling alone can help boost your score—studies have shown that when people strongly believe in themselves going into a standardized test, that confidence makes them perform better.

While this process should work for just about anyone with any test, only you know best how much preparation you need. Don't overstress yourself or spread yourself too thin. Preparation is important but so is your mental health, so don't let anxiety about preparing for the test become overwhelming. It's okay to take a break and let your brain process now and then!

You can also sign up for a class at a local or online test prep center. There are many prep companies and tutors that are nationally well known and others that are locally run. Some prep classes charge a hefty sum, and their reputations vary, so make sure you look for reviews. You can also see if your school, community center, or public library offers community classes or a course as part of your tuition or school curriculum. Your guidance counselor may also have information on other free resources.

Preparing for and Taking Standardized Tests

1. **SET A TIMELINE.** Figure out exactly what you need to study and plan it out in advance of your test date.

2. **KNOW THE TEST.** Spend time learning what the format of the test is, what question types to expect, how long you can expect the test to be, and how it's scored.

3. **LEARN THE DIRECTIONS AHEAD OF TIME.** Read the directions in advance so you know what to do in each section of the test. Usually, the directions contain details that can help you avoid making simple mistakes.

4. **BE ON TIME.** Some tests won't allow you to go through with the exam if you're late, so be sure to arrive on time or even early if possible.

5. **PACE YOURSELF.** You have a lot of questions to get through, so manage your time wisely. On certain tests, you may be able to skip a question and go back to it, but some tests will not allow that. If you find yourself spending more than a minute or two on one question, make your best educated guess and move on.

6. **THINK THROUGH ANSWER OPTIONS STRATEGICALLY.** It's important to weigh each of the answer options, but it can be overwhelming if it's hard to narrow it down. When in doubt, go with your gut instinct.

7. **LEAVE SPACE FOR QUESTIONS YOU SKIP.** Make sure to leave an open bubble row for any questions you skip. Correcting this is a mess!

8. **USE THE SPACE ALLOTTED TO YOU.** When working on an essay, give yourself time and space to express your ideas. If the prompt says 250–750 words, aim for more than the minimum 250 words. Use the space to fully develop your ideas in a way that isn't wordy or repetitive.

9. **PROOFREAD.** Take the extra couple moments to proofread what you wrote to avoid errors in spelling, grammar, or usage. If your response is riddled with errors that impede your ideas, it will lower your score.

10. **BREATHE.** Seriously, whenever you feel stressed, take a deep breath or three. It'll calm the nerves and help clear your head.

Financing Your College Plans

Getting financial aid can be intimidating. College is a worthwhile but very costly investment—everyone's heard the horror stories of crushing student debt and rising tuition costs. The truth is, sometimes, those aren't just stories—college is absolutely getting more expensive and financial aid is a big undertaking that requires significant planning and forethought. But don't let that stop you! While college is a very costly investment, it can also be worth it. For many, it is advantageous to look for scholarships and grants foremost and use student loans only to fill in the gaps. We don't want to scare you off. We just want to speak to you realistically and help you understand that a student loan may be your first big financial obligation as an adult. You want to go into the endeavor prepared, which is exactly what this chapter can do for you.

The Short and Sweet Version

If you know you want to go to college but don't necessarily have the money to cover it you've still got a lot of options. Your best option is scholarships and grants since you don't have to pay them back. Scholarships and grants can come from all kinds of sources (including directly from your school), and you have lots of free resources to look for them. By the way, don't trust any scholarship search engine or offer that makes you pay up front because it could be scam.

You might already know that you can get scholarships and grants for things like financial need, academic merit, athletics, creative talent, or affiliation with certain groups, but did you know that you can even get them for random things like using Duck® brand tapes to craft the ultimate prom look— no, seriously, that's a real scholarship called the "Stuck at Prom" Scholarship Contest, look it up! The key is to start sometime in your junior year (or even earlier!), look in a lot of places, and apply to anything for which you can meet the qualifications.

Your next best options after scholarships and grants are subsidized federal loans, which don't accrue interest during school, then unsubsidized federal loans, which do. Federal loans are good because they have favorable rates and conditions, plus there are lots of ways to pay them back. Only take out private loans if you really, really must. Usually, the maximum amount you're allowed to take out is based on your school's estimation of your total education expenses, including stuff like room and board (e.g., housing and buying food, that sort of thing).

Make sure you know everything you can about the conditions of any loans you take out so you can plan for how to pay them back in the future—you don't want them to sneak up on you! You can also consider things like getting general education out of the way at a community college or attending public schools in your home state to save on tuition. There are lots of ways to cover the cost of a degree.

THE CURRENT STATE OF FINANCIAL AID

It's in your best interest to prioritize figuring out what sorts of scholarships and grants are available to you since you can more or less think of scholarships and grants as "free money." You won't have to pay them back except under certain circumstances, such as not meeting a condition of a particular grant. If you can't get enough scholarships and grants to cover the costs of your education, you'd then be in a position where you'd have to take out loans—money you'll have to pay back, with interest!

All that said, financial aid can ease the financial burdens of college significantly, making it easier for those who might not otherwise have the opportunity to attend college to do so. Attaining financial aid can seem like an overwhelming challenge, but it is a very doable undertaking if you devise a strategy well before you start the college application process.

Modern Approaches to Funding

College *is* getting more expensive, but there is also growing competition among colleges to attract incoming students. As a result, financial aid is slowly becoming more comprehensive and readily accessible. In fact, some colleges and universities use financial aid not only as a method to help students fund their college education but also as a marketing and recruitment tool. This slow change is incredibly advantageous to you, the student. Why? Well, in the past, colleges offered need-based and merit-based financial aid only to students with demonstrated exceptional financial need

or academic prowess. Now, though, some schools offer what might be called "incentive-based" aid to encourage students to choose them over another college. This aid, which is not necessarily based on need or merit, is aimed at students who meet the standards of the college but who wouldn't necessarily qualify for traditional kinds of aid. Essentially, if a school offers you this kind of aid, they're using the money to sweeten the deal and persuade you to attend their school over another.

Another way that modern students are bucking the trend of taking out huge student loans is by using community college as a cheaper alternative to get core education requirements out of the way. Increasingly, many students are opting to attend community college for a year or two before transferring to a four-year college or university. This allows them to take their general education credits in courses like math and college composition for significantly cheaper than if they completed those same core classes at a more expensive college or university. It can also be a great way for students who had a lower high school GPA but are motivated to do well in college to prove that they are capable of college-level education. Grades a student receives at the community college level will likely be considered a better indicator of their aptitudes than high school grades by that point. State schools and public universities tend to cost less than private schools or out-of-state tuition, so many students are also shopping around to find schools with a more affordable price tag.

Still other students are opting to take gap years or enter the workforce for a while to save up money and avoid taking out loans. Then, once they've established a solid foundation for themselves, some of those students go on to attend college, while others may find that they prefer to stay in the workforce. In short, there are many different solutions to funding one's education and career path with or without financial aid. Recent high school graduates should feel empowered to make sensible financial decisions surrounding their college and career that best suit their long-term goals.

Don't Let Tuition Scare You Away!

During the application process, many students—especially those applying simultaneously for aid and to an expensive private school—start to freak out because of the price of their prospective schools. Don't let this be you! If you qualify for admission, don't let the "sticker price" of the college or program alone scare you away. There is always a chance that you may get enough financial assistance to pay for the education you want, so don't rule out a private institution until you have received its financial aid package. Private colleges, to attract students from all income levels, offer significant amounts of financial aid. In fact, private colleges generally offer more aid than their public-supported counterparts. This is partially because public schools have a lower tuition to begin with, so there is less need to offer additional aid, but it's also partially because private schools sometimes have large pools of money donated by alumni and other stakeholders, meaning they have a greater ability to give money to qualified students.

Some institutions, private or otherwise, may even have programs that make school free for students who fall under a certain income level. For instance, competitive schools including Duke University, Columbia University, Yale University, and Stanford University, among others, have programs that provide free tuition to low-income students who are accepted, so it is worth asking if your school of choice has a program like this.

If you are looking for ways to make a public education more affordable in general, try applying to public schools in your home state. In-state students have a much lower tuition rate and more aid possibilities than out-of-state students.

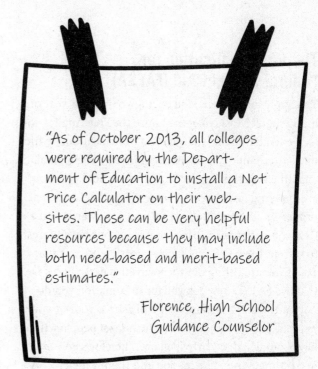

"As of October 2013, all colleges were required by the Department of Education to install a Net Price Calculator on their websites. These can be very helpful resources because they may include both need-based and merit-based estimates."

Florence, High School Guidance Counselor

FINANCIAL AID: THE BASICS

Given the rise in incentive-based aid, you and your family should be assertive in negotiating financial aid packages with the colleges to which you've been accepted. Even though it may seem pushy, it is generally wise to be a comparison shopper—that is, accepted students should wait until they've received all their financial offers from all the institutions to which they applied so they have a comprehensive picture of what kind of assistance is truly available. Then, students and their families can talk to their first-choice college to see if the college can match any better offers they might have received. While not all will be able to revise an offer, some financial aid offices have wiggle room and can adjust the offer to attract interested students.

To be eligible to receive federal/state financial aid, students must maintain satisfactory academic progress toward a degree or certificate. Note that the specific criteria for a given program is always established by each individual college or university, so students should familiarize themselves with their institution's expectations for eligibility. Students also need a valid social security number, and all eligible male students must register for selective service on their eighteenth birthday.

The Free Application for Federal Student Aid (FAFSA)

You apply for financial aid during your senior year of high school. Most colleges require the Free Application for Federal Student Aid (FAFSA), which cannot be filed until after January 1 of your senior year. The federal aid deadline is not until June 30th of the school year you are applying for. However, some aid packages, such as programs at individual institutions, are awarded on a first-come first-serve basis, so it is in your best interest to submit the FAFSA as soon as possible after January 1st. If you are filling out the forms this early, be aware that the FAFSA may ask you for information you do not know yet. For example, it will ask for your or your parents' current tax returns, which most people will not have completed by early January. Therefore, you should just estimate this information and submit the FAFSA as early as you can, rather than waiting for the accurate information. This is an acceptable practice in the FAFSA system for this very reason, as they will allow you to amend it later as needed.

You can apply for the FAFSA in two ways: either through paper application or online at **www.fafsa.ed.gov**. A word of caution: Do not go to any other website about the FAFSA that does not end in **.gov**, as it is likely a scam. You do not need to fill out the FAFSA through any kind of third party.

If you use the paper application, your form will be processed in about four weeks, but if you submit online, it will only take about one week to be processed. Once your application is processed, you'll receive a Student Aid Report (SAR), which will report the information from the FAFSA and show your calculated Expected Family Contribution (EFC)—the number used in determining your eligibility for federal student aid. Each school you listed on the application, as well as your state of legal residence, will also receive your FAFSA information.

The CSS/Financial Aid Profile®

If you are applying to some private colleges, higher-cost colleges, or scholarship programs, you may also have to file the CSS/Financial Aid Profile application, which you should complete sometime between September and January of your senior year. This form is less common,

"Students and their parents need to remember to get their financial application filed early enough so that if they run into problems, they can be corrected. Parents often make mistakes, such as not answering the question about the amount of taxes paid the previous year. Something as simple as that causes a lot of problems. If their financial information is recorded incorrectly, it can really mess them up. They should read all the information on the financial aid form, and if they have questions, they should ask someone. Speaking from my experience, if you can't get in touch with the college your child is thinking of attending, you may want to call a financial aid specialist at your local college. Any time an application doesn't go through the system smoothly, it can cause major problems. Though the applications are much simpler and are worded in layman's terms, I highly suggest applying online so that you minimize your chances of making a costly error filling in the paper form."

Lee, Financial Aid Officer

so your guidance counselor should mention it if it pertains to you; if you're not sure, you can always ask. Bear in mind that submitting the Profile application requires a fee.

Institutional Financial Aid Applications

Once in a while, certain institutions may have a third financial aid application that you can fill out. This is called the Institutional Application, and it is unique to each college that chooses to use one. Check the financial aid tab on the website of every college you are considering to determine the applications that each school requires.

"As a potential college student, you will have many people—parents, coaches, and counselors—helping and focused on your process along with you. Once in college, you will be more or less on your own, which means that deadlines to renew your aid can be easily missed. Some colleges outright deny renewal or halve the grants and scholarships if you are even a day late. It is your obligation, not theirs, to remind yourself of the deadline to renew. Remember that applications you will use to apply for financial aid as a high school senior will need to be submitted every year in college (except your senior year). Do not miss those deadlines while there. I have seen too many students miss those deadlines with huge consequences such as increased loans that they did not anticipate. Also, consider applying for aid even if your income is high, as some colleges award merit aid only if a need-based application is submitted. But you will need to balance this desire with the fact that most colleges today are not need-blind, meaning they will consider whether you need aid in their admission decisions."

Elodia, High School Counselor

Filling out these forms may seem tedious, but it is well worth it for a shot at financial aid. That said, you must reapply for federal aid every year, so make sure you really understand the application process and track it closely as it changes from year to year. Along those same lines, if you decide to transfer to another school, your aid doesn't necessarily go with you. You'll need to check with your new school to find out what steps you must take to continue receiving aid. For this reason, you should plan any transfer at least three months in advance. You certainly wouldn't want to be excited to transfer into your new school, only to find that your aid package is not accepted there. That would put you in a bind, to say the least!

Once you've filled out these forms, talk to the financial aid officers of those schools you intend on applying to. When it comes to understanding your financial aid options, the best place to get information is from the source. That personal contact could lead you to substantial amounts of financial aid. If there is ever a problem with your aid, it's also not a bad idea to go to the financial aid office directly so you can talk to a real human being who can guide you to a solution. On paper, you're one of many students, but if you go into the financial aid office, you may be able to get more direct help solving your individual inquiry.

APPLYING FOR FINANCIAL AID

Now that we've gone over the basics, it might be helpful to see a step-by-step guide of how to apply, as this is a first step most students will need to take before they even start making decisions about how to fund their education.

Steps for Applying for Financial Aid

1 You must complete the Free Application for Federal Student Aid (FAFSA) by June 30th to be considered for federal financial aid. Pick up the FAFSA from your high school guidance counselor or college Financial Aid Office or complete it online at **www.fafsa.ed.gov**. The FAFSA can be filed only after January 1st of the year you will be attending school. Submit the form as soon as possible after that date. Typically, to get the application submitted quickly, you will want to estimate income tax information, as it is easily amended later in the year.

2 Apply for any state grants. Most states use the FAFSA for determining state aid but be sure to check out the specific requirements with your state's Higher Education Assistance agency. Your high school guidance counselor can answer most questions about state aid programs.

3 Some schools (usually higher-cost private colleges) require an additional form known as the CSS/Financial Aid Profile. This application is needed for institutional grants and scholarships controlled by the school. Check to see if the schools you are applying to require the profile form. The form should be completed in September or October of your senior year. Additional information is available from your high school guidance office or online through the College Board at **www.collegeboard.com**. A fee is associated with this form. Some schools may require an institutional aid application. This is usually found with the admission application. Contact each college you are considering to be sure you have filed the required forms.

4 Complete all required financial aid application forms on time. Check to be sure you know the specific deadline. Financial aid funds are limited, and schools usually do not waver on their deadlines. Check and double-check all application dates to be sure you are filing on time.

5 Make sure your family completes the required forms during your senior year of high school. It will be much harder to complete them later and you may miss out on critical aid deadlines.

6 Always apply for grants and scholarships in addition to applying for student loans. Grants and scholarships are essentially free money. Loans must be repaid with interest. Whenever possible, opt for grants and scholarships first.

TYPES OF FINANCIAL AID

When you fill out the FAFSA, you're applying for all federal forms of aid, but your school will also use that information to determine if there are other types of aid you're eligible for. Therefore, you should apply, then make sense of the type of aid you're offered later. For most students, a combination of the sources listed here can make school much more affordable. Each type will be covered in more detail in the sections that follow.

Grants

Grants, like scholarships, are financial aid awards that do not need to be repaid. Grants usually go to students with financial need. But the term is also used for athletics (Division I only), academics, demographics, and special talents. Grants do not have to be repaid.

Like scholarships, grants are essentially free money that one can use to cover education costs. However, unlike scholarships, students don't always have to apply for grants. Instead, your school's financial aid office may automatically help you acquire grants you're eligible for or they may be offered to you directly. Talk to your high school guidance counselor and college financial aid office to make sure you have a full picture of the grants that might be available to you.

Scholarships

Scholarships, also called "merit aid," are awarded for academic success and potential, athletic excellence, or other special talents or abilities. Scholarships may also be awarded based on civic, professional, or union affiliation; religious affiliation; employment or volunteer experience; residence; military service; or nationality or ethnic heritage. Repayment is not required.

Programs

There are various service-oriented programs available to help students finance portions of their education in exchange for hours worked at their college or for nonprofit community-service hours. The Federal Work-Study program and AmeriCorps are the most well-known.

Student Loans

Government student loans have more favorable terms and conditions than private student loans and are sponsored by the federal or state government. You automatically apply for federal loans when you fill out the FAFSA, though state loans will vary based on the state you're from and/or where you'll be attending school. You can also get private student loans from commercial lending institutions. While these may have more favorable terms and conditions than other types of loans, they are typically still less favorable than federal loans. Generally, if you are offered loans from the state or federal government first, opt for those over private loans.

Private student loans are what you will most likely need to take out if you or your family does not meet the need criteria for federal aid or if the federal aid offered is not enough to cover your full expenses. Some families also take private loans to cover other necessary expenses related to education, such as cars and off-campus housing situations. Remember, though, that generally sound financial advice suggests you only take loans that you absolutely need. Good practice would be to make a budget of your expenses for the year, ensure you have enough aid to cover them, then stick to that budget. It's never too early to start good financial planning and doing so will make things so much easier down the road.

Unlike grants or scholarships, loans must be repaid, generally after you graduate or leave school. Be careful when taking loans because while it may seem like free money now, it is not the same as a scholarship or grant—that money will have to be paid back at some point in the future, with interest. While it may seem scary to contemplate paying back so much, remember that you are in school to get a more stable and lucrative career in the long run. If you work hard, study well, plan, and take the necessary steps to secure a good job, you will hopefully not have to worry about it being difficult to pay back the loan. If you do, or if unforeseen life circumstances put you in a financial bind later in life, there are also programs to help you navigate debt.

The important thing when deciding whether to take out loans is to understand the nature and expectations of a loan before you agree to it so that you can manage your money and plan accordingly for your future financial obligations.

TYPES OF FEDERAL AID

The world of federal aid can be a tangled web, but it's easier to navigate if you know exactly what is out there. Though many students end up taking out federal loans as a primary form of aid, there are a lot of different ways the federal government helps subsidize education.

Federal Scholarships, Grants, and Programs

Before taking out any loans offered to you, make sure that you are not eligible for other forms of federal aid first. Most of the time, you will be applied for programs like these when you fill out the FAFSA. Talk to your guidance counselor or a financial aid officer at the school you plan to attend to determine if there are any federal scholarships, grants, or other programs for which you might be eligible before closing the gap with loans.

Teacher Education Assistance for College and Higher Education (TEACH) Grant

In 2007, Congress created the TEACH Grant Program, which is available to students who plan to pursue a career in teaching at a public or private school that serves low-income families. The grant provides up to $4,000 per year to students who meet the criteria. Recipients of the TEACH Grant must work full-time for at least four school years, within an eight-year period, in a high-need field. High-need fields include the following:

- Bilingual education
- English-language acquisition
- Foreign language
- Mathematics
- Reading
- Science
- Special education

Other areas are listed in the Department of Education's Annual Teacher Shortage Area Nationwide Listing. If a recipient fails to meet the conditions outlined, the grant will be converted to a Federal Direct Unsubsidized Stafford Loan, which must be repaid with interest accruing from the date the TEACH Grant was disbursed. Colleges need to participate in this program, so you should contact schools directly for more information about this grant.

Federal Pell Grant

The Federal Pell Grant, intended to be the base point of assistance for lower-income families, is the nation's largest grant program. Eligibility for a Federal Pell Grant depends on your Expected Family Contribution (EFC). The actual amounts awarded with a Pell Grant depend on how much funding is appropriated by Congress each year. For the 2021–2022 school year, the maximum individual grant was $6,495. How much you specifically will receive depends not only on your EFC but also on your school's tuition and other costs, how much grant or scholarship money you may have already received, and whether you're a full-time or part-time student.

Federal Supplemental Educational Opportunity Grant (FSEOG)

As its name implies, the Federal Supplemental Educational Opportunity Grant (FSEOG) provides additional need-based federal grant money to supplement the Federal Pell Grant. Each participating college is given funds to award to especially needy students. The maximum award is $4,000 per year, but the amount a student receives depends on the college's policy, the availability of FSEOG funds, the total cost of education, and the amount of other aid awarded.

Iraq and Afghanistan Service Grant

A student who is not eligible for the Federal Pell Grant may be eligible for the Iraq and Afghanistan Service Grant if their parent or guardian died during service in Iraq or Afghanistan after September 11, 2001. The student must have been under 24 years old or have been enrolled in college when their parent or guardian died. The amount of the grant is equal to the maximum amount a Federal Pell Grant would award.

Federal Work-Study

Federal Work-Study (FWS) is a federally sponsored program that enables colleges to hire students for employment. If eligible, students work a limited number of hours throughout the school year. Many colleges use their own funds to hire students to work in the many departments and offices on campus. If you do not receive an FWS award, you should contact the Student Employment Office or the Financial Aid Office to help locate nonfederal work-study positions that may be available. If you don't qualify, your school may also have copious student employment opportunities outside of the federal work-study program.

AmeriCorps

Through AmeriCorps, many Americans engage in intensive service to meet community needs in education, the environment, public safety, homeland security, and other areas. Members serve with national nonprofit organizations like Habitat for Humanity, the American Red Cross, and Teach for America, as well as with hundreds of smaller community organizations, both secular and faith-based. Other members serve with AmeriCorps NCCC (National Civilian Community Corps), a team-based residential program for adults ages 18 to 24, or in low-income communities with AmeriCorps VISTA (Volunteers in Service to America). In exchange for a year of service, AmeriCorps members earn a Segal AmeriCorps Education Award of $4,725 to pay for college, graduate school, or to pay back qualified student loans. Members who serve part-time receive a partial award. Some AmeriCorps members may also receive a modest living allowance during their term of service. You should speak to your college's Financial Aid Office or visit the AmeriCorps website for more details about this program and any other initiatives available to students.

SCHOLARSHIPS 101

As mentioned, scholarships and grants should be your first stop when funding your education. Here is everything you need to know about tackling a search for scholarships.

Applying for Scholarships

Use the following tips to help make your scholarship hunt successful.

Start Early

Your freshman year is not too early to plan for scholarships. Choose extracurricular activities that will highlight your strengths and get involved in community organizations. Scholarship providers want to see student involvement, and some of the organizations you are involved in could even offer scholarships themselves!

Search for Scholarships

The best sources of scholarships can be found on the internet. Many great, free websites are available, so you should check sites like **www.finaid.org**, **StudentAid.gov**, and **www.petersons.com**.

Apply, Apply, Apply

Nobody is keeping track of how many scholarships you apply for and do not get. Even if you apply for twenty scholarships but only get a few, you will have still won yourself free money to put toward your college education.

Plan Ahead

It takes time and effort to get the transcripts and letters of recommendation that many scholarship organizations want to see. Ask for letters of recommendation early.

Be Organized

Store all your relevant scholarship information in the same place, whether this may be on in a folder on your computer or in a hard copy format. This will allow you to review deadlines and requirements every so often. You may also be able to reuse parts of one application as the base for another, such as with essays. However, remember to tailor each to the institution to which you're applying so it doesn't sound generic.

Follow Directions

Make sure that you don't disqualify yourself by filling out forms incorrectly, missing a deadline, or failing to supply important information. Type your applications and have someone proofread them, if possible.

ROTC Scholarships

The US Armed Forces (Army, Air Force, Navy, Marine Corps, Coast Guard, and Space Force) may offer up to a four-year scholarship that pays full college tuition plus a monthly allowance; however, these scholarships are competitive and are based on GPA, class rank, ACT or SAT scores, and physical qualifications. Apply as soon as possible before December 1st of your senior year. You can find more information on the websites of each branch of the US military.

Scholarships from Federal Agencies

Federal agencies—such as the Central Intelligence Agency (CIA), National Security Administration (NSA), National Aeronautics and Space Administration (NASA), Department of Agriculture, and Office of Naval Research—offer an annual stipend as well as a scholarship. In return, the student must work for the agency for a certain number of years or else repay all the financial support. These scholarships, in addition to being highly competitive, require very specific qualifications and skills, so see your guidance counselor for more information.

Robert C. Byrd Honors Scholarship

To qualify for this state-administered scholarship, you must demonstrate outstanding academic achievement and excellence in high school as indicated by class rank, high school grades, test scores, and leadership activities. Award amounts of $1,500 are renewable for four years. Contact your high school counselor for application information. Deadlines may vary by state, so contact your state's Department of Education.

Myths about Scholarships

Many high school students do not have a clear understanding of the scholarship and financial aid game. On top of that, while most high school guidance counselors do their best to have a full understanding of opportunities available to students, they are still only humans. It would be basically impossible for any one high school guidance counselor to know about every opportunity that's available to students or how financial aid and scholarships differ from school to school. Consequently, myths about scholarships tend to persist among high school students from generation to generation, so let's clear a few up.

What You Need to Know About Athletic Scholarships

For many student-athletes, athletic scholarships are the payoff for devoting countless hours to training, practicing, and competing. Colleges offer scholarships for a whole range of sports, but you must plan ahead if you want to get your tuition paid in return for your competitive abilities.

Four Common Scholarship Myths

Myth 1: Scholarships are rare, elusive awards won only by valedictorians and athletic prodigies.

The truth is that with proper advice and strategies, private scholarships are very much within the grasp of high school students who possess talent and ability in almost any given field. Thousands of high school students win scholarships each year, many of which are specifically designed for students who fill niches or meet specific criteria. If you look hard enough, you can find scholarships for students who knit, students who lost a parent in high school, students who overcame addiction, vegetarian students, and just about anything else you can think of. There are also plenty of oddball scholarships for any number of things ranging from creating a public service announcement to being a member of a particular fandom. The key is to search far and wide and to apply to anything for which you might qualify.

Myth 2: All merit scholarships are based on a student's academic record.

Being an all-around good student will absolutely help you get scholarships, but it's not the only way. Many of the best opportunities are in areas such as writing, public speaking, leadership, science, community service, music and the arts, foreign languages, vocational-technical skills, or other fields that don't directly translate to your GPA. If you don't have a stellar overall GPA but excel in one area, you can probably find scholarships for students who excel in that area.

Myth 3: You must be a member of a disadvantaged group to get a scholarship.

Some scholarships are indeed targeted at disadvantaged groups who are more likely to need assistance with college. This is a good thing because it helps make access to a college education open to a wider variety of people. However, if you are not in a disadvantaged group, there are still plenty of scholarships you might be able to find. For instance, some scholarships require membership in a specific national club or student organization (such as 4-H or the National Honor Society), while others simply require you to write the best essay or send the best sample project. Many scholarship opportunities are not exclusive to any one segment of the population.

Myth 4: If you have need for and receive financial aid, it's useless to win a scholarship from some outside organization because the college will just take away the aid that the organization offered.

It's true that if you receive aid, you can't receive more than the total cost of attendance (including room and board, books, and other expenses, not just tuition). If your financial aid award meets your total costs and you win an outside scholarship, colleges must reduce a different type of aid. Usually, they will reduce loans and work-study allotments before ever reducing free forms of money like grants and scholarships. This means that you won't have to borrow or earn as much at a job, which is ultimately a good thing—why take a loan and pay it back with interest later when you could have a scholarship or grant now? Plus, if you get a scholarship and the college reduces your aid, you're freeing up aid money for someone else who might need it, too, which is a net positive for the wider college community.

"Many students have the impulse to ask their English teacher for help proofreading college and scholarship essays and it's a good one! But remember that your 11th or 12th grade teacher has many students in the same boat and may or may not have the time to help each one, so use all the resources you have available, like other teachers, peers, librarians, parents, older siblings, etc. The more eyes you get on your scholarship application materials, the more feedback you'll have to work with."

Rob, High School
English Teacher

At the beginning of and throughout high school, ask your guidance counselor to help you ensure that you take the required mix and number of academic courses. Ask them the minimums for GPA, SAT score, and ACT score that must be met to play college sports at the Division I (DI) and Division II (DII) levels, then commit those numbers to memory. Also, ask your counselor about academic requirements because you must be certified by the NCAA Eligibility Center. This process must be started with your transcript by the end of your junior year. No such requirement exists to compete at the Division III (DIII) or club level.

Before you do all that, though, think. Do you want and need an athletic scholarship? Is this a commitment you are ready and willing to make? Certainly, it is a prestigious honor to receive an athletic scholarship, but some athletes compare having an athletic scholarship to having a full-time job. In fact, with DI and DII scholarships, you are effectively an employee of the school and therefore an athlete/student, rather than a student/athlete. Meetings, training sessions, practices, and games take away from studying and social time. Also, with very few full-ride scholarships available, you'll most likely receive a partial scholarship or a one-year renewable contract. If

Locate the colleges and universities that offer scholarships in your sport.

To successfully sell your skills to a college or university, you'll need to take three main steps:

Follow up on each lead.

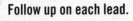

Contact the institution in a formal manner.

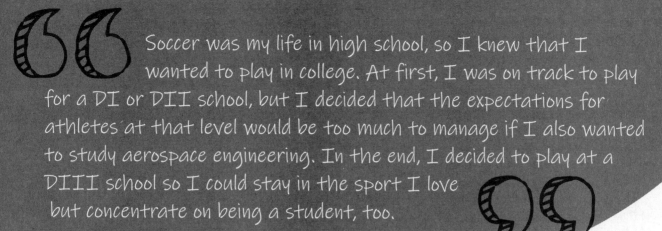

> Soccer was my life in high school, so I knew that I wanted to play in college. At first, I was on track to play for a DI or DII school, but I decided that the expectations for athletes at that level would be too much to manage if I also wanted to study aerospace engineering. In the end, I decided to play at a DIII school so I could stay in the sport I love but concentrate on being a student, too.
>
> Marisol, College Freshman

your scholarship is not renewed, you may be left scrambling for financial aid. So, ask yourself if you are ready for the demands and roles associated with accepting an athletic scholarship before pursuing this goal. It can be a great way to pay for school, but it absolutely comes with some strings attached.

If you decide that you want an athletic scholarship, you need to realize that there are thousands of other determined athletes trying to compete for that very same scholarship spot. Therefore, you'll have to really market yourself, or "sell" your abilities to college recruiters. As an athlete, you're the product, and the college recruiter is the buyer. What makes you stand out from the rest?

College recruiters look for a combination of the following attributes when awarding athletic scholarships: academic excellence, a desire to win, self-motivation, ability to perform as a team player, willingness to help others, cooperation with coaching staff, attitude in practice, attitude in games/matches, toughness, strength, growth mindset, and excellence.

The following four steps can help you in your quest to obtain an athletic scholarship:

1 CONTACT THE SCHOOL FORMALLY. Once you make a list of the schools in which you are interested, get the names of the head coaches and write letters to the top schools on your list. Then, compile a factual resume of your athletic and academic accomplishments. Put together 10 to 15 minutes of video highlights of your athletic performance, get letters of recommendation from your high school coach and your off-season or club coach, and include a season schedule.

2 ACE THE INTERVIEW. Just like when you are interviewing with an admissions officer, when you meet a recruiter or coach, be certain to offer a firm handshake and maintain eye contact. According to recruiters, the most effective attitude is one of quiet confidence, respect, sincerity, and enthusiasm.

3 ASK GOOD QUESTIONS. Don't be afraid to probe the recruiter by getting answers to the following questions: Do I qualify athletically and academically? If I am recruited, what would the parameters of the scholarship be? For what position am I being considered? It's okay to ask the recruiter to declare what level of interest they have in you.

4 FOLLOW UP. Persistence pays off when it comes to seeking an athletic scholarship, and timing can be everything. Even if you have not been offered a scholarship yet, so long as you don't go over the top, you should keep trying to persuade recruiters through follow-up letters and emails. There are four especially good times when a follow-up from your coach or a personal letter or email from you is extremely effective: prior to your senior season, during or just after the senior season, just prior to or after announced conference-affiliated signing dates or national association signing dates, and mid to late summer, in case other scholarship offers have been withdrawn or declined.

Winning a Scholarship with a Captivating Essay

You've already completed the standard rigors of high school: the SAT and ACT, doing community service, excelling in your classes, and writing your personal statement. Your one last hurdle could be a scholarship essay, where you try to convince the college or a source of aid that you are worthy of a scholarship.

The scholarship essay is an intensely competitive endeavor, regardless of how much you have excelled athletically or academically. No doubt that your GPA, standardized test scores, volunteer efforts, leadership roles, and community service are immensely important, but, again, you must remember that during the process of selecting an award recipient, pretty much all the applicants are going to be stellar on some level. So, as the scholarship awarding committee members look for a reason to select *you* over everyone else, they will use your essay to see what really sets you apart from the crowd.

Think of your scholarship essay as a supplemental personal statement. Use it as an opportunity to showcase your best self. Your scholarship essay serves many purposes, the primary of which is to show the scholarship awarding committee that you are able to do the following:

- Effectively communicate through the written word
- Substantiate your merit and unique qualities
- Follow directions and adhere to guidelines

A winning scholarship essay can mean up to tens of thousands of dollars for your college education, so we've provided you with the following tips to help you maximize the impact of any scholarship essay you might write.

Use Effective Written Communication

In an essay, every idea you want to share must come through the written word. It can be hard to breathe life into your writing, but there are a few proven ways to make your writing more effective, no matter the topic.

Be Passionate

An important common feature of all winning essays is that they are written on subjects about which the author is truly passionate. When you are genuinely enthusiastic about something—rather than feigning enthusiasm for the subject—the words and thoughts flow easily and your energy naturally shines through in your writing. Therefore, when choosing your scholarship essay topic, be sure it is something you truly care about and can show your affinity for—keeping both you and your reader interested.

Be Positive

Try to steer clear of essays that are too critical, pessimistic, or antagonistic. This doesn't mean that your essay can't acknowledge a serious problem, nor does it mean that everything has to have a happy ending. You can still talk about difficult topics, but it's important to show how those topics contributed to positive growth, even if only as a silver lining to a tragedy.

To put it simply, you should avoid focusing primarily on the negative. If you are writing about a problem, then offer solutions. If your story doesn't have a happy ending, then write about what you learned from the experience or how you would do

> Never underestimate the power of using strong verbs and adjectives. Don't just say something was good, say it was phenomenal, awe-inspiring, or impactful. Don't just say you tried, say you overcame, labored, or applied yourself. Be bold and specific with your word choices!
>
> Zhan, Writing Tutor

things differently if you had the hindsight you have now. Your optimism and hope for the future can help make the scholarship-awarding committee excited about giving you money to pursue your dreams. Use positive language and be proud to share information about yourself and your accomplishments.

Edit and Proofread Thoroughly

After you have a draft, do a first round of edits by yourself. Figure out whether your essay is concise enough and focused on a specific incident rather than a general message. After revising for content, move on to tweaking your grammar and structure for the best stylistic essay you can craft. Feel free to ask teachers or other trusted adults for some editing help, but make sure that the piece retains your own original voice.

Highlight Your Unique Qualities

Another important part of writing an effective essay involves conveying some aspect of who you are. What makes you you? How are you different than anyone else who might be submitting an essay? What have you experienced that others might not have, and how have those experiences shaped you? The less generic your essay, the more likely it is to be memorable. The following are some ways you can make sure to stand out.

Show a Slice of Your Life

While one goal of your essay is surely to explain why you should win the scholarship money, an equally important goal is to reveal something about you, some distinctive quality that makes it easy to see why you should win. Most likely, the rest of the scholarship application will include quite a bit of information about you. The essay is where you need to home in on just one aspect of your unique talents or experiences. It's not about listing out every single accomplishment (again, you probably did that on the application). Instead, it's about sharing a slice of your life—telling your story and

offering details about what makes you memorable.

Highlight Your Accomplishments

Your extracurricular activities illustrate your personal priorities and let the scholarship selection committee know what's important to you. Being able to elaborate on your accomplishments and awards within those activities certainly bolsters your chances of winning the scholarship. Again, though, be careful to not just repeat a list of what is already on the application itself. Instead, use your essay to focus on one or two specific accomplishments (or activities, talents, or awards) of which you are most proud and to offer a few details about them, such as the planning or work you put in to reaching your goal, the path you took to get to where you are, what the accomplishment meant for you personally, or what you learned from the experience.

Tell the Truth

It can be tempting to exaggerate or sensationalize, especially if you feel like you've had a pretty easy and uneventful life that doesn't offer you much to write about. Challenge yourself to dig deep and find a truth about yourself to focus on rather than lying or stretching the truth. A simple, truthful essay about overcoming an everyday challenge is more powerful than an exaggerated essay about an extreme hardship. On top of that, a lie is pretty easy to spot in most cases and being outright untruthful is unlikely to land you a scholarship. If you don't feel like you have a "big" topic to address, it's okay to focus on "little" things, like the time you overcame some test anxiety or stood up to a bully. What matters is that you're truthful and honest in sharing your, genuine thoughts and feelings.

Don't Go Overboard!

A tear-jerking story is rarely enough on its own to win. For one, it is likely to be one of many stories with tragic components that the scholarship selection committee will see. Another reason is that a tear-jerking story doesn't do much if it can't show how you, the author of the essay, have progressed as a person because of your experiences. Even if you can understandably say that what happened to you wasn't your fault, those who read the essay are still wanting to see how you took the opportunity to rise to the occasion and address the hardship. While it's just fine to write about why you truly need the scholarship money to continue your education, you'll want to avoid simply writing a laundry list of family tragedies and hardships without much context for how they shaped you into who you are today.

Instead of simply presenting a sob story, highlight how you have succeeded and what you have accomplished *despite* the hardships and challenges you faced. Show how the things you went through taught you courage, tenacity, resourcefulness, empathy, or any other quality. Keep in mind that everyone has faced difficulties, so what's different and individual to you is how you faced your difficulties and overcame them. That is what will make your essay significant and memorable.

Follow Directions

It may seem obvious, but if you can't follow the basic directions of an essay prompt, you aren't likely to stand out. Following the directions shows attention to detail and a willingness to be thorough, qualities which reflect well on scholarship applicants. Show how serious you are about the scholarship to which you are applying by taking the directions and prompts seriously.

Answer Both the Prompt and the Underlying Question

The goal of every scholarship selection committee is to determine the best applicant out of a pool of applicants who are all likely to be rather similar. If you pay attention, then you'll likely find that the essay question is an alternate way for you to answer the less obvious underlying question the scholarship-awarding committee wants to ask. For instance, an organization giving an award to students who plan to study business might ask, "Why do you want to study business?" But their real underlying question could be something more like, "Why are you the best future businessperson to whom we should give our money?" They may ask something like "Who is your role model?" But what they're secretly really looking for is "Who is creative enough to give us an answer we aren't expecting instead of just another essay on Elon Musk?" Remember, the person reading these essays has to read a bunch of them in a row. They are likely to see a lot of things repeat. You could very well be at the bottom of the stack when they're starting

to get bored. If you ask yourself what underlying questions the scholarship selection committee may be asking themselves, that might help you shape a dynamic essay accordingly.

Tailor Your Approach to Fit the Question

Be sure to not only connect your personal skills, characteristics, and experiences with the objectives of the scholarship and its awarding organization but also to address the specific question you are given. If it asks about your role model and you talk about an experience that shaped you, all you're really going to communicate is that you didn't take the application seriously enough to read it closely.

Similarly, don't try to reuse essays you used for other scholarships if they're not the same or a very similar question, and even then, you should make some modifications to suit the particular scholarship to which you are applying. If you have many scholarships to apply to and many ask a similar question, it is smart to use the same essay as a base for each. However, you'll want to edit thoroughly and modify each essay to highlight the qualities that each specific scholarship selection committee would be interested in. A generic essay that the selection committee can tell was sent many places is unlikely to get you a scholarship. One way to tailor your essay is to make sure the theme of your essay meshes with the overarching purpose or goal of the organization awarding the money. Once you have clarified the organization's central message or purpose, you can more easily see if and how your words tie into the organization's likely vision of who should win their scholarship.

Follow Formatting Guidelines

Like following directions for *what* to write, you want to make sure that you follow any directions about *how* to present the information you write. For instance, you may need to write the essay in a particular font and font size or with certain formatting expectations, such as single spacing or double spacing. There may also be a length requirement for the essay, such as a page or word count. A good rule of thumb is to never go over the maximum length but to not fall too short of it, either—use all the space you are provided and
no more.

Be Timely

If there is a deadline for your scholarship essay, make sure you send it on time or early! Even if you could get the scholarship selection committee to accept a late application, how would doing so reflect on your work ethic and attention to detail? Show how responsible and on top of things you are by getting your essay in early, if possible, and on time if not.

Scholarship Scams

Although most scholarship sponsors and scholarship search services are legitimate, schemes that pose as either have cheated thousands of families. These scams usually ask you to either pay for a scholarship search by an independent organization or pay a "processing fee" to a particular organization to receive its scholarship. If you must pay to locate scholarships, it's best not to trust the source!

The most obvious frauds operate as fee-based scholarship search services or scholarship clearinghouses. These fraudulent businesses may have a legitimate looking website but will usually ask you to pay for a scholarship search by an independent organization. There are plenty of free scholarship search resources, such as Peterson's scholarship search **https://www. petersons.com/scholarship-search.aspx**. Furthermore, if they "guarantee" that you will get a scholarship, be wary. A search engine cannot truthfully guarantee that a student will receive a scholarship, and students almost always will fare as well or better by doing their own homework using a reliable scholarship information source than by wasting money and time with a search service that promises a scholarship.

Another quieter breed of scholarship scam involves someone acting as a scholarship sponsor, charging a fee for students to apply to the scholarship, then pocketing the money from the fees and charges without delivering

Warning Signs of a Scholarship Scam

The Federal Trade Commission (FTC), in Washington, D.C., has a campaign called Project $cholar$cam to confront this type of fraudulent activity. Through this project, the FTC warns that scholarship hopefuls should be alert for these six warning signs:

"This scholarship is guaranteed or your money back."

No service can guarantee that it will get you a grant or scholarship. Refund guarantees often have impossible conditions attached. Review a service's refund policies in writing before you pay a fee.

"The scholarship service will do all the work."

Unfortunately, nobody else can fill out the personal information forms, write the essays, and supply the references that many scholarships may require. If a scholarship site doing all the work for you sounds too good to be true, that's because it is.

"The scholarship will cost some money."

Be wary of any charges related to scholarship information services or individual scholarship applications, especially in significant amounts. Before you send money to apply for a scholarship, investigate the sponsor. A popular scam, for example, is **FAFSA.com**. Avoid this domain and use the free **FAFSA.ed.gov** website instead.

"You can't get this information anywhere else."

Scholarship directories from Peterson's and other publishers are available in bookstores, your local public library, and high school guidance offices; they're also available as ebooks. The information is widely available for those who look, so there is no one worth paying for "exclusive" information.

"You are a finalist" OR "You have been selected by a national foundation to receive a scholarship."

Most legitimate scholarship programs almost never seek out particular applicants. Most scholarship sponsors will contact you only in response to an inquiry because they generally lack the budget to do anything more than this. If you think there's a real possibility that you have been selected to receive a scholarship, investigate closely and ensure the program or sponsor is legitimate before sharing any financial information.

"The scholarship service needs your credit card or checking account number in advance."

Never provide your credit card or bank account number on the phone to the representative of an organization that you do not know. Get information in writing first.

on any scholarship. A few of these frauds can inflict even greater harm by gaining access to individuals' credit or checking accounts with the intent to extort funds. Remember, someone who wants to give you a scholarship shouldn't need to be paid to do so. If they are asking for your personal banking information as a condition of applying to the scholarship and you can't get any legally viable information in writing, run away!

In addition to the FTC's six signs we presented, here are some other points to keep in mind when considering a scholarship program:

- Fraudulent scholarship operations often use official-sounding names, containing words such as *federal*, *national*, *administration*, *division*, *federation*, and *foundation*. Their names are often a slight variant of the name of a legitimate government or private organization. Do not be fooled just because an organization has a name that seems reputable or official, an official-looking seal, or uses a Washington, D.C., address. If you are ever unsure, your guidance counselor can help you evaluate if a website or service is legitimate.

- Be wary if an organization's only address is a box number or a residential address. If a bona fide scholarship program uses a post office box number, it usually will include a street address and telephone number on its stationery.

- Beware of telephone numbers with a 900-area code. These may charge you a fee of several dollars a minute for a call that could be a long recording that provides only a list of addresses or names.

- Watch for scholarships that ask you to "act now." A dishonest operation may put pressure on an applicant by saying that awards are on a "first-come, first-served" basis. Yes, it is true that some scholarship programs will give preference to earlier qualified applications (which is why we suggest applying early). However, if you are told that you must respond quickly but that you also won't hear about the results for several months, there may be a problem.

- Be wary of endorsements. Fraudulent operations will claim endorsements by groups with names similar to well-known private or government organizations.

- Don't pay money for a scholarship to an organization that you've never heard of before or whose legitimacy you can't verify. If you have already paid money to such an organization and find reason to doubt its authenticity, report (perhaps to your credit card company) that you think you were the victim of consumer fraud.

> " I had a Federal Work-Study job all through college. My first year, everyone on work study had to work in the cafeteria. After that, we could do whatever on campus, and I wanted to learn to sew, so I spent the next three years working in the theater and dance department sewing costumes. Funnily enough, that ended up helping me get a job in a wedding gown shop after graduation. "
>
> Phoebe, Recent College Graduate

Trust your gut and your common sense. If a situation seems fishy, you can't verify information online, and you are being asked to give private financial information, it is likely not an opportunity you want to pursue. If you need to report a scam or need more information, contact the FTC Consumer Response Center through the FTC's website.

MAKING SENSE OF STUDENT LOANS

This section explains the different types of federal loans available. Our advice is to pursue federal loans first before considering private loans, as they typically have better terms. If you are considering private loans, make sure you understand the terms of the loan before you commit. Private loans have a different set of rules

Subsidized vs. Unsubsidized Federal Loans

SUBSIDIZED

- No payments are due during the first six months after you leave school—this is called a "grace period."

- The maximum amount you can take out will be determined by the school you attend. They will calculate your projected expenses and compare that amount with your expected family contribution (EFC) and any other aid you receive, such as scholarships and grants.

- The Education department pays your interest while you're in school at least half-time, during your grace period, and during any deferments.

- As of the loaning period between July 1, 2021, and July 1, 2022, the interest rate was 3.73% for all subsidized loans.

- Only undergraduate students may take out subsidized loans.

UNSUBSIDIZED

- No payments are due during the first six months after you leave school—this is called a "grace period."

- The maximum amount you can take out will be determined by the school you attend. They will calculate your projected expenses and compare that amount with your expected family contribution (EFC) and any other aid you receive, such as scholarships and grants.

- Interest starts accruing (meaning "adding up") on your loan as soon as you take it out, even if you are in school. It will also accrue during any deferments. You can choose to pay the interest during these periods, but if you do not, it will be capitalized; in other words, it will be added to your loan's principal amount.

- As of the loaning period between July 1, 2021, and July 1, 2022, the interest rate was 3.73% for undergraduate students and 5.28% for graduate students on all unsubsidized loans.

- Both undergraduate and graduate students may take out unsubsidized loans.

Source: "Subsidized and Unsubsidized Loans," Federal Student Aid, US Department of Education, accessed March 29, 2022, studentaid.gov.

to follow than federal and state-sponsored loans, which are highly regulated. Not all federal loans are the same; in fact, the federal government sponsors numerous types of loans for both parents and individual students. Here is an outline of some of the different types.

Direct Subsidized Loans

Compared with direct unsubsidized loans, which we'll discuss next, direct subsidized loans have the most favorable terms of any type of federal loan. They are available to undergraduate students who can demonstrate financial need. Individual institutions use your FAFSA to determine exactly how much aid you need, and guidelines stipulate that the amount of your direct subsidized loans cannot exceed this number.

What makes a subsidized loan different from an unsubsidized loan is that the interest on the loan will be paid by the US Department of Education so long as you are enrolled in school at least half-time. They will also continue to pay that interest on your behalf for your grace period (a length of six months after you leave school) and any time you are in deferment, which refers to an agreed upon payment postponement period for which one must meet certain conditions, such as demonstrating financial need. We've outlined the difference for you on the preceding page.

Direct Unsubsidized Loans

As the provided graphic lays out, the main difference between unsubsidized loans concerns how interest accrues and the maximum amounts one can take. Generally, students take unsubsidized federal loans only if they cannot take subsidized (such as during graduate school) or if the amount they need exceeds the amount of subsidized funding they are offered. Unsubsidized loans continue to build

up interest while you are in school, during the six-month grace period following the end of school, and during any deferments. If it's possible to pay that interest during those periods, financial planners would recommend that you do so, as this is a way to keep the principal balance on the loan from going up before you start paying it back. However, if you're unable to pay the interest, it will simply be capitalized (added to the balance) after the fact.

Direct PLUS Loans for Parents and Graduate/Professional Students

Direct PLUS Loans are for parents of dependent students and for graduate/professional students. They are designed to help families with cash-flow problems who might need an extra boost to cover education expenses. No needs test is required to qualify, and the loans are available under the Federal Direct Loan Program. For the 2021–2022 school year, direct PLUS Loans had a fixed interest rate of 6.28%. Parents or graduate/professional students can borrow up to the cost of the education less other financial aid received. The repayment period begins once the loan is fully disbursed, and the first payment due date will be within sixty days of the repayment period begin date. Up to a 4 percent fee may be charged for these loans and deducted from the loan proceeds. A credit check will be performed, and the borrower must have no adverse credit to qualify for a Direct PLUS Loan.

Direct Consolidation Loans

If after your schooling you have multiple federal loans with different interest rates, you may decide to consolidate, or combine, those loans using an average interest rate calculated from their existing rates. Some opt for this because it allows them to have a single monthly payment rather than multiple loans they must address each month.

Other Student Loan Programs

Certain fields, like nursing or education, may have unique federal loan programs. Your institution should have resources to connect you to these types of programs, but you can always inquire about them as well.

Considering Private Loans

Almost every banking institution has some kind of private loan for students. Furthermore, the financial aid office at your college can help you make sense of which private loan options may be available to you. The terms and expectations of private loans depend entirely on the lending institution, so there is no blanket advice that one can give on what to expect. That said, always make sure you know the exact terms and conditions you're agreeing to when taking out a private loan. It is smart to shop around to find the loan with the most favorable terms for your needs. Remember also that most sound financial advice suggests taking out private loans for school only as a last resort.

Know Your Status: Independent vs. Dependent Students

One factor that has a big effect on how much money a student can take out is their status as an independent or dependent student. An independent student is someone who meets one or more of the following criteria:

- Over the age of 24
- Married
- A graduate student or a student in a professional program
- A veteran or current member of the military
- An orphan, emancipated minor, ward of the court, or anyone else who is legally unconnected to their parents
- Those with nonspouse legal dependents, such as children
- Those who are currently unhoused or who are at risk of losing housing

Dependent students, by contrast, are anyone who does not meet the criteria of being an independent student. Knowing your status is important. As of the publication date of this book, both independent and dependent students are not allowed to take out more than $3,500 a year in subsidized loans. However, the max amount in total loans a dependent student may take in the first year is $5,500, whereas for an independent student, the limit is $9,500. This means that an independent student is allowed to take out $4,000 more in unsubsidized loans in their first year than a dependent student.

The amounts you may take out shift based on your year of schooling and annual EFC, so make sure to speak with a financial aid counselor at your institution about how your status as a dependent or independent student may affect your total aid. Moreover, if you are a dependent student who can prove that you are not receiving any assistance from your parent(s) or guardian(s), as is often the case when people come from families who won't or can't support their education, a financial aid officer may be able to work with you on finding a way to get you listed as an independent student. There's no guarantee, but this is the kind of issue where it's worth talking to someone at your institution's financial aid office to see if there are ways they can help you.

> I had to pay for college entirely on my own. My financial aid officer helped me sign a form proving that I was legally disconnected from my parents and receiving no assistance so I could be considered an independent student. That way, I was able to get more financial aid.
>
> Colby, College Junior

Repayment Options for Federal Loan Borrowers

Here are some repayment options available to borrowers of federally guaranteed student loans.

THE INCOME-BASED REPAYMENT PLAN has a monthly payment capped at an amount that is intended to be affordable based on income and family size. The monthly payment may be adjusted once each year, and the repayment period may exceed ten years. To be eligible for this plan, payment under the standard ten-year repayment plan must exceed the monthly income-based repayment amount. Under income-based repayment, you may be eligible to have the outstanding balance of your loans canceled after a certain amount of time. In addition, public service workers making payments under an income-based repayment plan for ten years may have their balances canceled.

THE INCOME CONTINGENT REPAYMENT PLAN in the Federal Direct Loan Program bases monthly payments on adjusted gross income (AGI), family size, and the total amount borrowed. As your income rises or falls each year, monthly payments will be adjusted accordingly. The required monthly payment will not exceed 20 percent of the borrower's discretionary income as calculated under a published formula. Borrowers have up to twenty-five years to repay; after that time, any unpaid amount will be discharged, and borrowers must pay taxes on the amount discharged. In other words, if the federal government forgives the balance of a loan, the amount is considered to be part of the borrower's income for that year.

THE EXTENDED REPAYMENT PLAN allows loan repayment to be extended up to twenty-five years. The borrower must have more than $30,000 outstanding in Federal Direct Loan debt. Borrowers may opt to pay a fixed amount each month or make graduated payments that start out low and increase every two years. Because the monthly payments are typically less than they are with the standard repayment plan, this plan may make repayment more manageable; however, borrowers usually will pay more interest because the repayment period is longer.

THE STANDARD REPAYMENT PLAN requires fixed monthly payments (at least $50) over a period of up to ten years. The length of the repayment period depends on the loan amount. This plan usually results in the lowest total interest paid because the repayment period is shorter than under the other plans.

THE GRADUATED REPAYMENT PLAN allows payments to start out low and increase every two years for up to ten years. This option works well for those who expect their income to steadily increase over time. Although your monthly payment will gradually increase, no single payment may be more than three times the amount of any other payment. The repayment period is ten years.

Thinking Ahead:
Paying Back Your Student Loan

More than ever, loans have become an important part of financial assistance. While they used to be less common, it can be difficult to complete one's education without taking out at least some form of a loan. People are also speaking out more than they used to about how hard it can be to pay back student loans if you find yourself at a disadvantage later in life, and there is even a fair amount of debate in the contemporary world about whether it's fair to expect young people to take on such a huge financial burden right after graduating high school in the first place. The cultural climate around student loans can be confusing and anxiety-inducing as a result, so if you're facing the need to take out loans, you may feel worried. However, half the battle with student loans is knowing what to expect so you can plan ahead for what's to come.

Even with increasing debate around loans, most students find that they must borrow money to finance the rising costs of education. It is important to understand that when you accept a loan, you are incurring a financial obligation that will stay with you until you repay the loan in full, along with all the interest and any additional fees (collection, legal, etc.). Therefore, it's that much more important to budget in a way that allows you to take out the minimum amount you truly need in loans, thereby minimizing the amount you'll need to pay back later.

Upon graduating from college, dropping below half-time enrollment status, or leaving school, government-offered loan borrowers receive a six-month grace period before they must start repaying their loans. Normal loan repayment terms are ten to twenty-five years and depend on the loan repayment plan you choose. Private loans, such as from a bank or credit union, do not offer grace periods, and monthly payments are sometimes due as soon as funds are dispersed.

FAMILIES' GUIDE TO TAX CUTS FOR EDUCATION

Many tax benefits are now available for adults who want to return to school and for parents who are sending or planning to send their children to college. These tax cuts help give many more working Americans the financial means to go back to school if they want to choose a new career or upgrade their skills. Millions of families are eligible for the American Opportunity Tax Credit (formerly Hope Scholarship Tax Credit) and the Lifetime Learning Credit (LLC), as well as the taxable income deduction allowed for tuition and fees.

American Opportunity Tax Credit

The American Opportunity Tax Credit helps to reduce the cost of higher education by reducing the amount of income tax you must pay. The maximum credit at the time of this book's printing was $2,500 for qualified education expenses paid for each eligible student. Qualified expenses include tuition

and fees required for enrollment. For 2021, the credit was limited to families with a modified adjusted gross income (MAGI) of $80,000 or less for a single head of household or qualifying widower or $160,000 or less if married and filing jointly. Forty percent of the American Opportunity Tax Credit may be refundable, which means that if the refundable portion of the credit is more than your tax, you'll receive the excess as a refund.

The American Opportunity Tax Credit is available only for the first four years of postsecondary education and only for four tax years per eligible student, including any prior years in which the Hope Credit was claimed. To be eligible, a student must be working toward an undergraduate degree or some other recognized education credential and must be enrolled at least half-time for at least one academic period that begins during the tax year.

Student Loan Interest Deduction

Even if taxpayers do not itemize their deductions, borrowers can deduct up to $2,500 of interest paid on student loans each year. Unlike a credit, which reduces the amount of income tax you may have to pay, a deduction reduces the amount of income subject to tax.

YOU *CAN* FUND YOUR EDUCATION

When you get down to it, there are dozens of ways to pay for college. Work with your parent(s) or guardian(s) and anyone else who may be contributing to funding your education to find a solution that saves as much money as possible (get those scholarships and grants!) while being workable for all parties involved. If you are a low-income student, be persistent in periodically talking to the financial aid office at your college to find out what sort of opportunities exist for students in your financial situation. You might be surprised how much help is out there if only you have the tenacity to locate it.

PART

4

Success in College and in Your Career

CHAPTER 10

Academic Expectations in College

Now that you've completed the arduous college application process, it's time for the fun part. College is the payoff for the hard work you've put in throughout your high school years. Just like when you entered high school, you'll probably find that with a little self-confidence and effort, the unique social environment of a college campus makes it easy to carve out a space for yourself and find friends and mentors who can help you thrive. That said, the new, larger, more open environment of college can be a bit daunting for anyone. This chapter covers a few of the bigger questions you might have, such as how to choose your classes or major and what resources are available to you during your studies.

The Short and Sweet Version

You got through the chaos of applying and have been accepted to a great college. Congratulations! Once you start your first semester, you'll have to familiarize yourself with college-level academic expectations. As your teachers have probably told you over and over again, college is a totally different experience than high school. But how exactly?

For starters, you'll mostly get to choose the classes you take according to what interests you. While there are certain general education requirements you'll have to meet to graduate, you get to pick your major—meaning the degree you'll have by the end of your undergraduate education. This is on top of numerous electives that you can take just because they interest you. There are a ton of options, so take note of which topics you're excited to learn more about as you try new classes. If you're not sure about a major, use freshman year to explore different potential subjects you might like.

As you start taking classes, you'll notice that you don't spend nearly as much time in the classroom as you do studying and working outside the classroom. For many, this self-motivated learning will be the biggest change from high school. Instead of hours of direct instruction a day, you'll have lots of reading, writing, research, and problem-solving to do outside of class. This can be an adjustment for students who got used to the rigid structure that high school had to offer.

To help you adapt to more rigorous academic expectations, most colleges offer plenty of resources, like writing centers, tutoring centers, and other student support services. There are also offices designed to promote diversity, equity, and inclusion for students of color, LGBTQIA+ students, students with disabilities, and more. See what your college offers, and don't be shy about stopping by or getting involved. You might even make new friends or learn about important resources available to you.

CHOOSING CLASSES

One of the first academic challenges you will face is choosing your courses. In fact, you will probably be asked to choose courses for your first semester sometime before school even starts, though colleges generally allow you an "Add/Drop" period after classes start to move your schedule around. In high school, you probably had some degree of freedom over the courses you took, but the options were likely far more limited than they'll be at your college. In college, you will be able to take classes that you find enjoyable and will therefore have a lot of freedom when it comes to course selection. You'll also have some degree of say over when you take your classes and with which professors. For instance, if you've heard that one professor is better at a particular class than another or if you're hoping to get into an afternoon section instead of a morning section, you'll sometimes be able to choose which section of a course best suits you.

Even though you have more choices, you'll still need to figure out your college's degree requirements and take the courses required to graduate. Most students are assigned an advisor for their first year. Depending on how your specific college is structured and staff availability, this advisor could be your advisor for every one of your college years or for just your freshman year, or you may switch advisors or add a second advisor after declaring a major. Whoever your advisor is, they can guide you through the maze of requirements and help you select classes that both pique your interests and meet graduation requirements. During your first year or two at college, you and your advisor will primarily choose classes that meet general education requirements. In addition, you will select electives, meaning classes that fulfill your total credit hours required towards graduation but not necessarily your major or general education requirements, that sound interesting.

Early in your college career, it is a good idea to take a lot of general education classes. These classes, also known as "intro" or survey courses, are meant to expose you to new ideas and disciplines. Even if you've never taken an art history course before, you could take Art History 101 as a freshman. Perhaps you wished your high

> "My college has a lot of gen ed requirements that feel more like electives. For instance, I had to take a class about non-Western cultures but there were a lot of options to choose from, so I ended up taking one on Ancient Chinese Poetry and I just enjoyed it. I'm a geology major, so I wouldn't really have had reason to take it otherwise, but I enjoyed finishing up a lab write-up and then jumping into reading for my poetry class. It felt like a nice change of pace for my brain and now I have a new passion for poetry."
>
> Jesús, College Senior

school had a psychology class, but you've never studied that discipline. If so, then Intro to Psychology may be the course for you. Don't be afraid to schedule a fun class, as even the most intense program of study will let you take a few electives. You also may find that taking courses in a variety of fields opens you up to new ways of thinking, making it possible to think more creatively about all your subjects.

An added benefit of these general education classes is that they can help point you in the direction of a major—the area of study that you will primarily focus on throughout your college experience. Also, if your school offers minors, you may find that after a few electives in a subject that interests you, you're halfway to a minor and may as well complete it. Once you have selected a major, you'll probably be assigned another advisor for that degree program. This person will help you understand and meet the requirements for that major. You can find some information on your major, which is a crucial component of your college education, later in this chapter.

The first two weeks of each college term are generally known as the "shopping period." This means that you can sign up and sample an array of classes to get a taste of what they are about. After the first two weeks, you can add or drop classes based on whether you enjoyed them throughout the shopping period. During this period, you may also find yourself on wait-lists for classes you want to get into that may already be full. If, during this period, students who are in that class drop, then whoever is next on the wait-list will be notified. Therefore, even if you think your schedule is pretty set, you'll want to shop around in case you find a class you like better, a wait-list spot opens up, or you determine that a class isn't a good fit for you. Take advantage of this great opportunity to try out new courses without risk of committing to them and "shop" for the classes that will benefit you most.

Here's one final word on course selection in college. When you plan your schedule, take into consideration how much work you'll need to do not only inside class but outside of class. The humanities—such as history, English, philosophy, and theology—involve a significant amount of reading compared to other

fields, but they may also be less time intensive in other ways, such as by not having lab requirements. Math and science classes may involve less reading and instead focus more on solving problems, but they sometimes have lab requirements or will require a lot more study time to master concepts. Some courses may not be very homework intensive but could require you to commit to things outside of the classroom, such as film showings and volunteer hours. This is another good reason to shop around for courses—generally, on the first day, you'll get a rundown of what's expected for the course and can gauge the time commitment. Aiming for a combination of time-intensive and more straightforward or light classes will ensure that you have a more manageable workload.

CHOOSING YOUR MAJOR

You can choose from hundreds of majors—from accounting to zoology—but which one is right for you, and when should you declare a major? Choosing a major can occur at different points. Maybe you decided on a major while you were completing your college applications. Perhaps you chose a major first and then geared your college search towards certain colleges who offer the major you want to declare. If you already have a major or career in mind, then work with the advisor for your degree program to help you complete all the required coursework and to make sure that you're able to graduate in the time frame that works best.

Not every student knows which major they want to declare. Only a small percentage of high school students know what career they want and what major will help take them one step closer to their goals. Don't worry. You have time to figure out what major is best for you.

"Take as many survey courses as you can in your first two years. I took a huge range of intro classes during my freshman year, and the one I liked the most was Introduction to Anthropology. I'm now having a great time pursuing my anthropology major, and I didn't even know what anthropology meant in high school!"

Diego, College Graduate

Where Do I Begin?

Choosing a major usually starts with an assessment of your career interests. If you took the self-assessment test in Chapter 2 of this book, you should have a clearer understanding of your interests, talents, values, and goals. From here, you can try to think of which majors match up with your interests.

Declaring a major involves a lot of thinking ahead. Picture yourself taking classes, writing papers, making presentations, conducting research, or working in a field related to your major. Talk to people you know who work in your fields of interest and see if you like what you hear. See if you can shadow someone on the job or maybe even get a summer internship in that field. Also, try looking at career services or networking websites to get a feel for jobs that you would enjoy doing. What jobs sound interesting to you? Which ones pay the salary that you'd like to make? What level of education is required for the jobs you find interesting? The more exposure you get to the day-to-day realities of working in a field, the better you'll be able to determine if you can see yourself doing so in the future.

Majors and Related Careers

If you have a general idea of what field you may want to pursue, consult the following list of majors to see which ones coincide with your interests. We've provided brief synopses following each major to help you get acquainted with what to expect. After reading this, gather some more information from your advisor, professors, and fellow students. The specifics of a given major (including the name) may differ from college to college, so it's a good idea to also look at your college's department home pages. There you can find information about a department's philosophy and goals, faculty who work in the department, the kinds of jobs students from that department end up getting, the degree requirements, and the kind of courses offered in that major.

Agriculture

Many agriculture majors apply their knowledge directly on farms and ranches. Others work in a specific industry (e.g., food, farm equipment, or agricultural supply companies), for federal agencies (primarily in the Departments of Agriculture and the Interior), or for state and local farm and agricultural agencies. Jobs might be in research and lab work, marketing and sales, advertising and public relations, or media. Agriculture majors also pursue further training in biological sciences, animal health, veterinary medicine, agribusiness management, vocational agriculture education, nutrition and dietetics, and rural sociology.

Architecture

Architecture and related design fields focus on the built environment as distinct from the natural environment of the agriculturist or the conservationist. Career possibilities include drafting, design, and project administration in architectural engineering, landscape design, interior design, industrial design, planning, real estate, and construction firms; government agencies involved in construction, housing, highways, and parks and recreation; and government and nonprofit organizations interested in historic or architectural preservation.

Area/Ethnic Studies

This discipline often includes majors such as political science, international relations, geography, and more. The research, writing, analysis, critical thinking, and cultural awareness skills acquired by area/ethnic studies majors, combined with the expertise gained in a particular area, make this group of majors valuable in many professions. Majors find positions in administration, education, public relations, and communications in such organizations as cultural, government, international, and (ethnic) community agencies; international trade (import-export); social service agencies; and media and communication. These studies also provide a good background for further training in law, business management, public administration, education, social work, museum and library work, and international relations.

Art

Art majors most often use their training to become practicing artists, though the settings in which they work vary. This major can lead you to a strictly art-related career, such as that of the self-employed artist or craftsperson. However, many other fields also require the unique skills of a visual artist. These include advertising; public relations; publishing; media and communication; museum work; television, movies, and theater; community and social service agencies concerned with education, recreation, and entertainment; and teaching. In a digital world, graphic artists can find positions in any number of fields. A background in art is also useful to pursue a career in art therapy, arts or museum administration, or library work.

Biological Sciences

The biological sciences include the study of living organisms from the level of molecules to that of populations. Biology majors can find jobs in industry; government agencies; technical writing, editing, or illustrating; science reporting; secondary school teaching (which usually requires additional courses in education); and research and laboratory analysis and testing. A major in biological sciences also offers a strong foundation for further study in medicine, psychology, health and hospital administration, and biologically oriented engineering.

Business

Business majors comprise all the basic business disciplines and prepare students for life in the business world. At the undergraduate level, students can major in a general business administration program or specialize in a particular area, such as marketing or accounting. These studies lead not only to positions in business and industry but also to management positions in other sectors. Management-related studies include the general management areas (accounting, finance, marketing, and management) as well as special programs related to a particular type of organization or industry. Management-related majors may be offered in a business school or in a department dealing with the area in which the management skills are to be applied.

Communication

Jobs in communication range from journalism, copywriting, technical writing, copyediting, and programming to advertising, public relations, media sales, social media, and market research. Such positions can be found at radio and TV stations, publishing houses (book and magazine), newspapers, advertising agencies, corporate communications departments, government agencies, universities, and firms that specialize in educational and training materials.

Computer, Information, and Library Sciences

Computer and information science and systems majors focus on managing information using various programs and software. Data processing, programming, and computer technology programs tend to be more practical applications of this major, as these fields are oriented more toward utilizing technology in a corporate or organizational context. Career possibilities for computer and information science majors include data processing, information management and security, programming, and systems development or maintenance in almost any setting, including business and industry, banking and finance, government, colleges and universities, libraries, software companies and computer manufacturers, publishing, and communications. Library science gives a preprofessional background in library work and provides valuable knowledge of research sources, indexing, abstracting, computer

"I'm one of those people who knew what I wanted to do since I was very little, so that made choosing easier. If I was not 100 percent sure that I wanted to go into medicine, I would not have applied to a seven-year medical program. For students who are interested but not really sure that they want to go into medicine, they should first enjoy college and a good education—and then worry about medical school. That way, if they decide in their junior year that medicine is not for them, they have options."

Kaman, Pre-Med Student

technology, and media technology, which is useful for further study in any professional field. In most cases, a master's degree in library science is necessary to obtain a job as a librarian. Library science majors find positions in public, school, college, corporate, and government libraries and research centers; book publishing (especially reference books); database and information retrieval services; and communications (especially audiovisual media).

Education

Positions as teachers in public elementary and secondary schools, private day and boarding schools, religious and parochial schools, vocational schools, online schools, and proprietary schools are the jobs most often filled by education majors. However, teaching positions also exist in noneducational institutions, such as prisons, hospitals, and nursing homes. Education majors who become certified in TESOL (Teachers of English to Speakers of Other Languages) can also teach English abroad. Jobs are also available as educators and trainers in government and industry. Education majors can put their skills to good use in administrative (nonteaching) positions in employee relations and personnel, public relations, marketing and sales, educational publishing, TV and film media, test development firms, and government and community social service agencies. Increasingly, the business world also has positions for instructional designers, training specialists, and curriculum developers, all of which are positions uniquely suited to the skills of education majors.

Engineering and Science Technology

Engineering and science technology majors prepare students for practical design and production work rather than for jobs that require more theoretical, scientific, and mathematical knowledge. Engineers work in a variety of fields, including aeronautics, bioengineering, geology, renewable energy, and quality control and safety. Industry, research labs, and government agencies where technology plays a key role—such as in manufacturing, electronics, construction communications, transportation, and utilities—hire engineering majors as well as engineering technology and science technology graduates regularly. Work may be in technical activities (research, development, design, production, testing, scientific programming, or systems analysis) or in nontechnical areas where a technical degree is needed, such as marketing, sales, or administration.

Family and Consumer Sciences and Social Services

Family and consumer sciences encompasses many different fields—studies in foods and textiles as well as consumer economics—that overlap with aspects of agriculture, social science, and education. Jobs can be found in government and community agencies (especially those in education, health, housing, or human services), nursing homes, childcare centers, journalism, media, and publishing. Types of work also include marketing, sales, and customer service in consumer-related industries, such as tourism and recreation, hospitality, food processing and packaging,

appliance manufacturing, utilities, textiles, and more. Majors in social services find administrative positions in government and community health, welfare, and social service agencies, such as hospitals and clinics, nonprofit organizations, welfare agencies, and employment services. See the "Law and Legal Studies" section for information on more law-related social services.

Foreign Language and Literature

Knowledge of foreign languages and cultures is especially important in today's globalized world. Language majors possess skills that are used in organizations with international dealings as well as in career fields and geographic areas where languages other than English are prominent. Career possibilities include positions with business firms with international subsidiaries; import-export firms; international banking; travel agencies; airlines; tourist services; government and international agencies dealing with international affairs, foreign trade, diplomacy, customs, or immigration; secondary school foreign language teaching and bilingual education (which usually require education courses); freelance translating and interpreting (high level of skill necessary); foreign language publishing; and computer programming (especially for linguistics majors). A foreign language major can also be a springboard towards any number of careers in a country or area where the target language is spoken.

Health Professions

Health professions majors, while grounded in scientific inquiry, are more focused on applying the results of scientific investigation than on the scientific disciplines themselves. Allied health majors prepare graduates to assist health professionals in providing diagnostics, therapeutics, and rehabilitation. Medical science majors, such as optometry, pharmacy, and the premedical profession sequences are, for the most part, preprofessional studies that comprise the scientific disciplines necessary for admission to graduate or professional school in the health or medical fields. Health service and technology majors prepare students for positions in the health fields that primarily involve services to patients or working with complex machinery and materials. Medical technologies cover a wide range of fields, such as cytotechnology, biomedical technologies, and operating room technology.

Administrative, professional, or research assistant positions in health agencies, hospitals, occupational health units in industry, community and school health departments, government agencies (public health, environmental protection), and international health organizations are available to majors in health fields, as are jobs in marketing and sales of health-related products and services, health education (with education courses), advertising and public relations, journalism and publishing, and technical writing.

Humanities and Liberal Arts

The humanities and liberal arts are essentially the study of the ideas and concerns of humankind, including philosophy, literature, cultural studies, language, and history. Majors in these fields often focus extensively on critical thinking, theories of analysis, ethics, and soft skills such as communication, creativity, empathy, research, and problem-solving. While the career possibilities are endless for these majors, there is some bias against the humanities and liberal arts as being too general or not applicable to the workplace. Many careers in the humanities also require a graduate degree. While this shouldn't dissuade students from considering a degree in the humanities or liberal arts, it's important to consider that graduates with these majors sometimes have to be creative with their career paths. Career possibilities for humanities majors can be found in management and business, government and community agencies, advertising and public relations, marketing and sales, publishing, journalism and media, secondary school teaching (which usually requires education coursework), freelance writing and editing, and computer programming (especially for those with a background in logic or linguistics). This major can also be a stepping-stone toward any number of graduate degrees where creative analysis and research skills are highly valued.

Law and Legal Studies

Students of legal studies can use their knowledge of law and government in fields involving legislation, law enforcement, and the criminal justice system. Graduates find positions of all types in law firms, legal departments of other organizations, the court or corrections system, public service and government agencies (such as law enforcement agencies or offices of state and federal attorneys general), and police departments. Oftentimes, legal studies or prelaw majors go on to pursue law school.

Mathematics and Physical Sciences

Mathematics is the science of numbers and the abstract formulation of their operations. Physical sciences involve the study of the laws and structures of physical matter. The quantitative skills that are acquired through the study of science and mathematics are especially useful for careers involving computers and technology. Career possibilities include positions in industry (manufacturing and processing companies, electronics firms, defense contractors, consulting firms); government agencies (defense, environmental protection, law enforcement); scientific/technical writing, editing, or illustrating; journalism (science, weather, and climate reporting); secondary school teaching (usually requiring education courses); research and laboratory analysis and testing; statistical analysis; computer programming; systems analysis; surveying and mapping; and technical sales.

Natural Resources

A major in the natural resources field prepares students for work in areas as generalized as environmental conservation and as specialized as groundwater contamination. Jobs are available in manufacturing and industry (food, energy, natural resources, and pulp and paper companies), consulting firms, federal and state government agencies (primarily the Departments of Agriculture and the Interior and the Environmental Protection Agency), and public and private conservation agencies. See the "Agriculture" and "Biological Sciences" sections for more information on fields related to natural resources.

Psychology

Psychology involves the study of behavior and can range from the biological to the sociological. Students can study individual behavior, usually that of humans, or the behavior of crowds. Students of psychology do not always go into the obvious clinical fields, like those in which psychologists work with patients. Certain areas of psychology, such as industrial/organizational, experimental, and social, are not clinically oriented. Psychology and counseling careers can be in government (such as mental health agencies), schools, hospitals, clinics, private practice, industry, test development firms, social work, and personnel. Psychology and counseling majors also sometimes pursue the careers listed in the "Social Sciences" section.

Religion

Religion degrees are usually seen as preprofessional studies for those who are interested in entering the ministry. Career possibilities for religion also include casework, youth counseling, administration work in community and social service organizations, teaching in religious educational institutions (or teaching a religious studies class at a non-religious school), and writing for religious and lay publications. You do not have to be religious to pursue a degree in religious studies, though. The field also prepares students for the kinds of jobs that other humanities majors often pursue, particularly museum work involving religious antiquities.

Social Sciences

Social sciences majors study people in relation to their society. Like majors in the humanities and liberal arts, social science majors can apply their education to a wide range of occupations that deal with social issues and activities. Career opportunities are varied. People with degrees in the social sciences find careers in government, business, community agencies (serving children, youth, and senior citizens), advertising and public relations, marketing and sales, secondary school social studies teaching (with education courses), social casework, law enforcement, parks and recreation, museum work and preservation (especially for anthropology, archaeology, geography, and history majors), banking and finance (especially for economics majors), market and survey research, statistical analysis, publishing, non-profit organizations, and politics.

Technologies

Technology majors, along with trade fields, are most often offered as two-year programs. Majors in technology fields prepare students directly for jobs; however, positions are in practical design and production work rather than in areas that require more theoretical, scientific, and mathematical knowledge. Engineering technologies prepare students with the basic training in specific fields (e.g., electronics, mechanics, or chemistry) necessary to become technicians on the support staffs of engineers. Other technology majors center more on maintenance and repair. Work may be in technical activities, such as production or testing, or in nontechnical areas where a technical degree is needed, such as marketing, sales, or administration. Industries,

research labs, and government agencies in which technology plays a key role—such as in manufacturing, electronics, construction, communications, transportation, and utilities—hire technology graduates regularly.

Still Unsure?

Even if you've read through all these majors and still have no idea what you want to major in, don't worry! You don't have to know before you enroll in college. In fact, more than half of all first-year students are undecided when they start school. This statistic makes sense because many people prefer to get a feel for what's available at college rather than locking themselves into a decision without having sampled what their school has to offer. Most four-year colleges don't require students to formally declare a major until the end of their sophomore or beginning of their junior year, as colleges know that being exposed to new subjects and new ideas is a vital part of the academic experience.

Changing Your Major

Once you have chosen your major, you do not necessarily need to stick with your choice. Changing your major is generally allowed, although you may have to talk to your advisor for your school's specific procedures regarding this process. (If you are unsure of what you want to major in, bear in mind that it would make sense to figure out how changing your major works before selecting one.)

However, choosing a major sooner rather than later does have its advantages. If you wait too long to choose, or if you change your major multiple times, you may have to take additional classes to satisfy the requirements, which may cost you additional time and money. If it's your senior year and you're already almost done with your current major, it might not be worth the switch. Some schools may also allow you to declare two majors, provided you have the time and energy to complete the requirements for both.

Choosing a Minor

A minor can be a good way to show that you have devoted extra time to a particular subject without making the required time commitment necessary for a second major. Most departments have minor requirements that involve students taking some, but not all, of the courses required for a major. A minor can also be a good way to enhance another degree. For instance, someone who gets a degree in secondary education but minors in chemistry may do so in hopes of becoming a high school chemistry teacher.

You shouldn't add a minor if it causes undue stress on your schedule or requires you to devote extra time and money to your education. Minors do not carry the same weight as majors, so you shouldn't expect to be able to automatically get a job in a field just because you minored in it. In most cases, the name of your minor also won't appear on your degree the same way your major will, though it will likely appear on your college transcript. Nonetheless, a minor can be a helpful way to demonstrate competency in a second field of interest and is especially worth pursuing if, as is often the case with students who decide to add a minor, you find yourself halfway there through electives on accident anyhow.

CAMPUS RESOURCES AND SUPPORT

Once you get to campus, it's important that you get to know all the resources available to you. These services are designed to increase student retention by providing students with the support they need to be successful in college. As such, your tuition costs often include fees associated with these services, so most (if not all) campus resources should be of little to no cost to you thereafter. Here, we'll cover some common resources and support services you can expect to find on your campus.

Library

Every school typically has a library where you can find credible academic research for your studies. While you will often use the library's website to conduct most of your research, libraries offer a variety of helpful in-person services and assistance. For example, you might be able to schedule a research consultation with a librarian, who will walk you through the databases and collections available so you can locate the sources you need to write a research paper. You can also typically find print resources with information that may not be accessible online, such as local newspaper archives, rare historical books, and oversized art books. Libraries often host workshops or other informational seminars given by academic researchers so that you can learn more about a specific topic. Libraries also generally have designated study areas and quiet zones so that you can concentrate on your work. Low-income students may find that the library can help them access resources they might not personally have, such as laptops. You'll likely use the library for most of your coursework, so it's important to get familiar with what's available to you early on in your academic career.

Writing Center

If your campus has a writing center, you'll be able to work with writing tutors to get feedback and guidance on your assignments. Writing centers are often staffed by English majors and composition instructors, so they have experience and training in working with students on all different types of writing. Even if you consider yourself a good writer, a writing tutor can teach you a variety of skills and strategies for every phase of the writing process: how to brainstorm ideas and outline your paper, write a strong thesis statement, organize and structure your paragraphs, revise and proofread your drafts, and avoid plagiarism by citing and documenting your sources correctly. Also, each major or discipline often has its own style guidelines, and it can be challenging to learn how to write in a new genre or format, like a lab report or case study. Writing centers often have additional resources on how to write effectively within your major, so don't be afraid to stop by and see what's available. Remember, the best writers take feedback on their work and use it to make their writing even stronger.

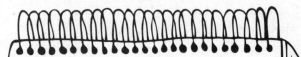

"Some students feel like they're just bad writers, but academic writing is a skill that requires time and effort to master. Remember that you're in college to learn and strengthen your skills, including writing. You'll do some kind of writing in most of your classes, so it's important to get familiar with the writing center, or whatever writing resources your college offers, early on in your academic career. Getting feedback on your work is incredibly helpful, and you can use that feedback to improve and refine your writing skills and build your confidence as a writer."

Justin, Writing Center Director

Career Services

Career services can help you create a résumé, write a cover letter, and find and apply to job opportunities. Oftentimes, you can work with a career coach to help you figure out which career is right for you. While this service will likely be most valuable to you in your final year of school as you prepare to enter the workforce, don't hesitate to visit early on in your academic career if you are having doubts about your career path. Additionally, some colleges make career services available to alumni, either at no cost or for a fee, so take advantage of these services if you are having trouble finding a job once you graduate.

Counseling Center

Counseling centers can provide you with the support or information you need to manage stress and prioritize your mental health. Most colleges offer free or low-cost counseling to students, usually in the form of a set number of sessions per semester. Additional sessions may be available to you for a fee, so contact your college's counseling center to learn more. If you are experiencing an emergency or mental health crisis, the counseling center will not be equipped to help; instead, please be sure to call 911 for immediate assistance.

Military/Veterans Office

Campuses often have a dedicated office for military or veteran students. This office usually coordinates benefits for students who are using the GI bill to cover the costs of attending college. Oftentimes, there are also additional academic or support services available to students who are veterans or in the military, so it's important to get acquainted with this office early on in your academic career or even before you enroll in your first semester.

Tutoring/Learning Center

Most schools offer tutoring in specific subject areas, including math, science, English as a second language (ESL), and more. Most colleges and universities include a certain number of hours of tutoring per semester as part of your tuition. Additional tutoring and other services may be available to you for a fee.

LGBTQIA+ Services

Some colleges have an LGBTQIA+ center or office, where students can connect with other students under the LGBTQIA+ umbrella, get involved in community initiatives, receive information about sexual health and wellness, and seek help in dealing with discrimination or harassment. Generally, most resource centers for LGBTQIA+ students aim to destigmatize and promote positive awareness of relevant issues through education, support, and other initiatives. If you have questions about sexual orientation or gender identity or if you are experiencing discrimination or prejudice, an LGBTQIA+ center can help connect you with resources and support.

Internship Office

If you are interested in completing an internship as part of your coursework, you'll likely need to visit the internship office at your school. An internship coordinator can help you find unpaid and paid internship opportunities in your field, fill out the appropriate paperwork, and register for the internship course. Please note that you will need to pay tuition if you are receiving course credit for the internship. Sometimes, internship services are folded into other resources, like enrollment, advising, or career services, so research what your school has to offer.

Study Abroad

For students who plan on studying abroad during their college years, the study abroad office can help you identify the program that's right for you and figure out how it can fit into your coursework. A study abroad program coordinator can also help you identify scholarships, grants, or other funding opportunities to help you pay for your study abroad experience. Programs may be connected directly to your school, coordinated through third parties, or some combination of both. The fees and guidelines associated with each program will differ and may include language prerequisites that will require you to get started on language courses in your first year of college, so make sure you speak with this office early in your college career if you think you might be interested in pursuing study abroad opportunities.

Registrar

The Registrar's Office generally handles issues pertaining to academic policies, such as the Family Education Rights and Privacy Act (FERPA), the Student Right to Know and Campus Security Act, and other policies pertaining to academic freedom, personal information and privacy, and more. The Registrar's Office also handles student records, including requests for official transcripts, registering for courses, filing a grade appeal, and paying tuition. Prior to your first semester, it will be important to know major deadlines for enrolling in, dropping, and withdrawing from a course. Generally, any time you want to make changes to your course schedule after a deadline has already passed, you'll need to work with the Registrar and fill out the appropriate paperwork. Depending on the situation, you may need to pay full or partial tuition or an administrative fee, and you'll likely need to get signatures from the instructor and department head.

"Being able to study abroad was the most important priority in my college search. I knew as a low-income student I had to find somewhere that made it possible, so I prioritized that when narrowing schools and ended up finding a school where my financial aid covered a year in Germany. It was honestly the single best year of my life to date, and I'm so glad I got to do it! I learned so much about who I am by seeing the world from a different vantage point. That's when I feel like I became the adult version of myself. If you can get the funding, I can't recommend studying abroad enough!"

Stacey, Liberal Arts
College Graduate

Financial Aid and Scholarships

The financial aid office can help you learn about the different types of financial aid, if you qualify, and how to apply. While some schools combine financial aid and scholarship support into one resource, other schools may have a dedicated scholarship office to help you locate and apply to merit-based and need-based scholarships. The financial aid office primarily helps you apply for grants, work-study opportunities, scholarships, and student loans and is responsible for disbursing your financial aid awards to you. If there is a problem with your financial aid disbursement, you'll work directly with the financial aid office to make sure everything is correct. Some financial aid awards come with stipulations for how many credit hours you must be enrolled in, so make sure you meet all the enrollment requirements.

Health Center

Most campuses have a health center where you can go for routine and preventative medical care, including immunizations, testing for sexually transmitted infections and diseases, wellness exams and physicals, and treatment for acute illnesses. How comprehensive a school's medical facilities are is often dependent on the size of the campus. Very large campuses may have their own urgent care or emergency facilities, while others will have smaller facilities and may need to refer you out to a more suitable medical facility for certain injuries or health issues. Mental health services are often either folded into the health center or operated through their own department, like a counseling services office.

Victim Services

Some campuses have an office dedicated to supporting victims of sexual assault, relationship violence, stalking, and harassment. At some schools, these services might be joined with other resources, like a campus health clinic or counseling center. We talk more about this topic in Chapter 11, but if you have experienced sexual violence, please reach out to someone who can help, whether that's a trusted adult, law enforcement, a local community organization, and so on.

Advising

As a student, you'll likely have a general advisor who will make sure that you are meeting general education requirements and a department-specific advisor who will make sure that you are meeting the specific requirements for your major, minor, and/or concentration. It's important to meet with each of your advisors once a semester, ideally before the deadline for dropping courses, to ensure that your course schedule helps you advance toward your degree.

Office for Diversity, Equity, and Inclusion

The office for diversity, equity, and inclusion is intended to handle issues of discrimination, harassment, and misconduct on campus. Depending on the college, there might be both a Title IX office and an office for diversity, equity, and inclusion. Title IX prohibits institutions that receive federal assistance from treating students differently on the basis of sex. Keep in mind that private undergraduate colleges are exempt from Title IX requirements. If you believe that you have been discriminated against due to your race, ethnicity,

> "My advisor was a lifesaver during my college career. He helped me register for classes, answered all my questions about electives, and made sure that I graduated on time. I always looked forward to meeting with him every semester, and I really appreciated his guidance when I needed advice.
>
> Chrissy, College Graduate

religion, national origin, disability, age, sex, gender identity, or sexual orientation, then contact the office of diversity, equity, and inclusion or its equivalent on your campus.

Federal TRIO Programs

TRIO originally referred to the three federal educational opportunity outreach programs designed to increase access to higher education for students from economically disadvantaged backgrounds. The original three programs, Upward Bound, Talent Search, and Student Support Service, are now eight programs designed to encourage students to pursue higher education regardless of their economic circumstances. To participate in TRIO programs, students must meet one of the following criteria: (1) neither parent graduated from college, (2) the student qualifies as low-income under federal income guidelines, or (3) the student has a documented disability on file with the college or university. Many undergraduate institutions offer TRIO student support services to promote student retention and increase graduation rates by making the transition to college more manageable. For example, TRIO student services may provide tutoring and workshops on academic skills and study strategies, assistance with financial aid and literacy, specialized general education courses for TRIO students only, community engagement initiatives and events, and more.

First-Year Experience (FYE)

Some colleges offer a first-year experience program, where students can transition to college alongside a cohort of other first-year students. FYE programs offer students a support system to help them adjust to the college experience and learn the skills necessary to succeed in college. These programs, which can offer a more structured first-year experience, typically involve personalized advising, smaller courses reserved for first-year undergraduate students, and events where students can get to know their peers and make friends.

ATTENDING COLLEGE WITH A DISABILITY

The Americans with Disabilities Act (ADA) requires educational institutions at all levels, public and private, to provide equal access to programs, services, and facilities. Schools must be accessible to students, as well as to employees and the public, regardless of any disability. To ensure such accessibility, they must follow specific requirements for new construction, alterations or renovations, academic programs, and institutional policies, practices, and procedures.

To comply with ADA requirements, many high schools and universities offer programs and information to answer questions for students with disabilities and to assist them both in selecting appropriate colleges and in attaining full inclusion once they enter college. Most colleges and universities have disability services offices to help students navigate the system. Students with specific disabilities have the right to request and expect accommodations, including auxiliary aids and services that enable them to participate in and benefit from all programs and activities offered by or related to a school.

If you have a disability that requires accommodations, you'll need to visit the disability services office at your school well in advance of your first semester. The disability services office will walk you through the process of providing documentation of your disability and requesting accommodations—such as a peer notetaker, alternative textbooks, assistive technology, or additional testing time—that will help you succeed in your coursework. The staff at the disability services office will also inform you of your rights and responsibilities as a student, so be sure to contact them with any questions or concerns.

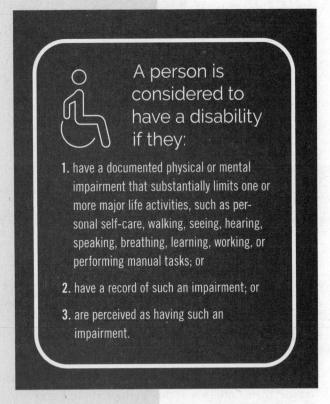

A person is considered to have a disability if they:

1. have a documented physical or mental impairment that substantially limits one or more major life activities, such as personal self-care, walking, seeing, hearing, speaking, breathing, learning, working, or performing manual tasks; or

2. have a record of such an impairment; or

3. are perceived as having such an impairment.

Physical disabilities include impairments of speech, vision, hearing, and mobility. Other disabilities, whether visible or invisible, may include diabetes, asthma, multiple sclerosis, heart disease, cancer, mental health issues, intellectual disability, cerebral palsy, learning disabilities, and more.

Learning disabilities refer to an array of biological conditions that may impede a person's ability to process and disseminate information. A learning disability typically impacts ability and performance in one or more of the following areas: oral expression, listening comprehension, written expression, basic reading skills, reading comprehension, mathematical calculation, or problem solving. Individuals with learning disabilities

also may have difficulty with sustained attention, time management, or social skills. Depending on the disability, a student may have trouble sustaining focus for as long as their peers or become more exhausted than peers after doing the same learning tasks.

If you have a learning disability, you deserve access to the support necessary to earn the same education as anyone else. No matter what college you end up attending, it's important for you to know your rights under the Americans with Disabilities Act, which prohibits discrimination based on disability. Some colleges help with schedules and offer transition courses, reduced course loads, general education requirement modifications, extra access to professors, and special study areas and dorms to help address your needs. If you find that the accommodations necessary for your disability are lacking, don't hesitate to request accommodations be put in place.

While the college is responsible for providing reasonable accommodations for students with disabilities, students must also provide the necessary documentation

"I broke my arm during a basketball game, and someone in one of my classes told me I should see what accommodations I'd be eligible for. I didn't know that the disabilities office could help with temporary injuries. I was approved for a notetaker and extended time on my quizzes and exams. It made a huge difference, and I was able to keep up in my classes even with a broken arm."

Amayrani, College Student

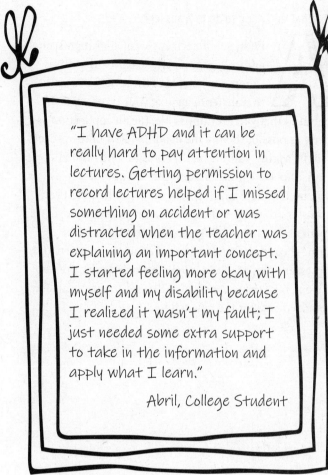

"I have ADHD and it can be really hard to pay attention in lectures. Getting permission to record lectures helped if I missed something on accident or was distracted when the teacher was explaining an important concept. I started feeling more okay with myself and my disability because I realized it wasn't my fault; I just needed some extra support to take in the information and apply what I learn."

Abril, College Student

and request accommodations in a timely manner. Note that students will often have to do this for themselves as adults. In certain cases, due to privacy laws related to college grades, accommodations must be sought by the student directly. There are numerous resources that can help students, families, and schools with the legal requirements for accommodating disabilities. They can also link you with other groups and individuals that are knowledgeable in students' rights and the process of transitioning into postsecondary education. Also, special interest, education, support, and advocacy organizations for persons with particular disabilities exist. Check with your guidance counselor or contact one of the organizations listed in Appendix B for more information.

TRANSFERRING

Circumstances shift, people change, and, realistically speaking, it's not all that uncommon to transfer. There are many reasons why students transfer, and among the most common transfers are students who move from a two-year school to a four-year college or university. If this is you, you'll be pleased to know that this path is becoming more commonplace. As a result, many two-year schools have revised their course outlines and established new courses in order to comply with the programs and curricular offerings of universities. Institutional improvements to make transferring easier have also proliferated at both the two-and four-year levels.

If you are interested in moving from a two-year college to a four-year school, the sooner you make up your mind that you are going to make the switch, the better position you will be in to transfer successfully (that is, without having wasted valuable time and credits). The ideal point at which to make such a decision is *before* you register for classes at your two-year school; an advisor or enrollment counselor can help you plan your coursework with an eye toward fulfilling the requirements needed for your major course of study.

But what if you are attending a four-year college and you find that it isn't what you thought it would be? Here are some common scenarios that may cause you to consider transferring to a different school:

- You can't stand being at the school.
- The courses don't match your interests.
- The campus isn't as ideal as you pictured it.
- The selection of extracurricular activities doesn't appeal to you.
- You thought you wanted to major in one subject but find that you are more interested in something else. However, the school doesn't offer a major in the subject you are interested in.
- The environment is not good for your mental health.
- You realize that you want to go to a college with lower tuition or better financial aid.
- You realize that being away from your family and support network is not good for your mental health.

Whatever the reason, if the college you picked is not the right fit for you, then consider transferring to a college that may be better suited to what you need. You'll need to plan, coordinate with your advisor, and apply to transfer to the school of your choice. Keep in mind that the key to a successful transfer is preparation, and preparation takes time—time to think through your objectives, what you want, and what you need. Find a trusted adult or advisor to help you.

Here are some commonly asked questions by students who are considering transferring schools—and their answers:

Q: Do students who go directly from high school to a four-year college do better academically than transfer students from community colleges?

 On the contrary, some institutions report that transfer students from two-year schools who persevere until graduation do *better* than those who started as first-year students at a four-year college.

Q: Why is it so important that my two-year college be accredited?

Four-year colleges and universities accept transfer credits only from schools formally recognized by a regional, national, or professional educational organization. This accreditation signifies that an institution or program of study meets or exceeds a minimum level of educational quality necessary for reaching stated educational objectives.

Q: What do I need to do to transfer?

 First, you'll need copies of your high school and college transcripts. Check the admission requirements of the school you wish to transfer to against your transcripts. If you find that you are admissible, file an application as early as possible before the deadline. Part of the process will be asking your former schools to send official transcripts to the admissions office—not the copies you used in determining your admissibility. Plan your transfer program with an advisor in your new department as soon as you have decided to transfer. Determine the recommended general education pattern and necessary preparation for your major. At your present school, take the courses you will need to meet transfer requirements for the new school.

Q: What qualifies me for admission as a transfer student?

Admission requirements for most four-year institutions vary. Depending on the reputation or popularity of the school and program you wish to enter, requirements may be quite selective and competitive. Usually, you will need to show satisfactory test scores, an academic record up to a certain standard, and completion of specific subject matter.

Transfer students can be eligible to enter a four-year school in a number of ways: by having been eligible for admission directly upon graduation from high school, by making up shortcomings in grades (or in subject matter not covered in high school) at a community college, or by satisfactory completion of necessary courses or credit hours at another postsecondary institution. Ordinarily, students coming from a community college, a two-year program, or from another four-year institution must meet or exceed the receiving institution's standards for first-year students and show appropriate college-level coursework taken since high school. Students who did not graduate from high school can present proof of proficiency through results on the General Educational Development (GED) test.

Q: Is it possible to transfer courses from several different institutions?

Institutions ordinarily accept the courses that they consider transferable, regardless of the number of accredited schools involved. However, there is the danger of exceeding the maximum number of credit hours that can be transferred from all other schools or earned through credit by examination, extension courses, or correspondence courses. The limit placed on transfer credits varies from school to school, so read the catalog carefully to avoid taking courses you won't be able to use. To avoid duplicating courses, keep attendance at different campuses to a minimum.

Q: Which is more important for transfer—my grade point average or my course completion pattern?

Some schools believe that your past grades indicate academic potential and overshadow prior preparation for a specific degree program. Others require completion of certain introductory courses before transfer to prepare you for upper-division work in your major. In any case, appropriate course selection will cut down the time to graduation and increase your chances of making a successful transfer.

YOU HAVE WHAT YOU NEED TO SUCCEED

Remember that no matter what college you attend, there will be numerous services and resources to help you overcome any obstacles you might encounter. Getting familiar with the different offices and student services early on can only help you during your academic career. Whether you're choosing a major, improving your writing, or managing your physical and mental health, make sure that you take advantage of the resources available to you. Finally, don't forget to enjoy the experience—it goes by fast!

CHAPTER 11

Preparing for College and Adult Life

Whether you're elated to finally have your freedom or shaking in your boots about the prospect of being on your own, you can be sure that there will be few periods in your life that come with as much change as does the transition from high school to adulthood. Day to day, week to week, things are going to be different than they were in high school. Depending on how far you move from home (if at all), the kind of job or college you take on, what you're doing day-to-day, and about a million other factors, your life as a recent high school graduate is in for a shake-up. Don't worry, though, because as with college and career, a bit of preparation can smooth out the bumps in the road ahead.

The Short and Sweet Version

Adjusting to adult life is challenging, as a college student or otherwise. Things can get pretty hectic as you try to balance your coursework or job duties while also trying to maintain a social life and figuring out how to live on your own or with roommates. You might find yourself exhausted as you hustle to stay on top of things, so it's important to learn some coping mechanisms and strategies for managing your time and stress level before it all gets too overwhelming.

A lot of the changes you're about to face are going to be so much fun! For instance, if you'll be living on campus, you can expect a rich social life full of clubs, events, and campus traditions. You'll also get to feel true independence in a way that was impossible in high school. You'll experience what it's like to live on your own with control over your schedule, your classes, your space, your social life, and more.

Yes, you'll have to take on a lot more responsibilities, too, and that can be a rude awakening. You'll need to make responsible decisions when it comes to drugs, alcohol, and sex. It will also be important for you to establish boundaries with the people in your life, whether it's with roommates, friends, or partners, so that you can take care of yourself and live out your values. If you're struggling with your classes, relationships, mental health, identity, stress, or anything else, make sure you reach out to someone you trust so you can get the help and support you need.

As you take the first steps into adulthood, try on new aspects of your identity, and figure things out for yourself, you're bound to make some mistakes. But throughout this process and during this exciting time in your life, you'll have a lot of wins, too. These first few years of adulthood are just the next step in your grand adventure!

MENTALLY PREPARING FOR ADULT LIFE

Even if you're the kind of person who feels like they have things together normally, don't be surprised if the weeks and months immediately following high school graduation feel weird or chaotic. Everything during this period is in flux. You might spend the summer trying to hang with friends before you or they go to college, working a part-time job to save money for when you move out, or getting your ducks in a row for a move across the country to start college or enlist in the military. Your parent(s) or guardian(s) might be freaking out in their own way as they prepare to let you leave the nest. Siblings and friends may seem distant or act weird as they cope with the reality that they might not be seeing you around as much.

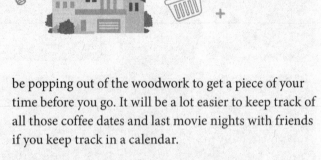

All of these things are likely to be going on, and through it all, you're supposed to mentally adjust to the idea that you're an adult now? How?! Well, there are actually a few routines you can ground yourself in to help make this transition period go smoother:

Move Your Body

Get exercise, go for a walk, dance in your kitchen with the speakers on full blast, whatever you have to do, just make sure to move your body. Studies have shown that even small amounts of exercise can help alleviate stress, depression, and other issues. It doesn't matter if you don't have time for a full workout; a quick walk around the block is enough to get the blood pumping and do the body good.

Use a Calendar to Manage Your Time

If you've heeded the advice in this guide, you're already accustomed to using a calendar for school and work by this point. Don't forget that you can use a calendar to schedule your social engagements, too! Especially if you are moving away from where you grew up, people will be popping out of the woodwork to get a piece of your time before you go. It will be a lot easier to keep track of all those coffee dates and last movie nights with friends if you keep track in a calendar.

Break Up Preparation into Pieces

You don't want to get to the weekend before you leave for college or have to move into your new apartment and have an entire place to pack, seventeen friends to say goodbye to, a rent check to mail, laundry to get done, and a hundred other tasks on your to-do list. Instead, figure out what tasks can be done earlier (such as packing winter clothes during summer) and do as much as you can in advance of crunch time.

Take Reflection Time

This is a big time in your life! Whether reflection looks like meditating, scrapbooking, looking at slide shows of pictures, journaling, or anything else, carve out space to reflect on your high school experience, express inner (or outer!) gratitude for the people, places, and moments that made it special, and start opening your mind to the possibilities of what's to come. Even if you aren't normally the type to meditate on your thoughts this way, doing so can give you a peaceful way to move from one life stage to another.

HOW TO SAY NO THANKS TO STRESS

High school can be stressful—with challenging classes, standardized tests, and the pressure of college or a career looming ahead. However, most high school students have their parents or other trusted adults at home as a built-in support network. When you move away from home, you must learn how to support yourself and build up your own new support network of local friends and mentors. This realization can be pretty overwhelming and trying to survive and thrive on your own can seem stressful. That said, here are some good habits to help you prevent stress before it escalates.

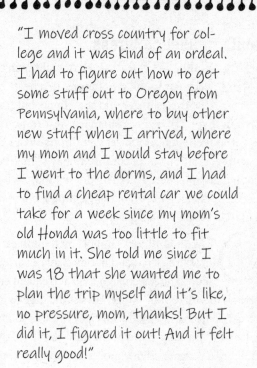

"I moved cross country for college and it was kind of an ordeal. I had to figure out how to get some stuff out to Oregon from Pennsylvania, where to buy other new stuff when I arrived, where my mom and I would stay before I went to the dorms, and I had to find a cheap rental car we could take for a week since my mom's old Honda was too little to fit much in it. She told me since I was 18 that she wanted me to plan the trip myself and it's like, no pressure, mom, thanks! But I did it, I figured it out! And it felt really good!"

Ace, College Freshman

Habits to Reduce Stress

 Sleep. Get at least seven or eight hours of sleep per night, if not more. In a hectic adult life, this is easier said than done, but it's well worth it. If you are trying to manage your responsibilities without enough rest to get you through your day, life will seem more out of control. It may seem like skipping an hour here and there doesn't matter, but it doesn't take long to run out of gas when you're not regularly getting enough sleep.

 Eat mindfully. It's important to both eat a nutrient-rich diet that represents a variety of foods and get enough food at frequent enough intervals to satiate your hunger. Resist the urge to give into fad diets, restrict food with rigid rules, or follow eating trends. Similarly, try to be mindful about not overindulging on sugars, highly processed foods, or certain fats, as doing so can make your brain feel foggy. Trust your body, feed it when it needs food, and try to incorporate a variety of wholesome nutrients into what you eat.

 Hang out with friends. It can feel like you don't have a lot of time to hang with your friends, but being with people you like and doing fun things is a necessary distraction. If you work too hard without these necessary social outlets, you'll burn out super quickly.

 Exercise. Fitting in at least 30 minutes of heart-pounding exercise is a great stress-buster, but so is getting in a long, leisurely walk. The point is to get moving in any way that feels good to you. When you exercise, your body releases endorphins, which can help you stress less, relax, and sleep better. Find lots of excuses to move your body. All movement counts!

Avoid vaping, smoking, drinking, or using excessive amounts of caffeine. Nicotine, alcohol, caffeine, and other mind-altering substances can actually make it harder for your body to fight stress. Alcohol and marijuana are both depressants that can impact your mood. Caffeine and nicotine are stimulants that can amp up your anxiety. For optimum brain function, these substances are better avoided.

 Simplify your expenses. Money can be a big stress factor. Try to make a budget and stick to it to reduce financial stress. If you are on a college campus, see if your school has resources for lower-income students. Otherwise, check to see what resources might exist in your county for those with lower incomes.

 Let your feelings out…don't just bottle them up. It takes time and energy to keep your feelings inside. Have regular conversations with your parent(s), siblings, friends, a counselor, or another trusted adult so that minor annoyances can be solved when they're still minor. It's particularly important to establish a clear and direct line of communication for roommate grievances, as this is a common source of stress. For those who live in college dorms, a resident advisor (RA) can help mediate if a roommate situation gets particularly tense.

 Organize your time. Prioritize and focus on dealing with certain parts of your life instead of trying to solve everything in one shot.

 Don't sweat the small stuff. One poor grade on a test or research paper will not ruin your entire life, as long as you don't let it. Take these difficulties in stride and learn from them so you can improve the next time around. Talk to your instructor and get connected with any resources you might need so you can get a better grade on your next assignment.

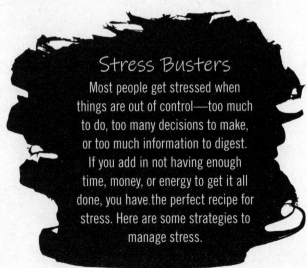

Stress Busters

Most people get stressed when things are out of control—too much to do, too many decisions to make, or too much information to digest. If you add in not having enough time, money, or energy to get it all done, you have the perfect recipe for stress. Here are some strategies to manage stress.

Habits to Manage Stress When It Arises

1 Alter the situation if you can and keep perspective if you can't.

Some things you can't control, and some things you can. Change the ones you can. If you can't change something, expending energy stressing about it won't help your situation. If you have too much on your plate and can't possibly do it all, figure out a way to put some things on the back burner. Maybe that means you need to be able to say no to extra demands or you need to devote less time to one aspect of your life. Concentrate on what is important. Make a list of your priorities from the most important to the least, then work your way down.

2 Avoid the situation—for now.

Step back and ask, "Is this really a problem? Do I really need to solve it now?" This doesn't mean you should procrastinate on things that need to get done. Think of this stress buster as buying some time, taking a break, catching your breath, getting advice, and airing out the situation so that you can deal with it when you're better prepared to handle it. Sometimes, it's as simple as just sleeping on it.

3 Accept the situation.

How you perceive your circumstances has a lot to do with how you make decisions about them. Put whatever is stressing you in the perspective of the big picture. How will this really affect me next year or even ten years from now? Remember to also consider whether the situation is temporary or permanent. If you know the stress will only last the next month and not a lifetime, it's easier to weather that month.

Quick Resets to Stress

In those moments when you are feeling like you're being pulled in a million directions, sometimes you just need a moment or two to reset. If you just need a quick distraction from unexpected anxiety or overwhelming feelings, use these ideas to help you reset.

Tips for Stressful Moments

- **PAUSE.** Pausing helps to slow down your instinctive reaction to stress. When we are overloaded, we often react first and think later. Pausing allows you to stop a potentially negative response and consciously say to yourself, "Hold on a minute." Pausing is often followed by breathing deeply, closing your eyes, and clearing your mind.

- **BREATHE DEEPLY.** Get in tune with the rhythm of your own breathing. Lie or sit down for 15 minutes, and just concentrate on relaxing. You can meditate or simply be silent for a while.

- **CLOSE YOUR EYES AND CLEAR YOUR MIND.** Visualize yourself in your favorite place: at the beach, under a tree, whatever works. Try and imagine yourself in the place with all your senses—what would you be able to see, smell, taste, hear, and touch?

- **DISTRACT YOUR MIND.** Take a walk or go for a jog. Take a shower. Listen to some soothing music. Turn on a guided meditation. Sometimes a quick, active distraction will clear your emotional reaction and allow you to think in a more rational manner.

- **WHEN ALL ELSE FAILS, WATCH A FAVORITE SITCOM OR A FUNNY VIDEO ON SOCIAL MEDIA.** Laughter really is the best medicine!

"I first figured out that I had ADHD and anxiety my freshman year because the workload just got so intense for me so fast. My psychiatrist said I had probably compensated with lots of coping mechanisms in high school, but college was just brutal by comparison. I'm glad I listened to my body and asked for help with how I was feeling. I learned that I wasn't imagining how hard it was to focus on lectures and that the scary sensation I'd feel before presentations was panic attacks, so now I'm working to manage all my symptoms and I can handle school so much better. If you ever feel like you're way more overwhelmed than you can manage, don't be afraid to talk to a doctor about what's going on with you. You have to take care of yourself and that includes your mental health."

Lydia, College Junior

TIME MANAGEMENT

Time can be an expensive resource when you waste it but when well-managed, time is a resource you can turn to your advantage. That said, even if you recognize the value of time, managing it is a challenge. When you live with enough time to fulfill all your needs and responsibilities, life is relaxed and balanced. To find that balance, you have to prioritize and plan. Decide what you want and what is important to you. Organize logically and schedule realistically. It may take practice and, ironically, a lot of time to become good at managing your time. If you are someone who hasn't had good time management historically, it could take even longer, but don't give up when you stumble. Instead, commit yourself to developing strong time management as a habit. After a while, it will get easier and easier to prioritize and to say no when you're overcommitted.

One of the greatest benefits of time management is that you can be in control. You have the same number of hours in each day; the key is in how to spend them. For some people, time management comes less naturally. People who have ADHD or who are juggling a lot of responsibilities, such as single parents, may struggle a lot more with time management than others. That doesn't mean it's impossible for those people to learn time management techniques; it's just important to recognize that if you are in that position, you might have to exert more discipline to manage your time. Doing so is ultimately worthwhile, though, for it allows you to feel in control of your own day-to-day life.

The tips on the next page are designed to help you spend your time wisely and to keep you in the driver's seat of your life.

Time Management Tips

- **UTILIZE A CALENDAR SYSTEM THAT WORKS FOR YOU.** Whether this is a paper planner or an electronic calendar, be sure to write down important deadlines so you can see a visual representation of what the next few days, weeks, and months look like. Plus, it feels good to cross accomplished tasks off your list! Hot tip: Color-coding your calendar can be a useful way to visually sort different types of events into categories.

- **BE REALISTIC ABOUT HOW MUCH YOU CAN REALLY DO.** Analyze how you spend your time now. What can you cut? How much time do you truly need for each task? Where in your schedule could you use time more efficiently?

- **THINK AHEAD.** How many times have you underestimated how long it will take to do something? Plan for roadblocks and give yourself some breathing space. It's never a bad idea to add a little "buffer" for important events, like leaving 10 minutes earlier than you think you need to make sure you're on time for an important meeting.

- **ACCEPT RESPONSIBILITY.** Once you decide to do something, commit yourself to it. Be consistent and specific about what you want to accomplish. Show up when you say you will so people know they can rely on you.

- **AVOID PROCRASTINATION.** There are a million ways to procrastinate and not one of them is good if you really want to get something done.

While procrastination is tempting, try to practice breaking work down into doable parts instead.

- **TACKLE THE HARDEST OR MOST UNPLEASANT TASK FIRST.** If you're dreading a task, get it over with when you have the most energy and are the freshest. Everything else will be easier from there.

- **LEARN TO SAY NO TO THE DEMANDS ON YOUR TIME THAT YOU CANNOT AFFORD.** Know your limits and don't be afraid to be assertive. The word *no* is a sentence all on its own. You don't have to offer an explanation if someone tries to pressure you to spread yourself too thin.

INDEPENDENT LIVING

As you consider moving away from home (either to a college dorm or your own place), you're likely pretty excited about the freedom that this experience can offer. When you're on your own, you can make your own decisions and rules. Your parent(s) or guardian(s) won't be able to exert the same level of day-to-day authority on you, even though they may check in every so often. However, the newness of living on your own will eventually wear off, and you'll soon realize that all the freedom you have comes with the burden of real responsibilities. Therefore, because living on your own is such a big decision, you should seriously weigh the options before you make the jump. Here are some ideas to keep in mind when you're considering if it's the right time to strike out on your own.

Things to Consider Before Moving Out on Your Own

- **Renting a place costs more than just rent.** Living on your own comes with a pretty obvious responsibility: paying rent. What you might not realize, though, is that moving out comes with far more financial responsibilities than just paying rent. Keep in mind that you have the added costs of utilities (like water, internet, trash, gas, electric, etc.), laundry, parking, and other expenses (such as giving first and last month's rent as a deposit).

- **Figuring out your medical insurance situation is important.** Your school or employer may offer plans to cover all (or some) of your healthcare expenses. Even so, you'll likely have to figure out some of this on your own. For instance, be sure you know how long you may remain on your parents' health plan, if applicable.

- **Food expenses add up quickly.** Groceries add up, but your food budget skyrockets the more you dine out. Your best bet to save money is to invest in cooking utensils, learn some basic cooking skills, and shop for ingredients you can keep as staples, like a pasta and sauce brand you know you like. Then, you can buy fresh ingredients like produce and dairy as needed. Cooking takes time and effort, so dining out sometimes happens, but try to make cooking a habit if you want to save on food expenses.

- **If you have a pet, your expenses go up.** We're not just talking food and supplies for the animal, but also things like pet deposits and pet rent, which can make your housing situation more expensive. Pets also need veterinary care, which could mean spending a few hundred dollars each year on check-ups and vaccinations alone. Find out what the pet policies are for any place you might be living. Usually, dorms do not allow any pet that isn't a service animal. Finally, it's harder to find places to rent that allow animals. Your options in your price range may be significantly narrowed, depending on the local rental market.

- **Managing money is complex.** Keeping track of all your expenses requires planning and organization. Using an app or software for budgeting helps, but you'll still need time and planning to set up a monthly budget and use it. On your own, you no longer have an "allowance" system, if that's something you had before. Instead, you'll have to figure out your own sources of income and keep track to make sure that you're bringing in more money than you're spending. Managing money in the real world is much more of a challenge, but it is certainly a rewarding opportunity for independence.

- **Making your own rules isn't all fun and games.** There can be a lot of growing pains learning time management and self-discipline. Juggling all the aspects of being independent is a tough task to accomplish. You'll have to consider your work schedule, maintenance of your living space and car, scheduling appointments, finding time for a social life, and much more. When you don't have someone around to help you with your schedule, you'll find yourself facing many pressures of living on your own that you may not have considered.

Remember, your parent(s) or guardian(s) can be your best source of help. Even though you're "on your own," don't be afraid to ask them for advice. They have lived on their own before (and have managed your life for many years), so they may be able to help you through those tough first few months on your own.

DRUGS AND ALCOHOL: ARE YOU AT RISK?

The legal drinking age in all fifty states is 21. At the federal level, it's also illegal to smoke or buy any tobacco product before age 18, and possession of any drug for recreational use is illegal, period. Some states have legalized marijuana for recreational use, but those that do also restrict its use to people 21 and over. So, if you drink alcohol before age 21; purchase or consume marijuana in states where it's not legalized or before age 21; smoke or buy cigarettes, cigars, vaping materials, or chewing tobacco before age 18; or take any illegal drugs, you could

- be arrested for driving under the influence (DUI)
- be convicted
- be required to pay steep fines
- have your driving privileges suspended or revoked
- get kicked out of school (that's any kind of school, college included)
- get fired
- go to jail
- end up with a criminal record

Keep in mind that many college dorm rooms also have strict rules about what is and is not allowed to be stored in the room or on a particular floor, so you could face extensive disciplinary action from your school if those items are found in your room, even if you did not consume them. Talk to your dorm roommates about your expectations regarding how to approach these rules as a room and don't be afraid to express concern if a roommate is breaking these rules without your consent.

How Can I Say No?

It's easy to preach about "just saying no" like the famous antidrug campaign you've maybe heard of, but in the heat of the moment, peer pressure can be a lot harder to resist. College parties tend to make using substances seem fun and exciting, so it can be difficult in the moment to remember your reasons for resisting the temptation to use drugs or alcohol. However, if you look closely at your college social circles, you'll

probably notice that a lot of your peers who do engage in these behaviors are suffering as a result. Whether it be hangovers, messy arguments, embarrassing antics, money difficulties from the cost of acquiring drugs or alcohol, legal trouble from getting caught, or even just generally doing too much partying when one should be studying, these behaviors can take a toll.

One thing that can keep you on the straight and narrow is thinking about all the work you've put in to get to college and recognizing that you want to be in your best form to continue to build on your successes. This makes it easier to say no to losing an entire weekend to partying hard and then dealing with the aftermath. Remember that friends worth having will respect your decision to say no. If a friend pressures you to drink or get high, don't spend time with that person—they're not a friend. Remember, too, the importance of never driving under the influence of anything. Take a rideshare, walk, whatever, but never operate a vehicle when impaired or get in a vehicle with someone who is.

Some Warnings and Cautions about Drugs and Alcohol

Despite the potential downsides, the reality is that some people will still choose to use drugs and alcohol. If you or your friends are partying and someone gets sick, make sure they get proper medical assistance. Keep an eye on your friends and make sure everyone is getting home safely. Even if you choose not to partake in these activities, they may still occur around you, so plan how you want to address related issues that come up when they do. Furthermore, if it seems that your or a friend's use of drugs or alcohol has become destructive, reach out to resources on campus designed to help students struggling with these issues. As one former user says, "It takes a lot more guts to stay sober, awake, and aware than to just get high [and] get numb." It's important to know that the potential for addiction is always there and to respond appropriately if you spot the signs of it. If a friend is trying to stay sober, be an ally and support that mission.

Along with the temporary pleasure they may give you, all drugs (including alcohol and nicotine) have a downside. Alcohol, for example, is a depressant. Even one drink slows down the part of your brain that controls your reasoning. This means your judgment becomes dull and impaired. Moreover, your body needs about an hour to burn up the alcohol in one drink (one shot of straight hard liquor, one glass of wine, or one 12-ounce beer). Despite rumors that coffee or water can help you get sober, the truth is that nothing will sober you up but the passing of time.

All of this means that alcohol and other drugs often contribute to smart people making bad decisions. Depending on what drug you take, how much, and what you do while you're on it, you're also risking confusion, nausea, headaches, sleep problems, depression, paranoia, decreased ability to defend against rape (especially "date rape"), unwanted pregnancy, sexually transmitted infections (STIs), having a baby with a birth defect, memory impairment, persistent psychosis, adverse medication reactions, lung damage, cancer, injuring or killing someone else, and even your own death.

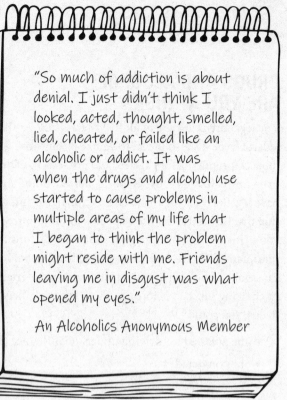

"So much of addiction is about denial. I just didn't think I looked, acted, thought, smelled, lied, cheated, or failed like an alcoholic or addict. It was when the drugs and alcohol use started to cause problems in multiple areas of my life that I began to think the problem might reside with me. Friends leaving me in disgust was what opened my eyes."

An Alcoholics Anonymous Member

Take a moment now, when your brain is razor-sharp, to decide if those consequences are worth the escape you get for an hour one night. Even though a single occasion getting drunk or high doesn't necessarily mean that you're an alcoholic or an addict, it always means at least some sort of loss of control. Some people may choose to take the risk anyhow, but it's important to recognize that impairment is always part of the package.

Do I Have a Problem?

On its website, the National Council on Alcoholism and Drug Dependence, Inc. (NCADD) offers a self-test for teenagers to determine how alcohol and/or drugs may be affecting their lives. If you are concerned about your use (or abuse) of alcohol and drugs, you may want to take this quick 20-question test at **https:// ncadd.org/for-youth/self-test- for-teens**. Here are some of the questions asked:

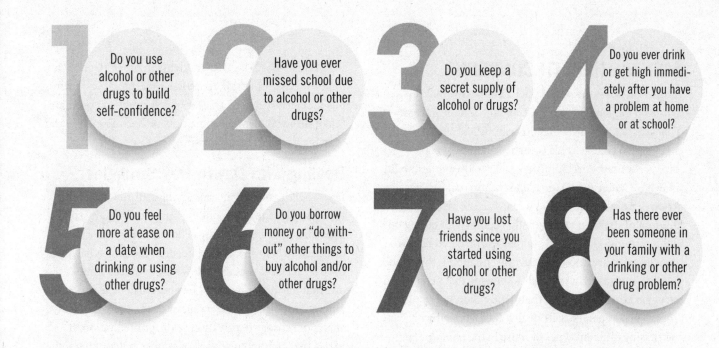

1 Do you use alcohol or other drugs to build self-confidence?

2 Have you ever missed school due to alcohol or other drugs?

3 Do you keep a secret supply of alcohol or drugs?

4 Do you ever drink or get high immediately after you have a problem at home or at school?

5 Do you feel more at ease on a date when drinking or using other drugs?

6 Do you borrow money or "do without" other things to buy alcohol and/or other drugs?

7 Have you lost friends since you started using alcohol or other drugs?

8 Has there ever been someone in your family with a drinking or other drug problem?

If you answered yes to any of these questions, there's a good chance you need help. If you have a friend who fits the picture, find a respectful way to bring up your concerns. Don't be surprised if your friend tells you to back off, but don't give up either. Also, if someone in your family has an alcohol or drug problem, be aware that you may be prone to the same tendency. According to NCADD, helping a friend or family member who is struggling with alcohol or drugs can be "heartbreakingly painful but, with help, it can be remarkably rewarding." It isn't easy, and you may want to ignore the problem and hope that it will just go away, but in the end, denying it will be "more damaging to you, other family members, and the person you are concerned about." Their advice: Don't wait—now is the time.

Where Can I Get Help?

If you think you have a problem, or if you think a friend has a problem, try Alcoholics Anonymous or Narcotics Anonymous. You may also want to find an NCADD affiliate, which can offer a range of services. For more information, go to **ncadd.org.**

In addition, health clinics and hospitals offer information and treatment. Organizations like the American Cancer Society can help you quit smoking. The graphic shows only a few of the places where you can get information and help; look online for more.

Where Can I Get Help?
Alcoholics Anonymous: www.aa.org

American Cancer Society: www.cancer.org

Narcotics Anonymous: www.na.org

National Council on Alcoholism and Drug Dependence, Inc. (NCADD): www.ncadd.org

Hope Line: 800-NCA-CALL (800-622-2255)

Student services on campus or city and county resources are available for people who are trying to separate themselves from substance dependence. If those resources don't work, sometimes the best first step is simply to talk to someone you trust. Your parents, trusted friends, counselors, doctors, or other confidants are good people to turn to for help in addition to all the aforementioned organizations.

MENTAL HEALTH CONCERNS

Addiction is not the only mental health issue that can come up for people your age. Late high school and early college is actually a very common time for mental health struggles to emerge. This is partially because people's brains continue developing into their mid-twenties, so it may have taken awhile for adult issues to make themselves known. Another reason has to do with the increased amount of stress and pressure that comes with taking on adult responsibilities. Still another reason could have to do with what are known as adverse childhood experiences (ACEs). Increasingly, research is showing that people who struggled through certain traumatic childhood experiences, such as parents getting divorced, enduring or witnessing different types of abuse in the home, or being around an addicted family member, are more likely to struggle with a broad range of health concerns in adulthood, both physical and psychological. The more ACEs a person has experienced, the more likely they are to struggle with mental and physical health issues in adulthood. Young adults with high ACE scores (tests can be done online) may find that living on their own for the first time gives them enough perspective to start recognizing the impact of ACEs on their current mental health.

In short, there are many different understandable reasons that young people may begin to recognize that their mental health is suffering when they strike out on their own. The important thing is to understand that there is nothing wrong with you as a person if you struggle with one of these issues. Mental health disorders are medical concerns like anything else; you wouldn't scoff at yourself for needing a physical therapist if you broke your leg so you shouldn't scoff at yourself if you need a therapist or medication to help you manage your depression, anxiety, ADD/ADHD, PTSD, or any other concern.

Dealing with a Mental Health Crisis

If you have a crisis, meaning an event that feels like an emergency, or if someone close to you is in crisis, reach out for help. For emergencies, you can call 911 to receive immediate assistance. After hours in dorms, an on-duty resident advisor (RA) or a member of campus security can get you in touch with the help you need. Resident advisors are fellow students who are trained to help deal with issues that arise with students in dormitories. For many, it is easier to talk to an RA first than to call campus security. It doesn't matter which route you take, just make sure you bring in some outside help. Don't try and manage a mental health crisis by yourself.

Dealing with Day-to-Day Struggles

If you have general concerns about your mental health, it's a good idea to reach out to your doctor. Many colleges also have a counseling center that is specifically designed to help students in need. In fact, most have drop-in services that can allow you to talk to someone that day or soon after. They may also have various amenities to help students relieve stress, such as massage chairs or sensory deprivation pods for meditation. It varies from school to school, of course, but looking into the counseling and therapy services available to you is a smart thing to do as soon as you get to campus—even if you don't end up needing them, it's good to know what's available. There should be lots of options on campus to help you address everything from a temporary event to a complex, long-term struggle.

If you ever feel like harming yourself or taking your own life, reach out 24/7 for free support:

1-800-273-8255 (National Suicide Prevention Hotline)

suicidepreventionlifeline.org (Lifeline)

Text HOME to 741741 (Crisis Text Line)

Call 911 or tell an RA or campus safety officer

You matter and your life matters. You deserve to live. Help is there if you need it.

The important thing is to make mental health a priority during this time. Don't ignore concerning behaviors if you feel them in yourself or spot them in people close to you. It's okay to lovingly talk to someone if you are concerned about them; you can even bring in an RA or a counselor to help you with the conversation. Take mental health matters seriously and look out for yourself and your friends.

SETTING AND HONORING BOUNDARIES

One aspect of adult life that doesn't seem to get talked about often enough is the importance of learning to both set boundaries and honor the boundaries others have set. Boundaries are important in all aspects of life. For instance, when you make a rule for yourself designed to create work/life balance, like "I won't answer phone calls from work after 6 p.m." or "I will save 3 hours on Saturdays for relaxation time," that's a boundary you have set with yourself and, where applicable, with others. By setting a boundary, you are saying what is and is not okay for you. It doesn't mean that you can't adjust your boundary later or have different boundaries for different people. It simply means that for now, this is the line you're drawing in the sand. The important thing about your personal boundaries is that you are the only one who can set and reset them.

Just like you want your boundaries respected, it's important that when someone sets a boundary for themselves, you respect it as well. For instance, if your roommate says, "I'm fine sharing groceries, but please don't touch my slice of cake," it would be objectively rude of you to then go eat their cake. If someone's boundary seems to violate yours, say if that same roommate said, "all cake that enters the fridge is automatically mine," then you have an opportunity to discuss how that violates your own boundaries and pose a discussion to reach a compromise. Learning how to assert and negotiate your own boundaries in relation to the reasonable boundaries of others is an important part of forming functional relationships as an adult, whether it be in your personal or professional life.

Keeping Consent in Mind

Consent is a form of boundary negotiation. When we talk about consent, what we mean is the act of asking permission to do a certain action to or with something or someone else. For example, if you wanted to borrow your friend's jacket, you would likely ask "Hey, can I borrow your jacket?" This is asking for consent. Your friend would then either say *yes*, meaning they consent to you borrowing it, or they could say *no*, meaning they do not consent to you borrowing it. Or they may consent, but with a condition (i.e., a type of boundary!), such as by saying "Yes, but please give it back by Friday, since I want to wear it this weekend." Consent discussions like this occur every day in a variety of contexts, so even though you may have heard consent discussed primarily in terms of sex and relationships, consent is important in all aspects of life. It's a framework that allows people to navigate each other's boundaries respectfully and securely.

Consent in Romantic Contexts

The reason that consent gets discussed so much in terms of love, sex, and relationships is that it's a place where consent is of the utmost importance, yet all too commonly overlooked. The topic of negotiating consent is an extensive one, but the basics boil down to this: it's important to ask for consent at the start of

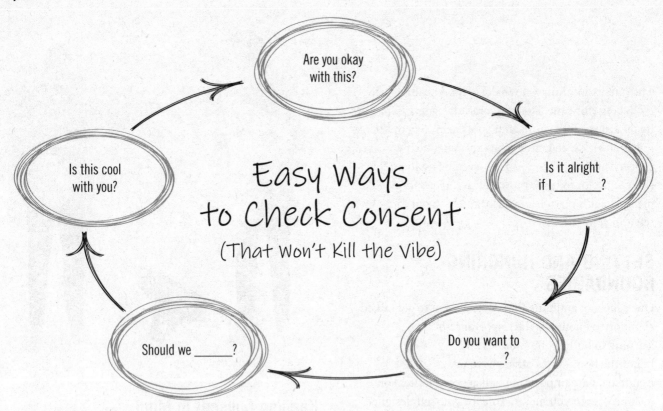

and throughout romantic encounters and relationships. Sexual contact without consent is sexual assault, plain and simple. This means that for someone to consent to intimacy, they must be conscious and of sound mind, meaning that they should not be impaired by drugs or alcohol. It also means asking directly if someone would like to receive a particular kind of contact from you. If you are ever in doubt, ask someone if they want the type of contact that you'd like to give them. It is your job to make sure you seek and receive consent from partners consistently throughout an encounter, including by watching their body language. If there is ever a question mid-encounter or you'd like to change to a type of contact that hasn't been discussed yet, check in.

Remember, you can always revoke consent. Just because you said "yes" before to some types of contact doesn't mean you can't change your mind and communicate that. For example, maybe you start engaging in mutual physical contact with someone at a party. After moving to another location, you decide you'd like to stop. Anyone who respects you and your boundaries will respect that decision, just as you should respect all boundaries communicated to you. This goes for any aspect of any encounter you're involved in.

Consent Outside of Romantic Contexts

Consent is also important in relationships that don't include a romantic context. For instance, if you have a friend who offers a lot of hugs but you're not much of a hugger, you have the right to tell your friend that you prefer high fives instead. Or maybe you have a friend who tends to tell others personal details about your life without your permission. You could absolutely have a discussion with that friend about what is okay for them to talk about (what you consent to) and what isn't (what you don't consent to). The more you think about consent in terms of all your social interactions (not just the ones that involve sex), the more you'll find that thinking about consent helps you foster both self-respect and respect for others. It helps you be more mindful of how honoring boundaries creates secure relationships and helps people build mutual trust. If thinking about your relationships in terms of consent seems new to you, know that it's a skill you can practice and improve upon over time. What's important is to keep at it until seeking consent is second nature.

Navigating Roommate Relationships

Unless you have had to share a room prior to moving out, a roommate relationship will probably be a completely new experience for you. This is especially true if you will be sharing a tiny dorm room with your roommate(s). Most people who live in the dorms will have one roommate, but you may have two or more, dependent on the size of your dorm room. There are a few different things you can do to make things easier on everyone who will be sharing a space.

Discuss Boundaries Early

On the first day you and your roommate(s) are together in your place, carve time out to have a sit-down discussion. Try and cover a variety of topics so that you can figure out which aspects of your lifestyles are compatible and which might not be. If you take the time to talk through important questions early on, it should nip most conflicts that arise in the bud. To assist with that task, the graphic on this page includes some questions you and any roommates can discuss on day one.

Questions for a First Roommate Meeting

- What time do you typically like to wake up on weekdays? What about weekends?

- What time do you typically like to go to bed on weekdays? What about weekends?

- Will you have any especially busy or early days in your schedule this semester?

- Do we want to establish "quiet hours" for our space and if so, what should they be?

- What expenses should be shared, and which expenses should be individual?

- What are your thoughts on sharing (or not sharing) groceries?

- How do we want to approach chores? What boundaries do you have about chores? For instance, is there one type of mess that bothers you much more than others?

- What should our policy be regarding guests? What about overnight guests?

- What communication style works best for you if a conflict arises?

- What rules would we like to collectively establish for our space and what should be the agreed upon consequence of violating a rule?

- What seems like a fair way to divide the space between us (especially if we don't have our own rooms)?

- Do you have any medical conditions or safety concerns you want me to be aware of as someone who is living with you?

- Is there anything you need to know about living with me? Is there anything you want me to know about living with you?

Once everything is on the table, decide together on some rules or guidelines for your shared space. If issues do come up, you'll have a common framework of agreements to come back to. You might even want to take notes or write up a formal roommate agreement that you can reference later.

Don't Let Issues Build Up

It's so easy to just go with the flow and not say anything when something with a roommate is bothering you. Nobody wants to rock the boat and most of us are conflict avoidant by nature, so we tend to bottle things up. However, stuffing your feelings down only makes it worse, namely because you'll resent your roomie more and more if they continue to do the same thing that they don't know drives you insane. A better policy? Learn how to bring up issues, both minor and major, calmly and early on rather than letting your frustrations build steam.

Two techniques that work well even if you're conflict avoidant or peeved in the moment are to avoid talking in extremes (the most, the worst) or absolutes (never, always) and to use "I" statements. If you phrase your frustration in terms of what you need and feel and avoid making it seem like the other person never does things right, you're less likely to make the person you're confronting defensive. Another tip is to offer a solution, when possible, rather than just identifying the issue. Consider these examples.

Effective Conflict Communication

- **INSTEAD OF:** "You never do the dishes and there are constantly disgusting pots and pans everywhere!"
  TRY: "I feel like I am cleaning significantly more dishes than I am dirtying and it's frustrating. It's awkward for me inviting friends over when there are often dirty pots all over the counter."

- **INSTEAD OF:** "You are the loudest person ever; turn your music down!"
  TRY: "I can't hear myself think and I really need quiet because I'm working on a paper. Could you please lower the volume?"

- **INSTEAD OF:** "Ugh, why do you never leave me any hot water?!"
  TRY: "I have class at 9 on Mondays and Wednesdays and really need to shower beforehand. Is there a chance we could work out a shower schedule?"

- **INSTEAD OF:** "Why the @#&%! are you on the phone at 6 a.m. every morning?!"
  TRY: "I noticed you've been making a lot of 6 a.m. phone calls, but I find it hard to sleep when that happens. Is there another time or place you could make those calls?"

A lot of times, handling something in the moment (or after you've had a little while to cool off and think on it) is better than waiting for weeks until the issue is such a nuisance that you snap.

Pick Your Battles

As important as it is to address issues head on, it's also important to choose your battles wisely. The person you are living with is not you and is not going to do things the same way you do. This is a reality of living with another human. Sure, if there are big issues to address, make sure to address them, but don't bring up every single little thing that annoys you about them, especially if it's inconsequential or something they

have no control over. If your roommate is stealing your chips, that's something worth discussing, but if you just don't like the way it sounds when they eat chips, get some earbuds.

Recognizing Abusive Behaviors

Unfortunately, the statistics for abuse among college-aged people are disturbing. While the tips we provide here are relevant to many different types of abuse, one of the most common forms of abuse experienced by college-aged people involves sexual violence or other forms of partner abuse. According to the Rape, Abuse & Incest National Network (RAINN), about 13% of all college students experience some form of sexual

WARNING SIGNS OF AN ABUSIVE PERSON

There are numerous red flags that you can watch out for when it comes to abusive behavior, including some not on this list. However, if someone has one or more of the common traits listed here, there's a good chance that you are dealing with an abuser.

- Over-the-top jealousy
- Frequent possessiveness
- Behaving in extremely controlling or highly unpredictable ways
- Harboring a bad temper
- Exhibiting cruelty towards animals, children, or other family members
- A tendency towards verbal abuse or "flying off the handle"
- Rigid or old-fashioned beliefs about gender roles, particularly regarding romantic relationships
- Disregard for their partners' sexual boundaries (sexual assault), including sabotaging birth control methods or refusing to honor agreements related to birth control
- Blaming their victims for their actions

- Sabotaging a victim's ability to work, go to school, and/or leave the house
- Hypervigilance about money and/or an insistence on controlling finances
- Making baseless accusations, particularly about flirting with others or the victim exhibiting "disrespect" towards the abuser
- Publicly embarrassing, shaming, humiliating, or demeaning their victims
- Harassing their victims, particularly at work or school
- Texting, calling, or visiting at too high a frequency, for too long of a duration, or at all hours of the night, particularly if their victim does not respond in between
- Engaging in cyberbullying behaviors against their victims

Source: National Coalition Against Domestic Violence, "Signs of Abuse," ncadv.org, accessed April 19, 2022, https://ncadv.org/signs-of-abuse.

SIGNS OF AN ABUSIVE PARTNER

An abuser will often…	This might sound like…
…deny that something happened or deny that what happened was all that serious.	"You're overreacting, lighten up." "I didn't push you that hard, you're fine." "I don't know what you're talking about.
…gaslight their victims, which means make their victims question their own reality.	"You're crazy, that never happened." "You're remembering it wrong; this is what actually happened…" "Oh, you're just confused, poor thing!"
…treat their victims like an object or like their personal property.	"Nobody talks to *my* girlfriend." "I made you, and I can ruin you." A friend saying, "My girlfriend gets mad if I'm not home by the curfew she gave me."
…appear successful or charismatic but be hiding low self-esteem and feelings of inadequacy or projecting their own insecurity onto another.	"I know you want to leave me for someone richer!" "I'll show you who's weak…" "Honey, girls like us just aren't attractive, we have to face it."
…blame their behavior on external circumstances instead of taking responsibility for it.	"Oh, come on, I was having a super stressful day." "You can't be mad—I was drunk!" "If you didn't get me so riled up, I wouldn't have screamed at you."
…act sweet and loving in between periods of being violent or cruel, usually to get back on their victim's good side.	"This time it's going to be different—I'm a new man." "That was a different person; I was wrong to ever take you for granted." "You mean the world to me—I could never do that again."
…appear deeply mistrustful, questioning their victims and making accusations.	"I know you're lying about just being friends with her; that's why I went through your phone." "Were you and your friends talking about me? I know you were. What did you say?" "I only keep a lock on the fridge because I know you can't be trusted."
…use threats to keep their victims complicit or quiet.	"How will you provide for the kids if you leave? You know a judge will give me custody." "If you tell anyone, I will hurt your cat." "No one will believe you, and you'll look pathetic."
…act different when others are around than behind closed doors.	Calling you names only when you're alone, changing to a kinder tone of voice or way of speaking in public, lying (or making their victims lie) to cover up what happens in private

Source: National Coalition Against Domestic Violence, "Signs of Abuse," ncadv.org, accessed April 19, 2022, https://ncadv.org/signs-of-abuse.

assault. More specifically, it is estimated that 26.4% of females, 6.8% of males, and 23.1% of transgender, genderqueer, or nonconforming undergraduate students will experience sexual assault. Of the sexual assaults that occur on campuses, more than 50% tend to happen between August and November when new students get to campus, and all students are at greater risk during their first year of college than in subsequent years. These statistics, while not meant to scare you, are sobering—the issue is pervasive, making it all the more important to maintain vigilance towards potential signs of abuse. Beyond sexual violence, abuse can take the form of emotional, verbal, psychological, or physical violence toward or coercion of partners, friends, roommates, employees, and loved ones, so know that while these tips are general, specific abusive behaviors could look different in different contexts. If you are ever unsure if the behavior you've witnessed or experienced is abusive, it is a good idea to make an appointment to talk to a counselor about it.

Speaking Up for Yourself and Others

It can feel really scary and, in certain cases, dangerous to speak up if you or someone you know is being abused or otherwise having their boundaries violated. If you are in a crisis, look out for number one and protect yourself by any means necessary. Don't just go with the flow to be polite if you sense something amiss; instead, trust your instincts and get out of the situation, if you can. In a noncrisis, when possible, it is commendable to use your voice to stand up for yourself or others, but know that there are also often ways to get support in the matter. Counseling services on campus, for instance, may have mediators, security officers, or other third parties that can help you navigate difficult situations, like helping a friend move out of her abusive partner's place. Don't be afraid to reach out to the various student services on campus (or, if you're off campus, to social services or other resources in your area) to get help taking on serious issues that may arise as you navigate adult life.

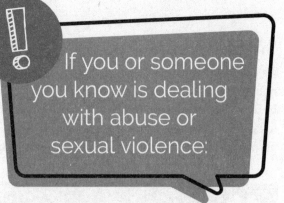

If you or someone you know is dealing with abuse or sexual violence:

- National Domestic Violence Hotline: 1-800-799-7233
- Text START to 88788
- RAINN Sexual Violence Hotline: 1-800-656-4673 or Live Chat at rainn.org
- Tell a mentor you trust and ask for guidance getting resources
- Reach out to counseling services on campus
- Contact the police or campus safety to make a report

You deserve to feel safe and secure in your relationships. Reach out to the hotlines above for free, confidential, anonymous help 24/7 or contact resources on campus. There *is* hope.

SAFETY ON CAMPUS AND IN LIFE

As you head towards adulthood, one thing you might not have thought about before is how different it will be to walk through life without a "grown-up" around to keep an eye on you. One minute you have to ask permission to go to the bathroom during French class and the next you're expected to live, work, get around, pay bills, sign important documents, and socialize as a fully independent adult being. Life without adults to oversee and monitor you can be exciting and fulfilling, obviously, but it can also be challenging and even, at times, dangerous. Keep in mind the following tips for avoiding rough situations.

TIPS TO KEEP YOU SAFER ON CAMPUS (AND ELSEWHERE)

- Walk like you're in charge and you know where you're going.
- When walking around at night, stick to well-lit areas.
- Travel with a trusted friend when possible. On campus, especially if you'll be walking alone, get an escort from security at night.
- If a person or group up ahead makes you nervous, cross the street immediately—and calmly—as if you'd intended to anyway.
- Call out to an imaginary friend, "Hey, Joe! Wait up!" and then run toward your "friend," away from whoever is scaring you.
- If it feels like someone might be following you, pretend to be on a phone call (or better, call a friend for real) and loudly but casually say where you are: "Hey, yeah, I'm just walking back from the library, I'm by the athletic center pond right now."
- Go right up to the nearest house and ring the bell. Pretend you're expected: "Hey Sam, it's me!" You can explain later.
- When you are in a social situation involving open containers, don't leave your drink unattended. When holding it, try to keep the opening covered with your hand or in your sight. Don't accept a drink you didn't see get made or opened.
- If someone assaults you, scream, kick where it hurts, scratch—anything.

- If someone threatens you physically, scream and shout, "No!" as loud as you can…more than once if you need to.
- Don't ever get in a car with someone you don't know well or trust, even if you've seen that person around a lot.
- Don't go home with people you don't know.
- Strike up a conversation with an innocent bystander if you feel threatened by someone else, just to make yourself less vulnerable for a few minutes.
- Wear a whistle around your neck or carry a personal alarm or pepper spray.
- If someone mugs you, hand over your purse, wallet, phone, jewelry, whatever—none of it is worth your life.
- Don't go along with something your gut says is wrong, no matter who says it's OK. Trust your instincts.
- Keep some essentials in both your home and car. Things like a flashlight, bottled water, nonperishable food, a first aid kit, a clean change of warm clothes, and a blanket can come in clutch when you least expect it.
- Always carry a charged cell phone.
- Take a self-defense course so you can defend yourself or someone else if something does happen.

Preparing for College and Adult Life

Of course, if something bad does happen to you, it's not your fault for failing to prevent it. Don't let yourself drown in guilt thinking that you should have or could have done more, because an attack or other crime is the fault of the perpetrator(s) alone. However, the tips mentioned here can hopefully help reduce your risk of falling into a dangerous situation and will help you better protect yourself if danger does come knocking.

Notes

You and the Workplace

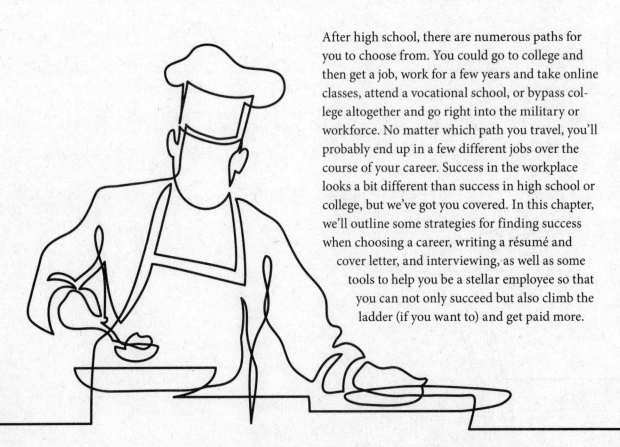

After high school, there are numerous paths for you to choose from. You could go to college and then get a job, work for a few years and take online classes, attend a vocational school, or bypass college altogether and go right into the military or workforce. No matter which path you travel, you'll probably end up in a few different jobs over the course of your career. Success in the workplace looks a bit different than success in high school or college, but we've got you covered. In this chapter, we'll outline some strategies for finding success when choosing a career, writing a résumé and cover letter, and interviewing, as well as some tools to help you be a stellar employee so that you can not only succeed but also climb the ladder (if you want to) and get paid more.

The Short and Sweet Version

You did it! You graduated high school, vocational training, or college and now, you're ready to enter the workforce. Congratulations on embarking on your career journey! Now comes the part where you have to find a job, nail the interview, and succeed in your new workplace. No pressure, right?

The good news is that just like success in high school or college, success in the workplace mostly involves knowing what to expect, planning ahead, organizing yourself and your schedule, and showing up with a positive attitude, ready to tackle your responsibilities. This chapter is loaded with tips on stuff like writing a résumé, maximizing the impact of your cover letter, interviewing well, and making a good impression with your coworkers. By the way, if you're considering staying in the military as a career or starting a new career there after college, you'll find more insights in Chapter 5.

One thing to understand is that for people your age, work no longer looks like it did for the last generation or those before them. What we call a "career" now may mean having lots of different jobs over the course of a lifetime, pursuing independent contract work alongside a "day job," or working remotely most of the time. Work is shifting and young people today will have to shift with it, but that's also the good news: there's more flexibility in the new normal, too.

Once you've perfected your application materials, used these tips to help you make a great impression on the job interview, and adapted to your new work environment, then you're off to a great start. Your prospects are bright, too—after implementing all the tools you've learned in this book, there's no stopping you from achieving what you set out to achieve!

CHOOSING A CAREER

As you make decisions about which jobs to pursue, keep in mind that the nature of work is changing. Some industries are thriving, others are stagnating, and some are mixed. There are a lot of factors at play here, with the COVID-19 pandemic being the most significant one. The COVID-19 pandemic has resulted in significant job shortages, primarily in service-oriented industries, such as healthcare, education, retail, and food service, as well as manufacturing and logistics. While it's hard to predict how long these shortages might last, their impact will likely be felt for years to come. When deciding on your career path, consider how the future of work might affect your choices and which industries and occupations are growing the fastest.

The Future of Work

When thinking about your own career path, consider that in our contemporary world, who does the work, when and where work is done, and how people work is all changing. When it comes to who does the work, corporations and organizations typically use some combination of full-time employees, part-time employees, and independent contractors. Full-time work usually comes with benefits, meaning paid time off, sick time, health insurance, a retirement fund, and more. Part-time work does not usually come with benefits, meaning that if you want to go on vacation or need to take a sick day, you will not be compensated for time that you didn't work. Some employers do provide part-time employees with benefits, but jobs at these employers will likely be more competitive as a result.

Independent contractors, sometimes also called freelance workers in certain industries, are contracted to do work for an employer but are not typically considered employees. Depending on the contract, benefits may or may not be offered. As a result, independent contractors are usually paid at higher rates to compensate for any additional expenses they incur from taxes, healthcare, etc. However, independent contractors may have to compete with other independent contractors to land jobs.

The COVID-19 pandemic accelerated trends related to when and where work gets done, meaning more employers have transitioned to offering remote work options or flexible work schedules. At the height of the pandemic, when people had to work from home for an extended period of time, companies quickly realized that employees could be just as productive, if not more so, from the comfort of home. Employers also recognized how having employees work remotely could save on major business expenses, such as office space, utilities, and other costs required to maintain an office workplace. During remote work, many workers saw the benefits of working remotely and avoiding long commutes to work in a physical office. While some jobs, like service-oriented jobs, cannot be done remotely, many office jobs simply require a computer and an internet connection, making it possible to work from anywhere. That being said, some types of work cannot be done remotely all the time, so many employers have opted for a hybrid work model, meaning employees can work partly from home and partly in the office. For the foreseeable future and depending on your career path, you can expect to see more and more remote and hybrid jobs, so you'll have more flexibility when it comes to choosing the work model that works best for you.

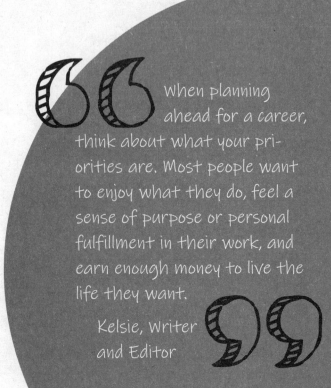

When planning ahead for a career, think about what your priorities are. Most people want to enjoy what they do, feel a sense of purpose or personal fulfillment in their work, and earn enough money to live the life they want.

Kelsie, Writer and Editor

Finally, keep in mind that how work is done has changed because of artificial intelligence, robotics, and automation. Some jobs have been, or have the potential to be, almost entirely automated. These jobs can be done by computers, robots, or other technology, requiring minimal human intervention. Other jobs are often done in tandem with some form of automated technology. Think of how easy it is to place an order online and pick it up from a local restaurant. You can customize your order through an app, then drive over, walk inside (or even wait curbside), and pick it up. You can complete the entire process with minimal human interaction. Jobs in the service industry, like cashiers, food-service workers, and customer service representatives, are particularly vulnerable to automation. As the capabilities of machines expand, other jobs will be susceptible to automation as well, but it's hard to predict which jobs will eventually be automated. Pursue the job you want, and as you progress through your career, be open to the idea of changing fields, acquiring new skill sets, or pursuing additional education as needed to secure a more stable position.

Growing Industries and Occupations

While technology has led to the automation of certain jobs, it has also created numerous industries and career paths that we could have never before anticipated. The technology sector has experienced incredible growth, resulting in innovative new jobs. You can expect that jobs related to artificial intelligence, information technology and security, cloud computing, software development, and social media will continue to increase for the foreseeable future.

Prior to the COVID-19 pandemic, the healthcare industry was already booming. However, as a result of the pandemic, a renewed focus on public health, preventing future pandemics, and researching treatments has ensured that the healthcare industry will continue to grow and evolve. New vaccines, treatments, and technologies have also radically changed what's possible when it comes to helping patients not only with COVID-19 but also HIV/AIDS, Alzheimer's, dementia, cancer, and other ailments. As science progresses, one can expect new fields and needs to emerge in this industry as a result. Recent shortages in these fields also mean that there is likely to be a lesser degree of competition for jobs in this industry than in others.

Similar to healthcare for humans, the world of veterinary care is changing as well. Attitudes about pet ownership and animal wellness have shifted dramatically, meaning many people want to give their pets the best food, supplements, and veterinary care possible. Specialties in veterinary medicine now include oncology, nutrition, sports medicine and rehabilitation, neurology, cardiology, and more. With more treatment options available, pets are living longer, healthier, and happier lives.

In response to climate change, renewable energy technologies have become more desirable. Occupations that focus on conserving energy, developing alternative energy, reducing pollution, or recycling will become increasingly more commonplace over time. Clean energy is also important in the manufacturing of homes and buildings and in designing more sustainable transportation methods. One can assume that any career that interacts with clean energy is sure to have some long-term sustainability in the 21st century.

In addition to these industries, there are a few sectors with conflicting forecasts. For example, prior to the COVID-19 pandemic, manufacturing was generally considered to be declining due to automation. However, worldwide lockdowns and travel bans have had a significant effect on the global supply chain, resulting in inflation and shortages of certain goods. Public opinion is moving toward reducing consumer dependence on imports by producing more goods in the United States, especially critical medical supplies such as face masks, vaccines, and pharmaceuticals. As a result, occupations in manufacturing and logistics might end up growing instead of shrinking, as was once predicted.

Similarly, while education itself isn't necessarily growing quickly, there has been a shortage of educators for years. While this shortage stems partially from frequently difficult working conditions for educators, aspiring teachers should rest assured that their career prospects are likely good as a result. Furthermore, remote instruction has resulted in the need for educational technologists who can use technology to design effective curriculum. Video has become an increasingly popular medium for remote education and training, so video producers and editors are in higher demand, too.

Tourism and the hospitality industry are always fluctuating in response to global influences, such as seasonal fluctuations, economic climate, political factors, and more. For example, tourism took a major hit due to travel restrictions intended to curb the COVID-19 pandemic. As a result, this sector tends to be more volatile, meaning there is more unpredictability when it comes to certain job forecasts. Sometimes, it just depends on which job you're looking at within a sector. Flight attendants, for example, have a much better job outlook than travel agents.

When looking ahead at how the future of work will continue to change, keep this in mind: You can always change your mind and pursue a different job or career. In the past, a worker would graduate from college, get a job, and stay at that job or company for decades before retiring. But with the advent of the internet, social media, and various technologies, changes happen more quickly and have a wide range of impacts on industries and companies alike. As a result, people tend to switch jobs more frequently than they did in the past.

As a worker in the 21st century, you'll likely have many jobs during your lifetime, and you might even change careers a few times. Don't let that scare you. As jobs become more nuanced and complex, it's okay to change your mind and decide that you might enjoy something else. In fact, while this cultural shift may seem less secure, it also has the potential to unlock limitless possibilities; for instance, you're less likely to get locked into a career path you hate or be unable to adapt if your life circumstances change. The key is to keep your options open and to be flexible. Figure out what you enjoy and how you envision your typical workday. Consider things like whether you enjoy working with people or on your own, how much money you need or want to make, how much responsibility you want to have, what kind of schedule you want to work, and whether you prefer working with your hands or sitting at a computer. You might also think about how certain career paths may look as your life evolves; for example, if you know for sure that you want to have children one day, you may consider which industries are accommodating to people with families. Then, decide what career path makes the most sense and what education or training you'll need.

"I've had to make a career pivot a few times. Initially, I got a Ph.D. to become a college professor. All the feedback I got during grad school was that I'd do great, but the full-time academic jobs dried up for everyone. I tried teaching high school, freelancing, tutoring, coaching, grading standardized exams, and an assortment of odd jobs, and I eventually landed in a full-time position that works for me. It's okay to take a leap and try something new. You'll land somewhere good if you work the skills you have."

Lacey, Writer and Editor

JOB HUNTING

When you've decided on a career path, you'll need to start looking for jobs in your desired field. A lot of the job search boils down to marketing yourself. You can use several approaches to market yourself successfully. Networking (the continual process of contacting recruiters, relatives, friends, and any other connections you might have) is a great way to get information about job openings. Job search engines will likely be your best option, but it's even better if you have a connection at the company or organization where you want to work. Referrals from friends, family members, and former colleagues can be a great way to get ahead in the job search. From the employer's perspective, hiring someone recommended by an employee is less risky than hiring someone unknown. Recruiters are also an increasingly valuable resource for matching applicants with positions or prospective employers. Everyone has a primary network of people they know and connect with frequently. Those acquaintances know and talk to networks of their own, thereby creating a secondary network for you and multiplying the number of individuals who know what you're looking for in a job.

It's hard to understate the value of networking during the job search. If you haven't created one yet, make sure that you sign up for a LinkedIn profile. As you progress through your career, LinkedIn allows you to stay in touch with your former coworkers, make new connections with recruiters and other people in your industry, and search for jobs. There are even specialized groups and forums where you can ask questions of other people in your field or get a referral for a position. You can also solicit endorsements or recommendations from your connections if you're applying for jobs and need someone to attest to your skills. A solid LinkedIn profile and a supportive network can help you stand out from the crowd when applying for your next job.

The following tips can help as you begin the job hunt:

- Job hunting takes time. For each job you apply for, you'll need to make sure you tailor your résumé and cover letter to the position.

- Prepare yourself for the fact that you'll likely receive far more rejections than acceptances. Remember that even if you get a *no* a dozen times, you only need one *yes*!

- Don't get discouraged when employers don't follow up. The best jobs will likely have numerous applicants, and even if the hiring manager has the best intentions, they probably can't respond to everyone.

- Consider taking a temporary job while you continue the job hunt. It will help pay the bills and give you new skills to boost your résumé at the same time.

- When possible, try to have a new job lined up before you quit your current job.

- Research the company before your interview to show that you understand the position, the company's needs, and the office culture.

- Keep careful records of your contact with prospective employers.

- Don't ignore any job leads—act on every tip you get.

- You don't have the job until you sign an offer letter, so try not to get your hopes up too high until then.

With all these thoughts in mind, you should be ready and confident to begin the process of marketing yourself, and that's a major part of being successful in your job hunt.

As mentioned, you can find jobs through your network of friends, family, and acquaintances as well as through job search engines. The following are some popular websites that not only aggregate job postings but also offer information on résumé writing, interviewing, and other important career advice.

indeed.com

glassdoor.com

linkedin.com

jobs.google.com

monster.com

careerbuilder.com

ziprecruiter.com

PUTTING TOGETHER YOUR RÉSUMÉ

The internet has made it easier to find jobs, so that means more competition. Now, with the rise of remote work due to the COVID-19 pandemic, you'll find yourself competing with candidates all over the country. Getting a job means marketing yourself: your skill set, your experience, and most of all, what you can offer to a potential employer. One of the most critical steps to getting a job is putting together a great résumé. A résumé is a document that provides a concise overview of your skills, experience, and education. Whenever you apply for a job, your résumé should be concise, persuasive, and tailored to the job posting. Here are some strategies for putting together a resume.

Parts of a Résumé

A typical résumé should include the following components:

1 HEADING: Centered at the top of the page should be your name, phone number, a professional email address (for example, abril.olivas@blakehighschool.com and not harrystylesfan32@email.com), and personal website or LinkedIn page (if applicable).

2 PROFESSIONAL PROFILE/SUMMARY OF QUALIFICATIONS: In a few sentences, summarize your experience and strengths, focusing on the types of jobs and careers you're pursuing. You should also include skills or core competencies that are directly relevant to the job you are applying for. This section will look different depending on the type and level of position you are applying for, so make sure this aligns closely with the job posting. Typically, a job posting will outline their minimum or desired qualifications, so look there to help you decide what to include in this section of your résumé.

3 EDUCATION: Beginning with your most recent school or program, include the date (or expected date) of completion, the degree or certificate earned, and the location of the institution. Don't overlook any workshops or seminars, self-directed learning, or on-the-job training in which you have been involved. If any courses particularly lend themselves to the type of work for which you are applying, include them. Mention grade point averages and class rank if they are especially impressive.

4 WORK EXPERIENCE: If you don't have any, skip this section. If you do, begin with your most recent employer and include the date you left the job, your job title, the company name, and the company location. If you are still employed there, simply enter your start date and "Present" (e.g., 2015–Present) for the date. Include notable accomplishments for each job. High

school and college students with little work experience shouldn't be shy about including summer or part-time jobs as lifeguards, babysitters, pet sitters, landscaping workers, servers, or retail associates. Showing that you have enough part-time experience is a good way to demonstrate that you are ready for the increased responsibility of a full-time job.

5 VOLUNTEER EXPERIENCE: If you don't have professional work experience, volunteer experience can be a good substitute on your résumé. Like you would with a work experience section, begin with your most recent volunteer position and work backwards. For each position, include the start and end dates of your position (or the start date and "present" if you still volunteer there, e.g., 2015–Present). You should also include your position title, the organization name, and the organization location. Include notable accomplishments for each position.

6 EXTRACURRICULAR LEADERSHIP OR RELEVANT EXPERIENCE: Maybe you haven't had a part-time job yet, but you served as Student Council Vice President or were the captain of your volleyball team. Those experiences with leadership are valuable to employers and are worth including. Furthermore, if you are applying to a position that is relevant to an extracurricular you participated in, make sure to mention it. For instance, you may be applying to work as a farm hand and have extensive experience with 4H. Employers will want to know if you've done something that helped you develop any relevant skills.

7 HONORS AND AWARDS: This section can help boost your résumé if you don't have a lot of work or volunteer experience. At the high school level, you might list National Merit Scholarships, President's Education Awards, school subject awards, and more. At the college level, this can include scholarships, grants, dean's list, honors societies, or other unique accomplishments.

8 LANGUAGES (OPTIONAL): If you speak a language other than English, add it to your résumé. When including languages on your résumé, you should specify your degree of fluency. If you only took a year of Spanish, then you probably wouldn't add it to your résumé. But if you are bilingual in both Spanish and English, then include both and specify your degree of fluency in each: native/bilingual, highly proficient, or proficient.

9 TECHNICAL SKILLS (OPTIONAL): Depending on the types of jobs you're applying for, you may or may not need this section. To get a good sense of whether you do, look at postings for the type of job you want. If there are several programs or tools you'll need to know for the position, then a technical skills section would be good to include on your résumé. If there are only a few important skills you'll need to know, you can just include those in your Professional Profile instead. This section doesn't refer to typical software experience, like Microsoft Word, but rather specialized technical skills required for the career you're pursuing. For example, if you're applying for a job as a photographer, you would list Adobe Photoshop in this section. If you're applying for a job as a web developer, you could include the different programming languages you know, like HTML or Python.

Sample High School Student Résumé

Xiaonan Li

Denver, CO 80210
720-555-0976

xiaonan.li@blakehs.com
www.linkedin.com/xli

Summary of Qualifications
Motivated and self-disciplined high school student with a 3.85 GPA and two years of experience in HTML and search engine optimization. Core competencies include:

- HTML
- IT Support
- Search Engine Optimization (SEO)
- WordPress

Education
Blake High School – Denver, CO

High School Diploma   (expected) 5/2022
GPA – 3.85

Volunteer Experience
Denver Public Library – Denver, CO   8/2021 – Present
Technology Support Assistant

- Provide one-on-one training in computer literacy to library patrons.
- Update announcements on library website.
- Troubleshoot hardware and software issues with library technology.
- Install and upgrade software on library computers.
- Improved library patron satisfaction score by 24%.
- Created reservation system for use of computers and 3D printers.

Blake High School – Denver, CO   5/2021 – Present
Assistant Web Developer

- Complete online tutorials and lessons in HTML and CSS.
- Implement SEO strategies when writing web content.
- Draft wireframes to design new web pages.

Honors and Awards
- **2021:** National Student Volunteer Award
- **2020:** National Merit Semifinalist
- **2019:** Perfect Attendance Award

Languages
- English—Native/Bilingual
- Chinese (Mandarin)—Native/Bilingual

Sample College Graduate Résumé

XIAONAN LI

Denver, CO 80210
720-555-0976

xiaonan.li@unwc.edu
www.linkedin.com/xli

PROFESSIONAL PROFILE

Skilled front-end web developer with two years of experience creating responsive websites for ecommerce shops. Core competencies include:

- HTML
- CSS and Bootstrap
- UI/UX Design

- JavaScript, jQuery, and React
- WordPress
- Search Engine Optimization (SEO)

EDUCATION

University of Northwestern Colorado – Steamboat Springs, CO

B.S. in Information Systems   5/2020
GPA – 3.85

CAREER SUMMAR

Lightbox, Inc. – Denver, CO   6/2020 – Present
FRONT-END WEB DEVELOPER

- Build custom ecommerce cart from scratch with full private API and website integration.
- Optimize existing front-end code for improved performance and responsiveness.
- Conceptualize and develop a new package structure, product database, and product API.
- Transition front-end framework from jQuery to React.

Frisco Community College – Frisco, CO   5/2018 – 5/202
HELP DESK TECHNICIAN

- Customized and managed forms and workflows in a Microsoft Dynamics CRM environment.
- Coordinated responses to customer requests in Jira.
- Reduced response time from 72 hours to 24 hours for customers by improving coordination with IT team.

LANGUAGES

- English—Native/Bilingual
- Chinese (Mandarin)—Native/Bilingual

Strategies for Writing a Résumé

Whenever you apply for a job, your résumé should be concise, persuasive, and tailored to the job you're applying for. Here are some strategies for putting together a resume.

1 TAILOR YOUR RÉSUMÉ TO THE JOB POSTING. Remember that your résumé is your opportunity to align your skills and experience with the needs of the employer. When you apply to a job, revise your résumé to emphasize the skills and experience they're looking for and use keywords from the job posting. A lot of companies use applicant tracking systems, which scan your résumé for keywords before sending your application to the next stage of review. You can get creative with how you fit these words into your résumé. For instance, if the job posting mentions the word *creative*, then you can fit that into the posting by mentioning your creative problem-solving, highlighting your creative mind, or mentioning experience in creative writing. It matters that the keywords can be found when the résumé is scanned, but it's up to you how you fit in those keywords—try to think outside the box so that you can do so while also showcasing who you are.

2 ILLUSTRATE AND QUANTIFY YOUR EXPERIENCE WITH SPECIFIC EXAMPLES. When you list your work or volunteer experiences, the goal is to show how you made a difference in your position. In addition to outlining your responsibilities, this is your chance to demonstrate how you effected change wherever you worked or volunteered. For example, instead of "Filed paperwork for multiple clients," highlight things you did that improved how the organization runs. If you recommended a better strategy for communicating with clients or for keeping track of paperwork, emphasize that in one of your bullet points: "Improved filing system to better organize records for 50+ clients." Quantifying your experience by providing numbers and percentages is even better because it provides specific evidence of how you made a difference in your position.

3 KNOW WHAT A RÉSUMÉ FOR YOUR CAREER PATH SHOULD LOOK LIKE. Everyone has a different opinion of what a résumé should look like. Depending on what field you go into, you'll need to research what employers look for when they review your application materials. Generally, a résumé should list your experiences in reverse chronological order to show the progression of your skills. For now, don't stress if you don't have much on your résumé. You'll add to and revise your résumé as you progress in your career, but meanwhile, focus on showcasing your strengths and experiences that are directly relevant to the position you want.

Tips for Writing Your Résumé

- Keep the résumé short and simple. Although more experienced applicants may use as many as two or three pages, recent high school or college graduates should limit themselves to one page.

- Use specific but concise bullet points to summarize responsibilities and accomplishments in different positions.

- Use keywords from the job posting to show you're a good fit for the position.

- Be honest: Don't lists skills or competencies that you don't actually have.

- Don't include information about salary or wages.

- Use present tense when describing the day-to-day responsibilities of a job you still work at. Use past tense to describe accomplishments you've completed at your current job or to describe a job experience you did in the past.

- Edit and proofread your résumé for grammatical errors and typos.

- For most jobs, your résumé should be a straightforward, black and white document with no pictures, clipart, etc. But if you're in a more creative field, consider using graphic design software to create a more visually appealing résumé.

- Update your résumé frequently, whenever you get a new job or learn a new skill. That way, it's easier to keep track of the jobs you've worked and the skills you've learned.

- Some jobs only require a résumé, but including a cover letter can help you showcase your writing skills and stand out above the competition.

ADDITIONAL JOB APPLICATION MATERIALS

In addition to your résumé, you'll likely be asked to submit other materials, depending on the type of job you're applying for. Here, we discuss how to write a cover letter, and we've included a sample cover letter for reference. Then, we discuss portfolios and skills assessments.

The Cover Letter

Usually, a résumé should be accompanied by a cover letter. A cover letter is an opportunity for you to speak more about your most impressive accomplishments, skills, and experiences. When you include a cover letter, not only are you giving your potential employer a sample of your writing but you're also showing that you care enough to illustrate how you're the best fit for the job.

Oftentimes, the hiring manager is listed on the job posting, but if not, include the phrase "Dear Hiring Manager" at the start of your letter. Although you'll want to keep your letter brief, introduce yourself and specify the position you're interested in and why. Be sure to mention who referred you or where you found the job posting. In the body of the cover letter, focus on drawing a clear connection between your experiences and accomplishments and the needs of the employer. For example, if the job requires you to have two years of experience in a technical support role, then be sure to discuss your relevant experience but in a way that shows you will anticipate and meet the employer's needs. Don't just say you have two years of experience in a technical support role. Explain how, in your two years in that role, you improved resolution times by 18% or increased customer satisfaction by 26%.

Finally, your cover letter should end with a call to action. Typically, this is where you invite the employer to contact you if they have any questions about your qualifications or if they want to schedule an interview. Even though your cover letter header should match the header on your résumé, be sure to mention your desired contact information in the closing paragraph of your cover letter. While some jobs invite you to contact them to follow up, most employers will discourage you from contacting them directly to check on the status of your application. Instead, if there's some kind of applicant portal, you may be able to check the status of your application there.

After submitting a job application, many employers unfortunately don't follow up with prospective applicants. This can be discouraging, but don't let it get you down—just keep looking. If you do get a response, you might be asked to complete a screening with human resources (HR) first to make sure that you meet the minimum qualifications. Ideally, you'll be invited to an interview with the hiring manager. Regardless, make sure to do your best at each and every stage of the hiring process.

> Think of a cover letter as a complement to your résumé. While a résumé is a comprehensive overview of your skills and experience, a cover letter gives you the space to write more in depth about a specific project, experience, or situation that highlights your most impressive qualifications. Try to outline a specific challenge or problem you experienced at work, discuss how you handled the situation, and emphasize how you were able to resolve the issue with positive results.
>
> Olive, Career Coach

Sample Cover Letter

Xiaonan Li

Denver, CO 80210
720-555-0976

xiaonan.li@blakehs.com
www.linkedin.com/xli

March 22, 2022

Dear Hiring Manager,

I am writing to express my interest in the Junior Web Designer position at Lightbox, Inc., which I recently found on LinkedIn. I am confident that my year of experience using HTML and CSS to design front-end web applications makes me an excellent fit for this position.

Currently, I volunteer as a Technology Support Assistant at the Denver Public Library. In this role, I am responsible for using HTML and WordPress to update announcements on the library website and help keep patrons up to date on changes at the library. I also provide support to library patrons who need assistance improving their computer literacy. This has given me extensive experience in troubleshooting technical issues with both hardware and software. In this role, I've also been able to institute a reservation system for our computer and 3D printers, which has made it easier for patrons to schedule one-on-one appointments for technical assistance and has helped increase patron satisfaction by 24%. This combination of experience makes me an excellent fit for the Junior Web Designer position at Lightbox because I will be able to both handle service requests from clients and make changes as needed to front-end web applications.

In addition to my role at the Denver Public Library, I am also an Assistant Web Developer at Blake High School. In this position, I have been completing tutorials in HTML and CSS while learning search engine optimization (SEO) strategies for writing web copy. As a result, I've been able to optimize our web content and increase our pages views by 56%. I am eager to continue improving my HTML and CSS skills as a Junior Web Designer, and I am confident that my background in SEO will be a valuable asset to Lightbox, Inc.

Thank you for taking the time to review my résumé and cover letter for the Junior Web Designer position. If you have any questions about my qualifications or if you believe there is a position that is more suitable for my qualifications, please contact me at 720-555-0976 or via email at xiaonan.li@blakehs.com. I look forward to speaking with you soon.

Sincerely,
Xiaonan Li

Portfolios and Skills Assessments

In addition to a cover letter, you may need to either complete a sample assignment or share your portfolio with employers. If the position requires you to use industry-standard software, a certain coding language, or some other specialized technical skill, you may be asked to complete an assessment or do a demonstration to provide evidence of your proficiency. If you're in a more creative field—writing, web design, graphic design, photography, video production, etc.—you'll likely need to have a portfolio of your work accessible to potential employers. A portfolio should include samples of work that are directly related to the position you're applying for, but you can also include some more unique samples to showcase the breadth and depth of your expertise.

THE JOB INTERVIEW

Hunting for jobs and compiling your application materials will eventually lead you to job interviews. A successful interview is an important step toward securing a job. It's okay, and even natural, to feel somewhat anxious before an interview, but here are some tips for acing the job interview:

- Dress professionally and appropriately for the job. The way you act and dress tells the interviewer plenty about your attitude and personality. Depending on the job you're applying for, business casual dress is typically sufficient for a job interview, although more formal positions or companies may require a suit. Consider a button-down shirt or blouse with slacks or a skirt; you could also opt for a dress. Don't forget to wear some nice, clean dress shoes.

- Arrive a few minutes early to show that you are punctual.

- Silence your phone.

- Shake hands with your interviewer and make eye contact.

- Speak up during the interview and give the interviewer the information necessary to make an informed decision.

- It is especially impressive if you can remember the names of people to whom you've been introduced. People like to be called by name, and it shows that you took the initiative to remember them.

- Bring extra copies of your résumé to the interview in case the hiring manager needs one.

- Sit up straight. Good posture is important.

The best way to prepare for the interview is to practice. Have a friend or relative play the role of the interviewer and go over some of the most commonly asked questions. The following is a list of interview questions you can expect to answer:

- **Tell me a little bit about yourself.** This is your chance to briefly pitch your qualifications for the job. Provide a few details about your education, previous jobs you've held, and extracurricular activities that relate to the position for which you're interviewing.

- **What did you like the most about your last job? What did you dislike the most about it?** You should always accentuate the positives in an interview, so focus primarily on what you liked. Be honest about what you disliked and then explain how facing the negatives helped you grow as an employee. Do not, however, be critical of your prior company. If you are shedding a negative light on your past company, your interviewer will wonder if you will do the same to your prospective company.

- **What are your career goals?** Be sure you've done some research on the company and industry before your interview. When this question comes up, talk realistically about how far you believe your skills and talents will take you and what actions you plan to take to ensure this happens, such as pursuing more education.

- **What are your biggest strengths?** Try to connect your description of a strength with the requirements for the job. When it comes to strengths, don't exaggerate, but don't sell yourself short either. Be proud of your best qualities but give specific examples to prove yourself. Much like a résumé or cover letter, instead of just saying "I'm a team player," show that you work well in a team environment by describing a challenging all-staff project at work where you were able to coordinate with your coworkers effectively and beat the deadline.

- **What are your biggest weaknesses?** This can be an intimidating question, but it's designed for your employer to get a better sense of where you might need additional support or improvement in the position you're applying for. Sometimes, employers don't have the bandwidth to train you on certain things, so it's better that they know this in advance. If you're asked this question, be honest. If there's a certain technology listed on the job posting that you don't have experience with, let them know that you haven't used it but that you're an eager and fast learner. Keep in mind that this question isn't the time to admit to any serious failings that would be a major red flag for the employer. It's also a good idea to demonstrate how you are working on improving any shortcomings you mentioned, if possible.

- **Tell me about a time when…** These questions are used to see how you respond to a given stressor or common situation in the workplace. For example, you might be asked how you handled a situation with a difficult coworker or a demanding client. Have a few scenarios ready to discuss. In these examples, you should clearly indicate the problem or issue you encountered, how you resolved it, and what you learned from it.

Remote Interviews

If you're interviewing remotely using video conferencing software, there are a few extra things you should be aware of:

- Test out your camera, microphone, and internet connection in advance to make sure they work. The interviewer will likely want you to be on camera, so be prepared for this.

- Make sure that you conduct the interview in a quiet, clean, and professional space. Test out what will be visible on camera and make sure that everything within view is something you would want a prospective employer to see. Adjust the lighting as needed. Minimize interruptions from roommates and pets as much as possible.

- Make sure your software is on the most current version so that it doesn't start installing updates at an inopportune time.

- Log in to the meeting room 10 minutes early to make sure that the link works. You don't need to stay in the meeting room until the meeting starts, but it's important to make sure that everything works the way it should prior to the interview.

- Use your first and last name as your username when you log in to the meeting room. Make sure your software isn't attached to an email address you don't want a prospective employer to see.

- Dress professionally on the top and bottom. In case you need to get up during the interview, you don't want to be wearing sweatpants (or worse, no pants at all).

- Close any unnecessary tabs or windows in case you are asked to share your screen.

- Keep a notebook with any notes you've taken nearby. You can also take notes during the interview if you have an idea for a question to ask the employer.

- Smile and nod to communicate that you are focused and interested. Remember, your face is the only thing the interviewer will really see of you, so your facial expressions will have to communicate your feelings and reactions.

Asking Questions

In an interview, you can ask questions of the employer too. In fact, the interviewer expects you to ask questions to determine if the job is right for you, just as the employer will be trying to find out if you'll be successful working for them. When you ask questions, it shows that you're interested and want to learn more. If the types of questions you ask indicate that you've done your homework regarding the job and the company, your interviewer will be impressed. Avoid asking questions about salary or fringe benefits, questions that might be perceived as adversarial, or questions that show you have a negative opinion of the company. It's all right to list your questions on a piece of paper to reference during the interview; it's the quality of the questions that's important, not whether you can remember them. The following graphic illustrates a few sample questions that you should consider asking if the topics don't come up in your interview.

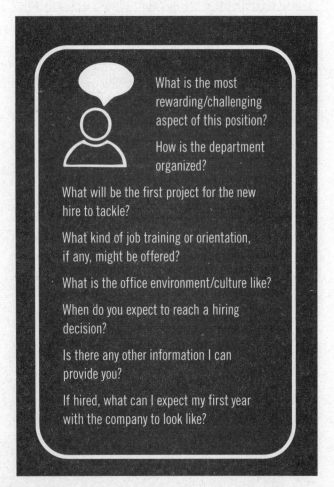

What is the most rewarding/challenging aspect of this position?

How is the department organized?

What will be the first project for the new hire to tackle?

What kind of job training or orientation, if any, might be offered?

What is the office environment/culture like?

When do you expect to reach a hiring decision?

Is there any other information I can provide you?

If hired, what can I expect my first year with the company to look like?

Following Up

After the interview, follow up with a thank-you note (usually via email) to the interviewer. Not only is it a thoughtful gesture, but it also helps you stand out among a sea of candidates and shows that you have a genuine interest in the job.

ON THE JOB

Don't expect to earn six figures in your first job or two. Remember, your first few jobs give you valuable experience that can help you in future jobs or higher-ranking positions. Once you get your first job, you'll need to keep your superiors happy and instill trust in your coworkers. The following are some ways for you to do just that.

Minding Your Office Etiquette

Those who succeed in the workplace do so because they know how to present themselves in a professional situation. Those who fail are generally flustered or unaccustomed to a professional environment. They don't realize that when they're working in an office with a group of people, they have to go out of their way to get along and follow the unwritten rules of that workplace. When you first enter a new work environment, there may be a specified dress code that you will need to follow. If there isn't, you'll need to take note of how others dress, then try to match the tone. For instance, if you work in a business office, are people dressed formally or in a business casual style? Or maybe you are working in a golf pro shop. Are the employees wearing polos and slacks, or are shorts or skorts allowed? It's fine to want to be an individual, but your attire has to fit in when you're in a business setting.

A lot of people new to the workplace don't grasp how important office etiquette is. Your ability to follow the norms of office etiquette, however, can make or break a job. You can have all the technical talent, but if you're not up on how to properly conduct business and refuse to conform to the company's norms on how to speak and dress, your job might not last long. When it comes to getting a job, first impressions are important, and engaging in bad office etiquette can ruin the impression you make. The best advice is that if you're not sure what the policy is, ask your boss or coworkers. They will be pleased that you were concerned enough to ask.

Mentors: Finding a Friendly Face at Work

Even for the most seasoned employee, the first few weeks at any job can be tough. Hopefully, your job will offer some sort of orientation or workplace mentorship program. Even so, you may want to seek out an "unofficial" mentor who can help you adjust, acclimate, and grow.

In her book, *Learn, Work, Lead: Things Your Mentor Won't Tell You,* author Terri Tierney Clark, a graduate of Smith College and Dartmouth College's Tuck School of Business with over 20 years of senior-level business experience, offers these thoughts about mentors:

"Mentors are trusted advisors who help you with career decisions and advise you on steps to take to advance your career. You can talk easily with mentors, and they make your career journey smoother. Managers can be mentors, but you don't have to have a reporting relationship to take advantage of the benefits of a mentoring connection. You could develop a rapport with someone you've worked with on a project or you can have several mentors who bring you diverse perspectives."

"A true mentor will know you well enough that [their] advice encourages you to capitalize on your talents and overcome your weaknesses. Simply having a mentor will make your work more enjoyable. Everyone likes a champion to cheer them on, and when that cheerleader is an accomplished business professional, all the better."

"But finding a good mentor isn't a matter of merely *encountering* one. You have to put forth an effort to get to know a colleague and afford them the opportunity to get to know you."

Clark cautions against simply asking someone to be your mentor. She notes, "*Mentor* is just a word that institutionalizes a relationship. You need the relationship first so don't ever ask anyone to be a mentor. That would be like asking someone to fall in love with you. A potential mentor is either going to want to continue spending time to help you with your career or not. Their interest in advising you will be a function of their impression of your potential, the depth of your relationship, and possibly what you can offer in return."

The good news, according to Clark, is that oftentimes, without much effort on anyone's part, mentors just happen. She adds, "Often a superior and [their] direct report develop a great rapport that turns into a mentoring relationship. If you have identified people who you believe would be great advisors, but you don't come in contact with them much, you will need to use your networking skills to develop the relationship. It's easy to connect with a potential mentor by asking for advice or feedback. Just ensure you are asking legitimate questions that also show you have put a great deal of thought into the issue. Be yourself and diligent about building the relationship. Then you will turn the corner into a comfortable rapport that feels more and more like a close friendship in which both individuals want to see the other succeed."

Who knows? You could become a mentor yourself one day after you've been in your career for a while. Maybe you'll be able to help some new employee who looks kind of bewildered and in need of a friendly coworker because you'll remember what it was like to be that new person.

But finding a good mentor isn't a matter of merely encountering one. You have to put forth an effort to get to know a colleague and afford them the opportunity to get to know you.

Terri Tierney Clark, Author

WHAT EMPLOYERS EXPECT FROM EMPLOYEES

Most employers use their job postings to outline the necessary qualifications to do a job well. Most of these minimum qualifications include some pretty standard soft skills, meaning the fundamental skills and qualities you'll need to succeed in the workplace.

- **COMMUNICATION:** Possessing strong oral and written communication skills means knowing how to express yourself thoughtfully, clearly, and effectively for your intended audience. Just as importantly, it means understanding how to be a good listener.

- **TEAMWORK:** Cooperating with others not only helps you get the job done quicker but also builds a strong and successful team. At some point in your career, you will find yourself in a group dynamic trying to complete a task. In this scenario, knowing how to work closely with your colleagues can be the difference between success and failure.

- **GROWTH MINDSET:** If you have a growth mindset, you acknowledge the areas in which you need improvement and you seek out the training or education necessary to improve yourself. Constructive criticism is usually necessary for any employee to learn how things should be done. Employees with a growth mindset consider feedback a valuable tool for their own personal and professional development. In turn, employers often recognize and value employees who are eager and willing to learn.

- **TIME MANAGEMENT:** The ability to plan, prioritize, and complete a task in a timely fashion is a valuable skill. Your employer will expect you to use your time wisely in order to perform your job duties. If you struggle with managing your time effectively, try out a few creative solutions to help you focus, minimize distractions, and complete the task at hand.

- **CRITICAL THINKING:** In a work environment, it's important that you know how to exercise good judgment by thinking clearly and rationally. Oftentimes, this requires you to gather, analyze, and evaluate available evidence and make an informed decision. As part of critical thinking, you'll need to be open-minded and willing to consider other points of view in order to make the best decision.

- **PROBLEM SOLVING:** Companies are looking for creative problem solvers. When you notice that something isn't working, it's important to identify and define the problem in order to find a solution. Then, you must explore your options and make a decision as to which action is the best solution and why. Effective problem solvers should also be able to learn from their successes and mistakes by reflecting on what went well and what could have gone better. You can learn these techniques by talking with others about how they solve problems as well as observing others in the problem-solving process.

- **RESPECT:** In addition to being kind and courteous to your coworkers, employees need to be respectful and understanding of a coworker's unique experience and perspective. This might involve putting yourself in the other person's shoes to gain a better understanding of their experience. Remember that each of your coworkers is a human being with their own thoughts and feelings and that they are deserving of respect. It is especially important to listen when a fellow employee points out any biases you might have on a given topic. Be open and willing to listen to their perspective, as it likely took some courage for them to bring it up.

- **ADAPTABILITY:** It's important that you are able to adapt to a changing work environment. You will likely be expected to work under pressure or manage workplace stress. Staying calm, cool, and collected will help you to think critically and make reasonable decisions based on experience and knowledge.

- **INITIATIVE:** Don't wait to be told exactly what to do. Show some initiative and look around to see what needs to be done.

- **HONESTY:** Always be honest. Dishonesty shows up in many different ways, ranging from stealing time or property to divulging company secrets. Nothing good will result from dishonesty in the workplace.

- **DEPENDABILITY:** Arrive at work on time every day and meet your deadlines.

Never fail to show pride in your work. By making these traits a part of your personality and daily performance, you'll demonstrate that you are a hard-working and qualified employee—and you may find yourself rocketing up the corporate ladder.

YOU'VE GOT YOUR WHOLE LIFE AHEAD OF YOU

As we've hopefully made clear throughout this book, this should be an incredibly exciting time in your life. Sure, there are lots of decisions to be made, like whether you'll go to college, pursue a trade, or enter the workforce straight out of high school. In order to help you make informed decisions, we aimed to provide you with practical advice about the challenges you'll face as you embark on your journey toward a satisfying and fulfilling career, including student loans, independent

living, and finding a job. As you weigh your options, consult supportive family members, friends, and mentors throughout the process. They can offer you helpful advice and encouragement as you weigh your options. Remember that everyone will have a different opinion on what you should do and how you should do it. Ultimately, you know yourself best, and the final decision is up to you. While that can seem daunting, it should also be empowering.

Going forward, remember that you have the freedom to choose what you do next. Perhaps more importantly, remember that you also have the freedom to change your mind. If you ever feel stuck, overwhelmed, or unhappy, you can always go back to school, change careers, or try something new. Don't be afraid to make mistakes or change your mind. The possibilities are endless, and there are numerous paths you can take to live the life you want, even if what you want changes as you get older. Embrace the excitement and know that you'll figure things out eventually. We can't wait to see what you do next!

PART

5

Appendixes

High School to College Timeline

This timeline is designed to show you at a glance when to complete the most important steps of the process. For a more in-depth breakdown with added steps and details, see Chapter 3.

9TH GRADE

- ☐ Meet with your guidance counselor and request your school profile or planned course of study.
- ☐ Start trying out some extracurricular activities, like sports, clubs, student council, etc.
- ☐ Focus on getting good grades and working on areas where you need improvement.
- ☐ Begin to casually research different careers or colleges that might interest you.

10TH GRADE

- ☐ Figure out which tests you'll need to take—ASVAB, PSAT/NMSQT, SAT, ACT, etc.—and mark them in your calendar.
- ☐ Participate in college and career fairs or other similar activities.
- ☐ Start keeping track of your accomplishments, like any awards or honors as well as extracurriculars and volunteer work, on your résumé.
- ☐ Meet with your guidance counselor to make sure that your coursework is on track to prepare you for college.
- ☐ Find a mentor who can support and guide you.
- ☐ Start researching the types of schools you're interested in, like community colleges, four-year-colleges, trade or vocational schools, etc.
- ☐ Consider visiting local college campuses.
- ☐ Start saving money for college, moving out, or other plans.
- ☐ Consider getting a summer job, performing community service, or finding volunteer work during the summer.

11TH GRADE

Fall

- ☐ Meet with your guidance counselor to talk through your college or career plans to make sure you're on track.
- ☐ Consider taking the PSAT/NMSQT in October to help you prepare for taking the SAT in the spring. The PSAT can also help you qualify for the National Merit Scholarship Program.
- ☐ Continue participating in college and career fairs or other similar activities.
- ☐ Continue researching the types of colleges you're interested in, like community colleges, four-year-colleges, trade or vocational schools, etc.
- ☐ Start planning visits to colleges you're interested in.
- ☐ Start thinking about potential career paths that you might want to pursue and doing intentional research about them.

Winter

- ☐ Make a list of colleges that meet your most important criteria.
- ☐ Start gathering information about the different colleges you're going to apply to.
- ☐ Start organizing your spring testing schedule so you know when to register for the SAT and ACT.
- ☐ Talk with your parent(s) or guardian(s) to get a sense of your financial situation and to understand what support you'll have when you graduate high school.
- ☐ Create a filing system for the print and online college materials you'll receive.

Spring

☐ Make an appointment with your guidance counselor to review your course selections for senior year.

☐ Take the tests you need and discuss your scores with your guidance counselor.

☐ Start working on your college essay and reach out to your English teacher, guidance counselor, or your mentor for assistance.

☐ Start considering who to ask to write your recommendation letters for college.

☐ Inquire about scheduling personal interviews at the colleges you're interested in.

☐ Consider getting a job or performing community service or other volunteer work during the summer.

☐ Figure out the fees and deadlines for your college application process.

☐ Start applying for scholarships and grants if you haven't already.

☐ Plan college visits.

Summer

☐ Send thank you notes to anyone you interviewed with for college or a job.

☐ Reach out to students or alumni of the colleges you're most interested in.

☐ Start working on college applications.

☐ Compose rough drafts of your college application essays and get feedback.

☐ Develop a financial aid application plan.

12TH GRADE

Fall

☐ Make a calendar to keep track of deadlines for college, financial aid, and scholarship applications.

☐ Resist senioritis and keep your grades up.

☐ Meet with your guidance counselor to make sure you're in a good position for senior year.

☐ Reach out to your mentor to discuss your top college choices.

☐ Apply early to your top colleges.

☐ Write your college application essays.

☐ Send online recommendation forms to the teachers you have chosen.

☐ Retake the ACT or SAT if needed and make sure your score reports will go to the colleges that need them.

☐ Start submitting your college applications.

Winter

☐ Continue attending college and job fairs at your school.

☐ Focus on getting good grades so you can send a strong mid-year grade report to colleges.

☐ Fill out the Free Application for Federal Student Aid (FAFSA) and if necessary the CSS/Financial Aid Profile.

☐ Make sure you've sent out any college applications and financial aid forms.

☐ Meet with your guidance counselor to verify that all your forms are in order and have been sent out.

☐ Save email confirmations of each of your college application submissions, including recommendations and test scores.

Spring

☐ Watch your email and snail mail between March 1 and April 1 for responses from colleges that offer rolling admissions.

☐ Keep an eye out for financial award notifications between April 1 and May 1.

☐ Compare financial aid packages and don't be afraid to ask your top choice if they can match your best package.

☐ Make your final choice and notify all colleges of your intent by May 1.

☐ Get ready to attend new student events and orientations at the school you'll be attending.

☐ Meet with your guidance counselor to make sure you've completed all the tasks on your to-do list for your school of choice.

☐ Follow up with the teachers who wrote you recommendation letters and let them know what school you'll be attending. Don't forget to write them thank you notes.

Summer

☐ If needed, be sure to apply for a Stafford loan.

☐ Make sure you're scheduled for your college's orientation.

☐ Get your courses scheduled for your first semester.

☐ If you'll be living with people, reach out to your future roommates once you know who they are.

Additional Resources
for Underserved
Student Populations

RESOURCES FOR STUDENTS OF COLOR AND OTHER MINORITY POPULATIONS

In addition to religious organizations, sororities and fraternities, and college minority affairs offices, minority students can receive information and assistance from the following organizations.

American Indian Higher Education Consortium (AIHEC)

AIHEC's mission is to support the work of tribal colleges and the national movement for tribal self-determination through four objectives: maintain commonly held standards of quality in American Indian education; support the development of new tribally controlled colleges; promote and assist in the development of legislation to support American Indian higher education; and encourage greater participation by American Indians in the development of higher education policy.

aihec.org

ASPIRA

ASPIRA's mission is to empower the Puerto Rican and Latino community through advocacy and the education and leadership development of its youth.

aspira.org

Education USA

Education USA is a division of the United States Department of State devoted to providing resources for international college students as well as servicing international student advising centers in at least 175 countries and territories at the time of printing. Students who are interested in studying in the US from abroad can use these resources to determine what opportunities might be available to them and to figure out which US schools might be a good fit for their education abroad experience.

educationusa.state.gov

Gates Millennium Scholars (GMS)

GMS, funded by a grant from the Bill & Melinda Gates Foundation, was established in 1999 to provide outstanding African American, American Indian/Alaska Native, Asian Pacific Islander American, and Hispanic American students with an opportunity to complete an undergraduate college education in all discipline areas and a graduate education for those students pursuing studies in mathematics, science, engineering, education, or library science. The goal of GMS is to promote academic excellence and to provide an opportunity for thousands of outstanding students with significant financial need to reach their fullest potential.

gmsp.org

Hillel International

Hillel's mission is to serve as a supportive community for Jewish college students all over the world. Through both their international organizations and local Hillel chapters at a variety of schools, they help students integrate Jewish traditions into college life, counter antisemitism they might face, and develop meaningful support communities.

hillel.org

Hispanic Association of Colleges & Universities (HACU)

HACU is a national association representing the accredited colleges and universities in the United States where Hispanic students constitute at least 25 percent of the total student enrollment. HACU's goal is to bring together colleges and universities, corporations, government agencies, and individuals to establish partnerships for promoting development of Hispanic-serving colleges and universities; improving access to and the quality of postsecondary education for Hispanic students; and meeting the needs of business, industry, and government through the development and sharing of resources, information, and expertise.

hacu.net

Hispanic Scholarship Fund (HSF)

HSF is the nation's leading organization supporting Hispanic higher education. HSF was founded in 1975 with a vision to strengthen the country by advancing college education among Hispanic Americans. In support of its mission, HSF provides the Latino community with college scholarships and educational outreach support.

hsf.net

Informed Immigrant

Informed Immigrant's mission is to provide immigrants in the US with resources on any topic that pertains to their status, whether they are documented or not. In addition to numerous guides on topics like Deferred Action for Childhood Arrivals (DACA), COVID-19, and immigrant mental health, they have a specific guide for undocumented high school and college students to help them understand their rights and the resources available to them.

informedimmigrant.com/guides/students

INROADS

INROADS is a national career-development organization that places and develops talented youth from African American, Hispanic American, and Native American populations in business and industry and prepares them for corporate and community leadership.

inroads.org

Jackie Robinson Foundation

Founded in 1973 by Rachel Robinson, the Jackie Robinson Foundation has advanced higher education by providing generous, multi-year scholarship awards coupled with a comprehensive set of support services to highly motivated JRF Scholars and Extra Innings Fellows attending colleges and universities throughout the country.

jackierobinson.org

Muslim Students Association (MSA) National

MSA National's mission is to provide Muslim students with safe campus spaces for community and support. In addition to supporting MSA chapters at schools across the country, MSA National also provides resources on topics that affect Muslim students, such as fighting Islamophobia on campus, establishing campus prayer rooms, eating halal in campus dining, and observing Islamic holidays while living on campus, among others.

msanational.org

National Achievement® Scholarship Program

The National Achievement Scholarship Program is a privately financed academic competition conducted by National Merit Scholarship Corporation (NMSC). It was established in 1964 specifically to encourage Black American youth to continue their education, increase educational opportunities for academically accomplished Black American students, and encourage colleges to broaden their recruiting efforts.

nationalmerit.org

National Action Council for Minorities in Engineering (NACME)

NACME is an organization that aims to provide leadership and support for the national effort to increase the representation of successful African American, American Indian, and Latino women and men in engineering and technology and math- and science-based careers.

nacme.org

National Association for the Advancement of Colored People (NAACP)

The purpose of the NAACP is to ensure the political, educational, social, and economic equality of all citizens; to achieve equality of rights and eliminate race prejudice among the citizens of the United States; to remove all barriers of racial discrimination through democratic processes; to seek enactment and enforcement of federal, state, and local laws securing civil rights; to inform the public of the adverse effects of racial discrimination and to seek its elimination; and to educate persons as to their constitutional rights and to take all lawful action to secure the exercise thereof, and to take any other lawful action in furtherance of these objectives, consistent with the efforts of the national organization.

naacp.org/our-work/youth-programs

National Association of Multicultural Engineering Program Advocates (NAMEPA)

NAMEPA is a platform for identifying best practices among university programs in the diversity space. Training opportunities are available for K–12 students and teachers and counselors to increase diversity in the STEM fields. NAMEPA helps ensure that its student members have access to the information, services, and tools to pursue the lucrative field of engineering, including scholarship opportunities, and encourages underrepresented engineering students to become active in student organizations and develop leadership skills.

namepa.org

The National Urban League

The National Urban League's Education & Youth Development division strives to improve educational opportunities for African American and underserved students. The division has developed a number of programs to prepare students for success after graduation. Among these is Project Ready, which provides academic support and encouragement for middle school and high school students. The division expanded the program in 2009–2010 to create the Middle School Transitions Project, which helps students in grades 5 through 8 make the jump from middle school to high school, and STEM, which works to provide urban students with the resources they need to excel in science, technology, engineering, and math (STEM).

nul.org

United Negro College Fund (UNCF)

The UNCF serves to enhance the quality of education by raising operating funds for its 39 member colleges and universities, providing financial assistance to deserving students, and increasing access to technology for students and faculty at historically Black colleges and universities.

uncf.org

RESOURCES FOR STUDENTS WITH DISABILITIES

The following resources can help students, families, and schools with the legal requirements for accommodating disabilities. They can also connect you to other groups and individuals that are knowledgeable in students' rights and the process of transitioning into postsecondary education. Note that special interest, education, support, and advocacy organizations for persons with particular disabilities also exist. Check with your guidance counselor or contact one of the following organizations for more information.

ACT Services for Examinees with Disabilities

ACT is committed to serving examinees with documented disabilities by providing reasonable accommodations appropriate to the examinee's diagnosis and needs. ACT has established policies regarding documentation of an applicant's disability and the process for requesting accommodations.

act.org/content/act/en/products-and-services/the-act/registration/accommodations.html

American Foundation for the Blind (AFB)

AFB's mission is to support initiatives that remove barriers to education for the blind and visually impaired. Their website includes information on different types of accommodations recommended for sight-impaired learners as well as lists of resources.

afb.org/blog/entry/accessible-education-resources

Association on Higher Education and Disability (AHEAD)

AHEAD is a professional association committed to full participation of persons with disabilities in postsecondary education.

ahead.org

Attention Deficit Disorder Association (ADDA)

ADDA is an international non-profit—501(c)—organization founded over thirty years ago to help adults with Attention Deficit/Hyperactivity Disorder (ADHD) lead better lives.

add.org

Children and Adults with Attention-Deficit/Hyperactivity Disorder (CHADD)

CHADD is a national nonprofit organization that improves the lives of people affected by ADHD through education, advocacy, and support.

chadd.org

Council for Learning Disabilities (CLD)

CLD is an international organization composed of professionals who represent diverse disciplines. CLD fosters collaboration among professionals, development of leaders in the field, and advocacy for policies that support individuals with learning disabilities at the local, state, and national levels.

council-for-learning-disabilities.org

Education USA Resource List

In addition to their more general purpose of supporting international students who come to the US to study, Education USA offers a resource list for international students with disabilities. It includes a host of information to help students with disabilities understand their rights and accommodation access when coming to the US for school.

educationusa.state.gov/resources-student-disabilities

HEATH Resource Center at the National Youth Transitions Center

The HEATH Resource Center at the George Washington University Graduate School of Education & Human Development is an online clearinghouse on postsecondary education for individuals with disabilities. Their site functions as a resource center for education support services and opportunities.

heath.gwu.edu

The International Dyslexia Association (IDA)

IDA is a nonprofit education and advocacy organization dedicated to issues surrounding dyslexia. They have more than 40 branches throughout the United States and Canada and global partners in 21 countries.

dyslexiaida.org

Learning Disabilities Association of America (LDA)

LDA's mission is to create opportunities for success for all individuals affected by learning disabilities, offering cutting-edge information, practical solutions, and a network of resources.

ldaamerica.org

National Center for Learning Disabilities (NCLD)

NCLD's mission is to improve the lives of the one in five children and adults nationwide with learning and attention issues—by empowering parents and young adults, transforming schools, and advocating for equal rights and opportunities.

ncld.org

National Deaf Center

In addition to other resources for deaf individuals and their families, the National Deaf Center provides resources on accommodations that are available to students who are deaf or hard of hearing. Their "Accommodations 101" info page includes the different types of accommodations commonly used for deaf students and tips on keeping schools accountable for ensuring these accommodations are provided.

nationaldeafcenter.org

National Federation of the Blind (NFB)

While there are a host of resources on their homepage to help the blind and visually impaired, NFB put together a "Self-Advocacy in Higher Education Toolkit" for students who are planning to attend college. It has everything blind or visually impaired students need to know about their legal rights to ensure their school makes appropriate accommodations, while also offering resources for navigating college life with a sight impairment.

**nfb.org/programs-services/
advocacy/advocacy-resources/
self-advocacy-higher-education-toolkit**

SAT Services for Students with Disabilities (SSD)

The College Board is committed to making sure that students with disabilities can take the SAT, PSAT/NMSQT, PSAT 10, and Advanced Placement exams with the accommodations they need. All reasonable requests are considered.

accommodations.collegeboard.org